ViaCAD Tips, Tutorials, and Techniques

280 Tips To Boost Your Productivity With ViaCAD

Timothy D. Olson

ViaCAD Tips, Tutorials, and Techniques

Edited By: Megan Olson

ViaCAD Tips, Tutorials, and Techniques

Copyright

First Edition

ISBN-13:
978-1466275133

ISBN-10:
1466275138

Trademarks

Warning and Disclaimer

VIACAD TIPS, TUTORIALS, AND TECHNIQUES

About the Author

Tim Olson, President, Evolution Software. Evolution Software leads the development efforts for Encore's CAD products that target the retail and professional digital design markets. These products were originally acquired from CADSoft Solutions (CSI) in 2006. As former founder of CSI, Olson guided the company into providing high-quality commercial CAD software rebranded under such names as CADD Pro, AeroCADD, Concepts Unlimited, Concepts 2D/3D, ViaCAD, Vellum Solids, Cobalt, TurboCAD Mac, TurboCAD 2D/3D, and Shark.

Prior to founding CSI in 1994, Olson was Chief Engineer for Lockheed's Advanced Programs Design Methods group where he was responsible for the development of an internal CAD program, one of the first associative hybrid CAD systems to evolve onto workstation technology in the early 1980's.

Table of Contents

INTRODUCTION
WELCOME

You do not need to be a rocket scientist to use computer aided design these days. Thanks to an amazing number of advances in computer hardware and software technology, affordable CAD tools such as ViaCAD are now well within the reach of anyone wanting to explore the benefits of 3D digital design. In fact, with ViaCAD's friendly user interface, it's not unusual for a new user to launch ViaCAD and start designing immediately!

Considering this, it is understandable that many users may not want to waste hours trying to decipher a technical manual, when all they are really looking for are quick to find and easy to understand tips that will increase their proficiency. The goal behind this book is to provide you with a variety of such easy-to-understand tips that will give you a new awareness of ViaCAD -- all without forcing you to slave hours over an overly technical manual.

Who Should Read This Book

This book is written with a wide range of ViaCAD users in mind, varying from beginning to advanced users. You will find tips, tutorials, and technical notes that apply to the ViaCAD family of products which include ViaCAD 2D, ViaCAD 2D/3D, and ViaCAD Pro. And since the Shark products extend upon the ViaCAD feature set, Shark users will find many helpful tips as well.

What is Covered in This Book

This book is divided into two parts that include Tips and Tutorials.

Part I: Tips

The heart and soul of the book, this section is full of great tips presented as questions for quick and easy searching. Tips cover user interface, drafting, surface and solid modeling, rendering and display, photo realistic rendering, and sharing data. To quickly search for the answer to a specific question, you can flip to Appendix of Questions in the back of the book to find a listing of every question.

Part II: Create This! Tutorials

The tutorial section holds step-by-step instructions for beginners and intermediate users to create models using ViaCAD. These tutorials allow you to apply many of the tips from Part 1 in actual design situations, giving you the opportunity to learn by example. Beginning with instructions on how to create a basic paper clip, this section proceeds to guide you into progressively more challenging designs, including instructions for designing a hair dyer and y-pipe.

Conventions Used in This Book

Callouts are made when the documentation is specific to a particular product. Since ViaCAD 2D is a 2D product, documentation pertaining to 3D features do not apply to this product.

Mouse Command	**What you do:**
Press	Press and hold down the mouse button.
Click	Quickly press and release the mouse button.
Point and click	Position the cursor and then click the mouse button.
Double-click	Click the mouse button twice in rapid succession.
Drag	Move the mouse while holding down the button.
Control-click	Press the control key and the mouse button. If you have a two button mouse, press the right button (Right-click).

How to Contribute to This Book

We welcome your feedback concerning *ViaCAD Tips, Tutorials, and Techniques*. If you would like to contribute a tip or tutorial please contact the author by email at tips@evo-soft.net.

Part I Tips

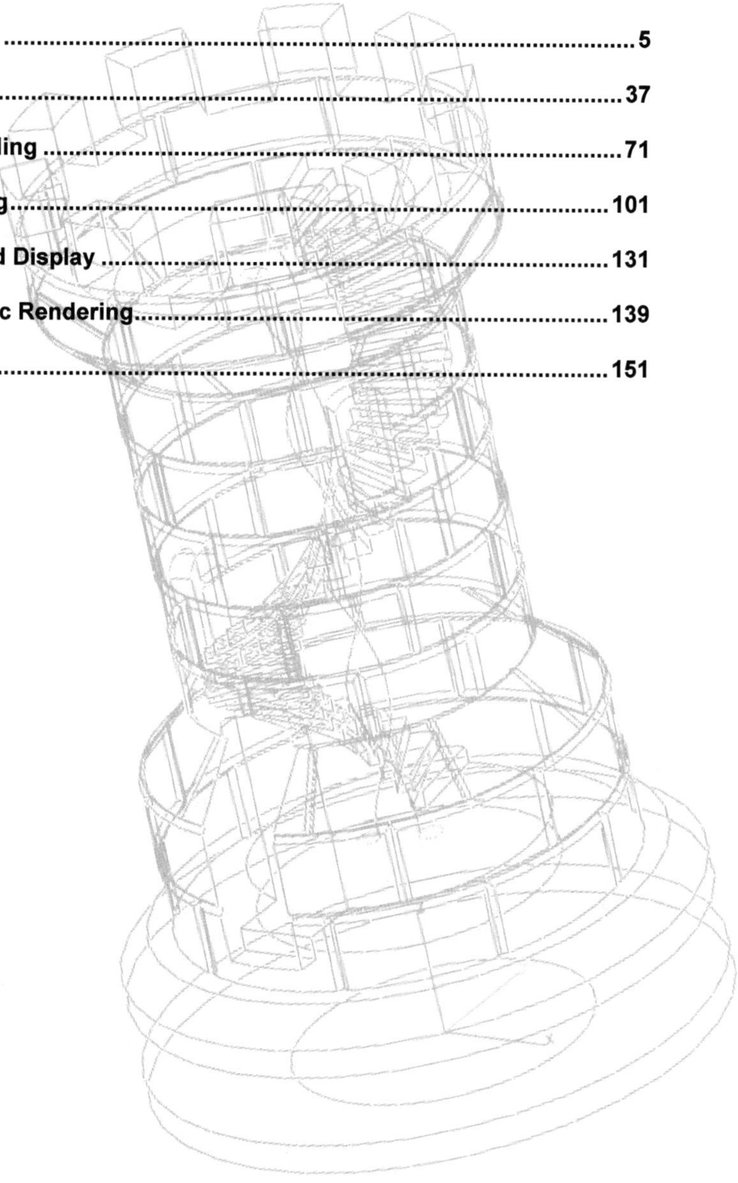

1 CHAPTER 1
USER INTERFACE

Overview

Getting comfortable with the user interface can significantly improve your productivity. This chapter covers some of the key user interface components of the product such as the start up screen, aspects related to selecting and modifying objects, and information regarding the Gripper, WorkPlanes, snaps, tool palettes, preferences, layers, and performance.

Top Ten Tips

What are your top ten tips for new users?

If you are a new user to ViaCAD, below are ten tips that will help you get started faster and immediately improve your productivity.

Tip #1. Mouse Functions
Left Button

Click to specify locations or select objects
Click Left Button along with the space bar to pan drawing

Right Button (Optional)

Click in drawing area to get view contextual commands
Click on object to get object contextual commands
Press Control Left Button to emulate Right Button (Mac)
Press to terminate a sequence of points (spline and polylines)

Wheel Button (Optional)

Scroll the wheel forward or backwards to zoom at the cursor
Reverse the zooming direction in the Preferences dialog box
Press and hold the Scroll wheel to rotate the view. If something is selected, that becomes the point of rotation.
Double click to zoom extents

Many CAD users use a three button mouse as it can significantly increase your productivity by placing view operations quickly at your finger tips.

Tip #2. Viewing Data
View Orientations

Access the View Menu to change the view to Top, Left Side, Right Side, Front, Back, Isometric, and Trimetric views

View Tool Palette

Access the View Tool Palette to dynamically pan, zoom, and rotate the view.

Display Modes

Select wireframe, hidden lines, or shaded display modes from the lower left corner of the primary tool palette.

Mouse Functions

Use the mouse functions from Tip #1 to zoom, pan, and rotate.

Tip #3. Selecting Objects

Arrow Tool 

Select left to right to pick objects only if their extents lie within selection box.

Select right to left to pick objects if any portion of the object lies within the select box.

Double click on the Arrow Tool icon to select everything in the drawing.

Deep Select Tool 

Use to select nested objects such as objects within groups or faces within a solid.

Selection Masking

Use the Window: Select Mask dialog box to filter selected objects by type, color, or layer. The mask settings stay in effect until a new tool is chosen.

Tip #4. Modify Objects

Arrow Tool 

Use the arrow tool to dynamically move the entire object or to move selected defining points.

Nudging 

In Preferences: General set the Nudge distance to a non zero value. Pressing the arrow keys will now move selected objects. Pressing Shift Arrow key will multiple the nudge distance by 10.

Deep Select Arrow Tool 

Use to modify nested objects such as objects within groups.

Automatically turns on and off displays object handles.

The Gripper

Graphical user interface used to translate, rotate, and scale objects.

Gripper attributes located in Inspector dialog box.

Data Entry Window

The Data Entry Window is located at the top middle of the screen.

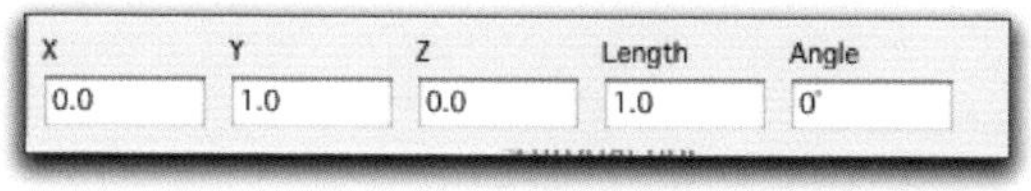

Use the Data Entry Window to explicitly create or modify geometry through parameter fields. These fields are accessible with your mouse-cursor by clicking within the box, or by hitting the Tab key to toggle between the boxes. You can enter easy, as well as complicated, mathematical expression in the Data Entry window.

3" +2cm

14+cos(45)*3

Alignment Locking

Press the “x”, “y”, or “z” key to constrain the snap along an alignment.

Snap Filters

Display the Window: Snaps dialog box to turn on and off snap filters such as endpoints, midpoints, centers, and along axis construction lines.

Snap Settings

Display the File: Preferences: Snaps dialog box to adjust the snap radius and angles.

Tip #5. Keyboard Shortcuts
View Orientation Keys

A Right Side View

S Front View

D Top View

F Isometric View

G Trimetric View

View Zooming Keys

W Zoom to user specified area

E Zoom to object extents

Construction Lines

Shift H Horizontal construction line at cursor.

Shift V Vertical construction line at cursor.

Tip #6. Work Planes
AutoWork Plane Orientation

The Work Plane will automatically adjust to be parallel to the viewing plane if the user defined work plane is perpendicular to the view plane.

Work Plane Display

From the menu, select WorkPlane: Show Work Plane to see the current orientation of the Work Plane.

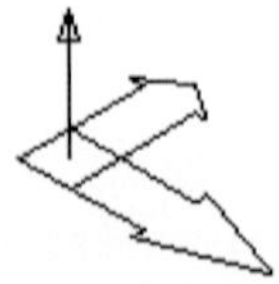

"C" Key

Press the "C" key to assign the work plane with respect to the current snap information.

If your cursor is over a curve, the Work Plane normal is assigned to the curve tangent at the current snap point.

Snaps

Snaps are projected into the work plane unless they reference another object point or alignment.

Tip #7. Tool Palettes
Tear Offs

The main tool palette has tear away tool palettes. Press, hold, and move the mouse to tear away a tool palette. Tool palette positions are remembered from session to session.

Sub Tool Options

Some tools have further sub tools accessible from the large icon in the upper left area known as the Tool Bar. By default these are on and displayed whenever a tool with more options is accessed. You can move this palette to another screen position.

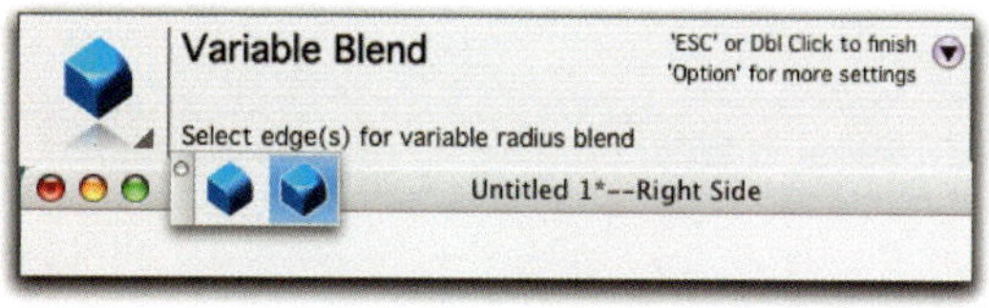

Horizontal or Vertical Orientation

Press the Right button over the title bar of any tool palette. You will receive a menu of options that control the horizontal or vertical orientation of the palette.

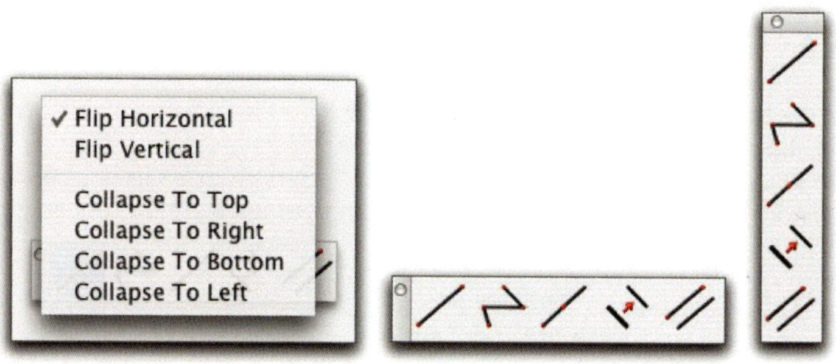

Palette Collapse

Press the Right button over the title bar of any tool palette. You will receive a menu of options that control palette collapsing. Palette Collapse will automatically open and close a window to its title bar as you move the mouse into the window.

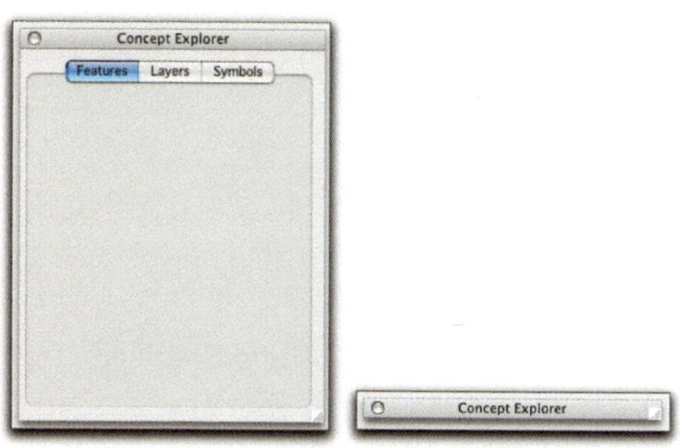

Tip #8. Setting Text and Dimension Attributes

Setting Text Font Size 

Select the Text tool. Be sure no text objects are selected. Then pick the desired font size, style, and color using the Inspector. The next time you create a text, the text will have these default attributes.

Setting Dimension Font Size 

Select the Dimension tool. Be sure no dimension objects are selected. Then pick the desired font size, style, and color using the Inspector. The next time you create a dimension, the dimension will have these default attributes.

Eye Dropper Tool 

Use the Eye Dropper Tool to copy text and dimension attributes from one object to another.

Tip #9. Training Videos

One of the best ways to get up to speed with ViaCAD is to explore the training videos that are included with the application. Each training session includes a video, a step by step PDF, and an example file. Training videos cover everything from the user interface to creating photo realistic renderings. You can access the training videos from the application Help menu.

Tip #10. Other Resources

MasterViaCAD.com
The MasterViaCAD.com site contains a variety of resources to help a new or experienced ViaCAD user become more productive with the application. At this site you will find training videos, feature videos, product announcements, and other resources. Visit this site at www.MasterViaCAD.com.

User Forum
The user forum is a great place to meet other users of ViaCAD. Use the forum to discuss design strategies, discover tips from users, and to see other ViaCAD projects. Visit the forum at forum.punchcad.com.

CAD Blog
Visit the Punch!CAD blog for more tips, tutorials, and product announcements related to ViaCAD and Shark.

Technical Support
Encore provides technical support for ViaCAD and Shark at:
http://support.encore.com/technicalsupport/
This site also includes a knowledge base system for questions regarding registration and system compatibility. You can also email or call Encore technical support from this location.

Startup Screen

What are some of the key components on the startup screen?

A very important part of the user interface is the startup screen and its key components. We will make reference to many of these features throughout the rest of the book, so try to familiarize yourself with these components as much as possible.

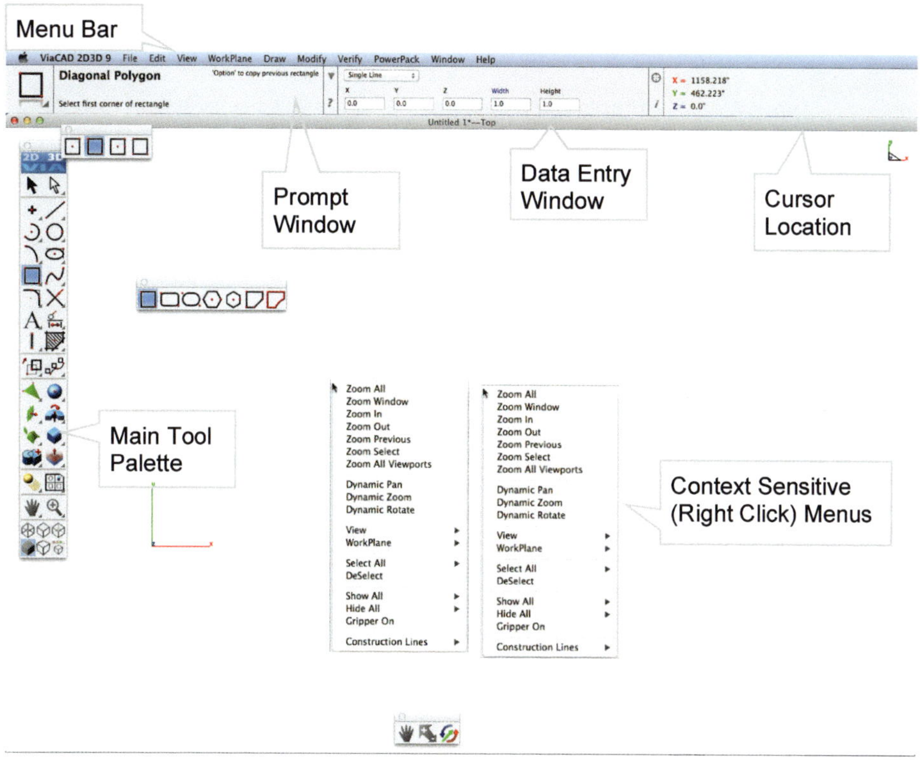

Figure 1.1

- *Menu Bar* - The Menu Bar provides access to the File, Edit, View, WorkPlane, Draw, Modify, Verify, and Window commands.

- *Prompt Window* - One feature that is often underused is the Prompt Window. Located at the top of screen under the Menu Bar, this feature displays information about the currently selected tool, including the tool name, instructions on the proper way to use the tool, and options if available. One useful aspect of the Prompt Window is its ability to guide you through tools that require multiple steps. It will guide you through each step, one at a time, until you have completed the task. The option-clicks are another helpful component of the Prompt Window that allow you to perform another task on-the-fly while continuing work on the original one. For example, it permits you to create an arc while you are using the *Multi Line* tool or to copy an object when you are using the *Move* tool.

- *Data Entry Window* - The Data Entry Window is used to specify values and parameters related to the current tool. It also provides graphical icons to access precision point and the Inspector. To utilize the Data Entry Window, use your cursor by clicking within the box or by hitting the Tab key to toggle between the boxes. You can enter easy, as well as complicated, mathematical expressions in the Data Entry Window. Examples include: 3" + 2cm, 3*25.4, 3+ sqrt (25), and 14+ cos (45)*3.

- *Main Tool Palette* - This is the location from which you can access tools for creating and manipulating curves, surfaces, and solids. Small gray arrows on the Main Tool Palette indicate that a tear away menu is available for more tool options.

- *Cursor Location* – This display shows where the next snap will be placed. It takes into consideration projections into the WorkPlane and any LogiCursor snaps.

- *Context Sensitive Menus* – Pressing the right mouse button will display one of two context sensitive menus. Clicking on an entity displays the menu on the right in Figure 1.1. Clicking on an empty area displays the menu on the left in Figure 1.1.

Selecting Objects

How can I quickly select everything in the drawing?

The obvious tool to select everything in the drawing is the *Select All* option under the Edit menu. However, a quicker way to select everything is to double click on the *Arrow* tool.

Note that *Select All* requires the current tool be the *Selection* or *Select Deep tool.* I find this tip most helpful when combined with such tools such as transform, modify attributes such as color or layers, and the trim tools.

Is there a way to select by object color or type?

You can filter objects by type, color, or layer using the Select Mask dialog box. The Select Mask dialog box can be found under Window on the Menu Bar.

These mask settings will stay in effect until a new tool is chosen. For example, clicking on the *Line* tool will turn back on all selection attributes. Hold down the control and shift key for selecting multiple items.

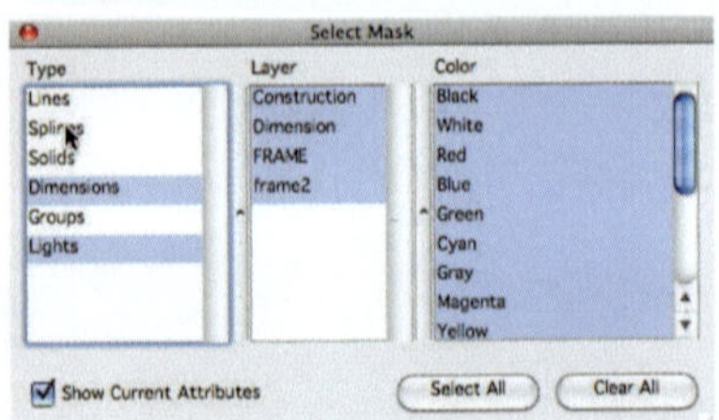

Figure 1.2 – Select Mask

How can I add specific types to the current Select Mask?

You can add or remove items to the Select Mask by pressing the appropriate key listed below while moving your mouse down.

- On a Mac: Hold down the Apple key.

- On a PC: Hold down the Control key.

Can I select an entire object by boxing just a portion of it?

Yes, to select an object you simply need to form a selection fence by pressing and holding the left button while moving from **right to left** over the object. This will select the entire object even if only a portion of it lies in the selection fence.

Here the blue selection fence only includes a portion of the circle.

Upon release, the entire circle is selected. However, the line is not selected, as no portion of it lay in the selection fence.

Figure 1.3 –Box Selection

How can I select one object when it's already part of a group?

To select nested objects, such as objects within groups, use the *Select Deep* tool.

You could use this tool, for example, if you wanted to change the pen properties of a particular object within a group. In Figure 1.4 below, the outer lines of a group are selected and changed to a different color.

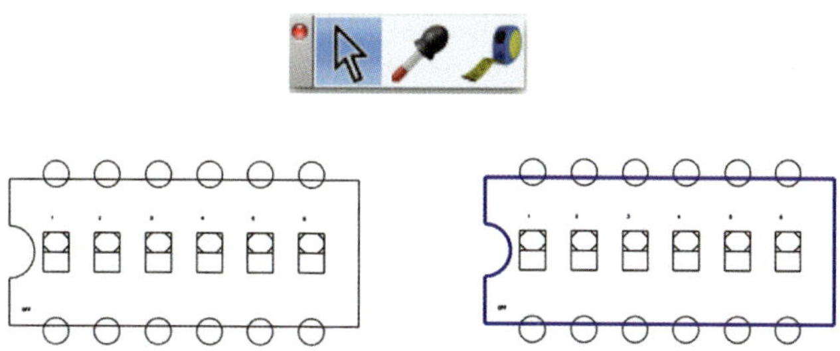

Figure 1.4 – Use Select Deep tool to select nested objects

Is it possible to select a specific face and change its color?

Yes, use the *Select Deep* tool and pick the face you want to change. Then select the desired color from the Pen Attributes tab found in the Inspector dialog box.

Don't forget you can hold down the Shift key if you would like to select multiple faces.

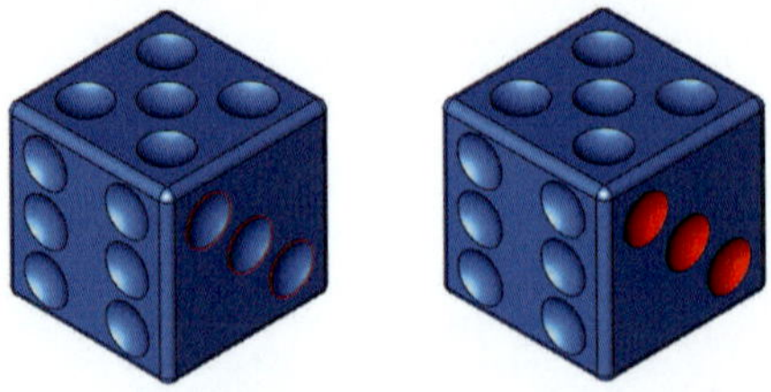

Figure 1.5 – Using Select Deep tool to select a face

How can I move overlapped object end points?

- Method 1: One option is to hide the object you do not want to move using the *Hide* tool and then use the *Show tool* when you're done modifying.
- Method 2: Another option is to use *Select Deep* tool with the following steps below:

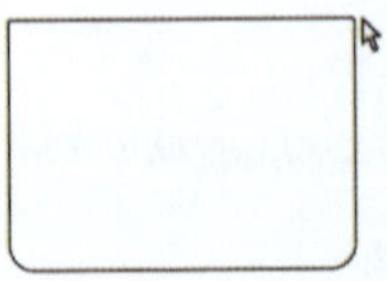

Step 1: Pick the *Select Deep* tool and click on the point you want to move.

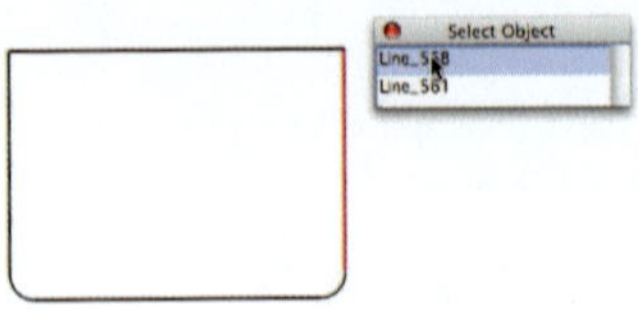

Step 2: After you click on the shared endpoint, the ambiguity dialog box will appear displaying the two objects by name.

Step 3: Select the object you want to move. In this case, Line 558 should be selected.

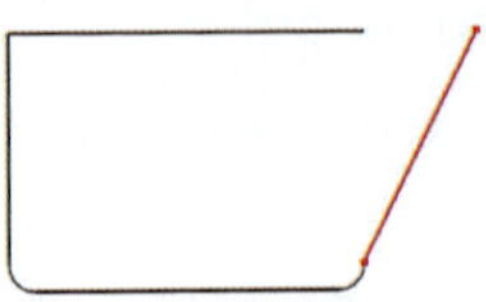

Step 4: Press and hold the mouse down and move the desired line end point to a new location

Why does Select Chain sometimes fail with the Extrude Solid tool?

Be sure to hold down the Shift key when choosing the first curve and continue to hold down the Shift key until you select the Select Chain option from the Edit menu. If you fail to do this, you will get the "Curves not planar" or "Gaps Detected" error dialog box.

You can avoid hitting the Shift key by moving your cursor over one of the curves and pressing the right button. This will display a popup menu with the "Select Chain" option. This will select the curve your mouse is over in addition to chained curves.

Modifying Objects

How can I nudge objects using the Arrow keys?

- First, go to the Preferences dialog box. For PC users, Preferences is found under File on your Menu Bar. For Mac users, Preferences can be found under Application on your Menu Bar.
- In Preferences, go to the General category.
- From the General menu, set the nudge distance to a non-zero value. Now pressing the Arrow keys will move selected objects the designated distance.

By pressing the Shift key with the Arrow key, you can multiply the nudge distance by 10.

Is it possible to modify an object's selected points by an explicit xyz value?

A lesser-known feature of the Verify XYZ command (found under Verify on the Menu Bar) is that it can be used not only to verify a location but also to modify that location. Thus, it is possible to modify an object's selected points by an explicit xyz value with this command.

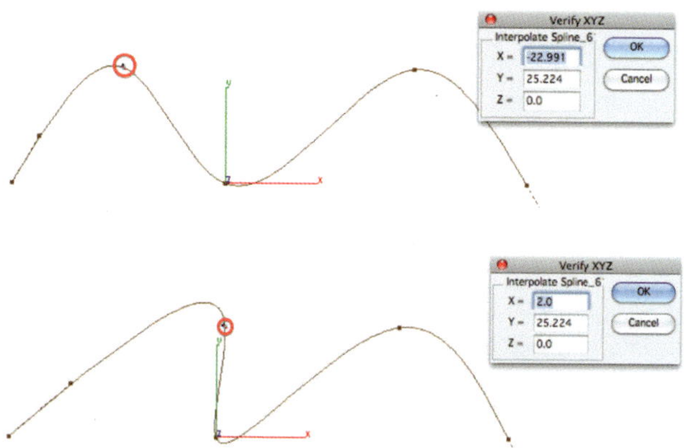

Figure 1.6 – Using Verify XYZ to move a selected point

Another method to modify an object's selected points by an explicit xyz value is to use the Gripper. Refer to the Gripper section for more information regarding this useful tool.

How can I display the Inspector?

The Inspector dialog box can be displayed by several different methods:

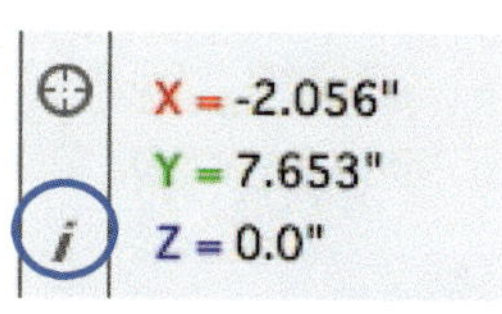

Figure 1.7 – Displaying the Inspector

- Method 1: Pressing the "i" symbol located to the left of the XYZ Cursor Location display.
- Method 2: Going to Window on the Menu Bar and selecting Inspector from the pull down menu.
- Method 3: Right clicking on an object and selecting Inspector from the pop up menu.

What are some of the features of the Inspector?

The Inspector tabs from left to right are:

- *Object Properties* - Change parameters of an object such as the line start or end point.
- *Pen Properties* - Change the color, line weight, or line style of an object.
- *Fill Properties* - Change the color or fill pattern associated with a polygon or hatched object.
- *Text Properties* - Change the text font, size, or style.
- *Dimension Properties* - Change the dimension attributes such as formatting and spacing.
- *Gripper Properties* - Change the size or location of the Gripper.

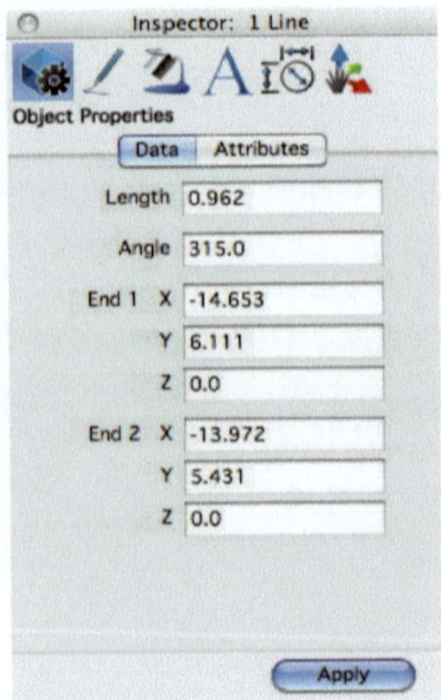

Figure 1.8 – Inspector Dialog Box

What does the Objects Properties tab do?

The Object Properties tab located in the Inspector serves two primary purposes:

1. It provides a means to inquire data parameters of attributes.
2. It allows you to edit data parameters of attributes.

The first purpose of the Object Properties tab is to display the current properties of the selected items, including information about lengths, angles, coordinates, patterns, weights, and arrowheads. If, for example, you wanted to find the radius of a circle on the screen, or if you wanted to know what layer a particular arc is on, you would simply select the object and read the information in the tab.

Did You Know?

The Object Properties dialog box does not go away after you press the Apply button; it remains open so that you can select new items and edit them as necessary.

Whenever more than one object is selected, the tab will display all the fields that contain data that is common to all selected objects. For instance, if you were to select a line and a circle and then open the Object Properties tab, you would see attributes that are common to both objects but no other information.

The second purpose of the tab is to modify object attributes. If you wanted to change the weight of a line, for example, you would change the value of weight in the Object Properties data entry field and hit the Apply button.

What does a blank field in the Object Properties dialog box mean?

If you have more than one object selected, common fields with different values will be blank. If all the selected objects share a common value, that value will be displayed. This is shown in Figure 1.9 below in which two lines share the same length but not the same angle or endpoints. The common value of 5 is displayed while the other fields appear blank in this example.

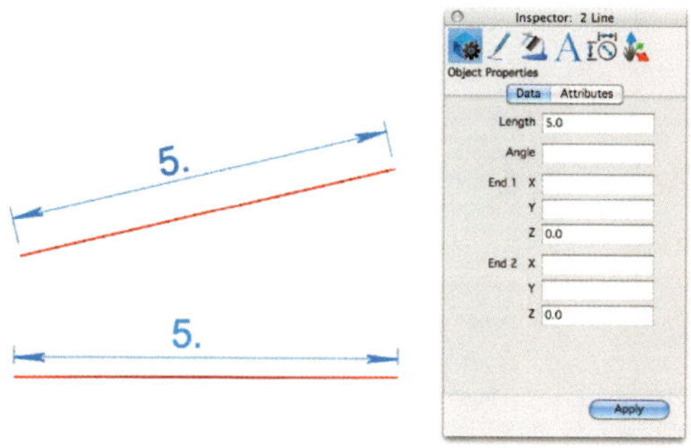

Figure 1.9

What does the * symbol mean in a dialog box?

The * symbol indicates that you can digitize a point in your drawing and have the xyz location of that digitized point automatically filled into the dialog box.

For example, the Linear Duplicate dialog box shown in Figure 1.10 below uses several * fields to define the Offset and Spacing values. If you click on the * in the Offset X text field and then move your cursor over into the drawing area, you can calculate the difference between the two digitized points that you select. This distance (1 inch in the example below) will automatically be filled into the Offset X, Offset Y, and Offset Z text fields.

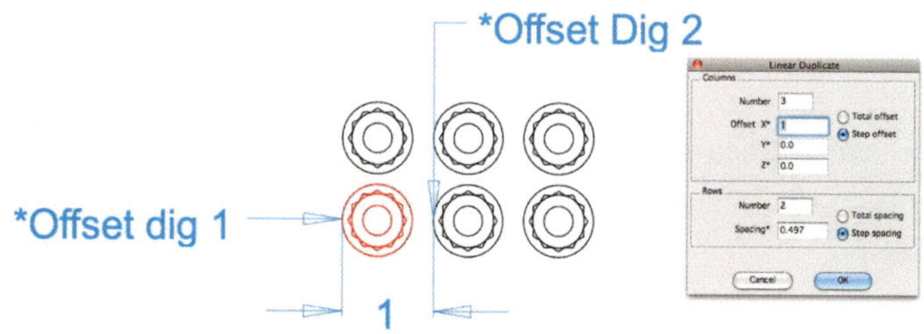

Figure 1.10

What can I type into a text field?

Text fields allow you to type data into dialog boxes. Something many users may not know is that text fields also accept mathematical, trigonometric, and exponential operators in the forms shown in Table 1.1. These operators can be used to edit objects, make entries in the Status Line, and specify values in dialog boxes.

Math operators are case-sensitive so be sure to type them in **lower case** when you use them.

Table 1.1

Operator	Example	Operator	Example
Addition	3+.450	Log (Base 10)	log(7.25)
Subtraction	3 - .500	Natural Log	ln(8.5)
Multiplication	3*.725	Remove Fractional Part	truncate(6.125)
Division	3/5.25	Absolute Value	abs(-47+16)
Square Root	sqrt(8.75)	Smallest Larger Integer	ceiling(5.25)
Parenthetical	3/(5*2/4)	Largest Smaller Integer	floor(12.75)
Scientific Notation	4e3	Negative Value	neg(11.12)
Sine of Angle	sin(15)	Round	round(11.12)
Cosine of Angle	cos(30)	Random #	rnd(3)
Arctangent	atan(30)	Fraction	1 1/2 + 3/4

Is there another way to quickly delete objects?

Yes, rather than selecting the item before hitting the Delete key, hold the Delete key down **first**. Then, select an item using the *Arrow* tool, and the object will be deleted from the drawing. In this manner, you can delete multiple objects very quickly by eliminating a keystroke for each delete operation.

This feature works equally well with fence-selections. Beginning with all objects deselected, hold down the Delete key and drag a Selection Fence around a group of objects you wish to delete. As soon as the mouse is released, the objects in the fence will disappear.

You can mix-and-match fence-selections and clicking to delete objects.

The Gripper

The Gripper is an intuitive, graphical widget that assists you in translating, rotating, and scaling an object freely in 2D or 3D space. In addition to freely moving your object, the Gripper also provides precision movements through the Data Entry Field.

How do I enable the Gripper?

The Gripper is enabled via the last tab in the Inspector dialog box. Enabling the Gripper turns on a graphical coordinate system that attaches to selected objects. The Gripper box also provides options for filtering out movements and setting the size.

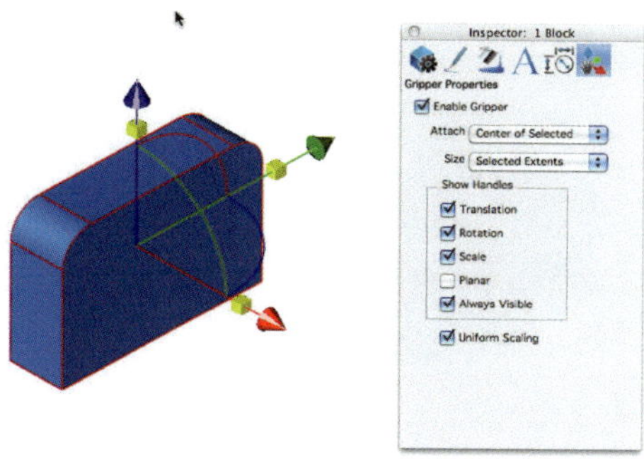

Figure 1.11

What do each of the Gripper handles do?

The Gripper displays nine different handles for different operations. For example, it displays arrows for translation, squares for scaling, and arcs for rotation. Pressing over one of these graphics activates its particular function.

How can I control the Gripper axis?

By default the Gripper uses the "Center of Extents" axis attachment mode. If an object axis exists (as in a group), it will use that axis first.

Another option is to use the "User Axis" mode loacated under the Attachment menu pull down. This option allows you to specify the Gripper axis through modifying handles or through axis options like reset and align to object. This means with the "User Axis" you can specify the center of roation and adjust the scaling to be a location other than the center of extents.

What does the 'Object to Axis' option do?

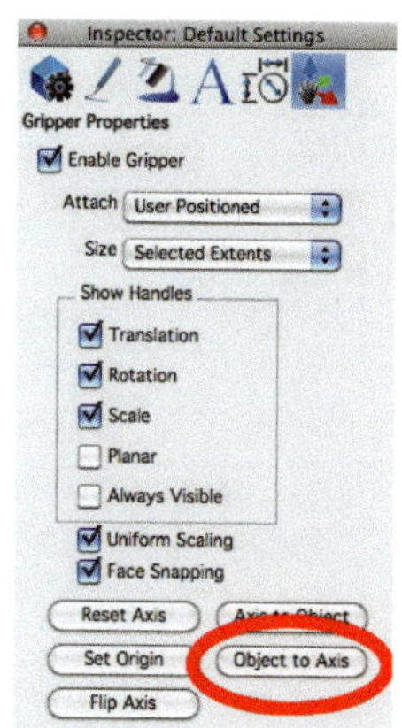

The Object to Axis command can be found under the Gripper properties tab when the Attach method is set to User Positioned. The location of the command is highlighted in Figure 1.12 to right.

This command allows you to transform an object from its coordinate system into the Gripper coordinate system. When using this tool on a solid, the object coordinate system is determined by whether you select an edge or face using the following rules:

- Edge — Edge is aligned to the Gripper's x-axis.
- Cylinder Face — Cylinder axis is aligned to the Gripper's

- x-axis
- Planar Face — Face normal is aligned with the Gripper's x-axis.
-

Figure 1.12 – Object to Axis Command

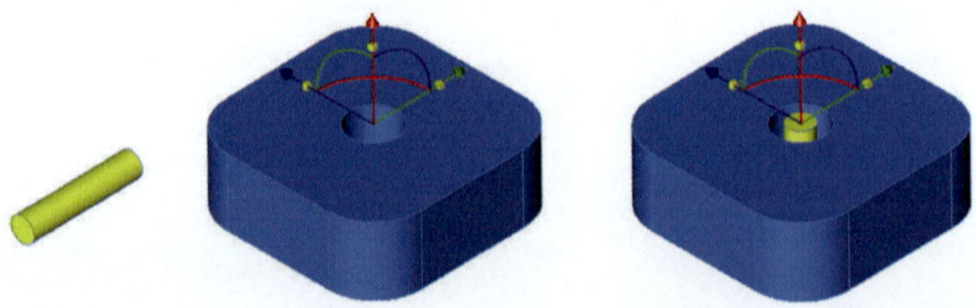

Before Object to Axis *After Object to Axis*

Figure 1.13

What does the 'Axis to Object' option do?

The Axis to Object command can be found under the Gripper Properties tab when the Attach method is set to User Positioned. The location of the command is highlighted in Figure 1.14 to left.

The Axis to Object command allows you to set the Gripper's axis to an object's axis. By default, the Griper's axis attaches to the object's center of extents, parallel to the *global* coordinate system. By using the Axis to Object command, the Gripper axis will now align itself with the *object's* coordinate system. Therefore, this command is useful for performing translations and rotations relative to the object. Figure 1.15 below illustrates this difference.

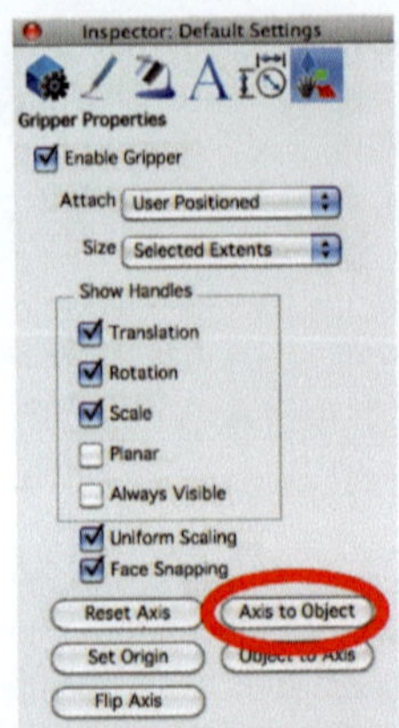

Figure 1.14 – Axis to Object Command

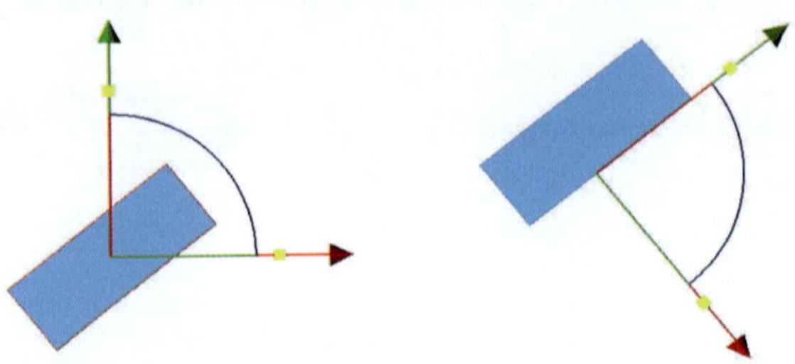

The default axis aligned to global coordinate system. *The Gripper's axis aligned to the object's coordinate system*

Figure 1.15

How can I rotate a face with the Gripper?

Use the *Deep Select* tool to pick a face to rotate. Then, perform a rotate using one of the Gripper's red arc rotation handles.

You can precisely rotate a face by first clicking without dragging on the rotation handle and then typing in a value into the Data Entry Window.

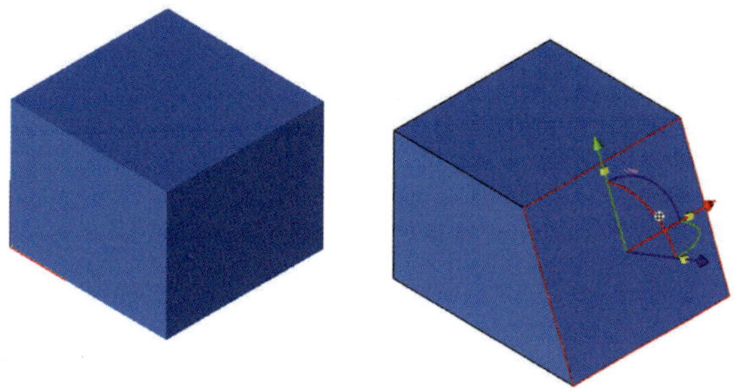

How can I copy a feature with the Gripper?

Use the *Deep Select* tool to select the faces associated with the feautres you want to copy. Then, hold down a copy key and drag the faces to a new location. Upon release, the copied faces are merged into the body.

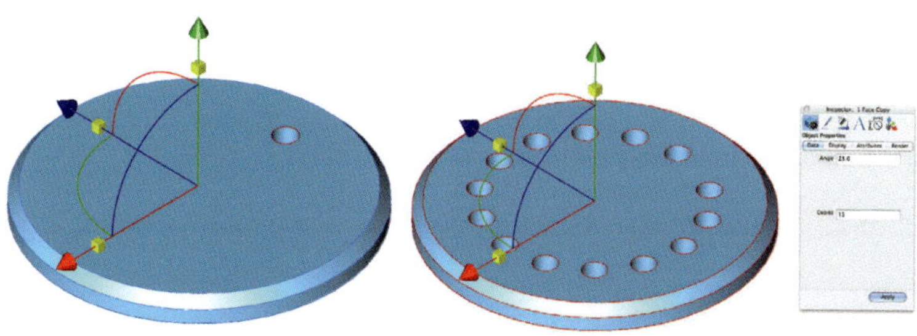

Figure 1.16

After you copy faces, you can go to the Data Entry Window to do a linear or polar array.

WorkPlanes

A WorkPlane assists you with creating objects in 3D. The WorkPlane defines the coordinate system associated with planar objects such as polygons, circles, and ellipses. A collection of tools for manipulation and displaying WorkPlanes can be found under the menu bar.

How can I see my current WorkPlane orientation?

To see the current orientation of the WorkPlane, go to your menu and select WorkPlane Show. Figure 1.17 is the graphical symbol for a WorkPlane aligned with the xy plane.

The Grid is always displayed with respect to the WorkPlane orientation.

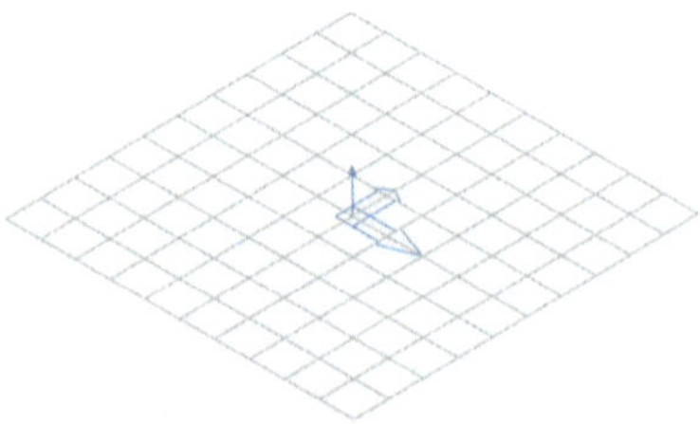

Figure 1.17 – WorkPlane Grid

How do snaps work in reference to the WorkPlane?

Snaps are projected into the WorkPlane unless they reference another object point or alignment.

Can I align the WorkPlane to a curve?

Yes, to align the WorkPlane to a curve move your cursor over a curve until LogiCursor indicates you are on, and then press the "C" key. This will extract the tangent from the curve the cursor is over and assign it as the WorkPlane normal. Hitting the "C" key toggles the WorkPlane through the below orientations:

1. Top
2. Right Side
3. Front
4. Viewing Plane
5. Perpendicular to Curve

How can I change the WorkPlane?

Select an edge or endpoint of any object and then press the "C" key to either see what your current WorkPlane is or to change the work plane.

Pressing the "C" key repeatedly flips from one plane to the next.

Snaps

How can I lock my snaps to a specific axis?

Press the "X", "Y", or "Z" key to constrain the snap along the x, y, or z alignment axis.

Where can I adjust snap settings for LogiCursor?

You can adjust snap settings such as the radii and angles of your snaps in the Snap dialog box. This dialog is found under Preferences. (For PC Users, Preferences can be found under File on your Menu Bar. For Mac Users, this is under Application on your Menu Bar).

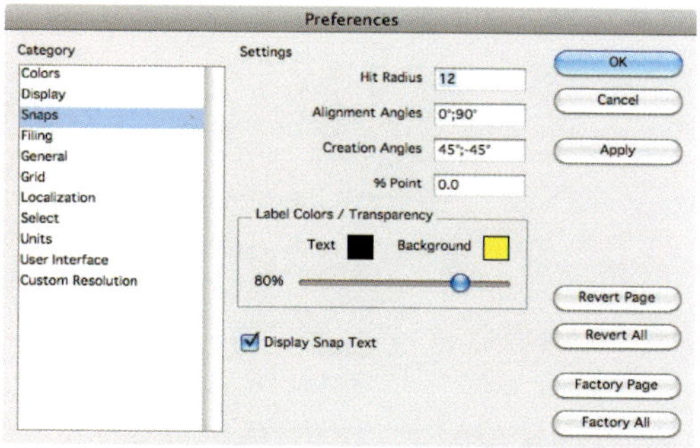

Figure 1.18 – Snap dialog box

Mac Users can also use this tool to adjust background color, transparency, and text color for snap text.

Where can I change the snap filters?

In addition to adjusting snap settings in the Snap Dialog box, you can also turn on and off snap filters here. This includes endpoints, midpoints, centers, and along axis construction lines.

How can I find the apparent intersection of two lines?

You can find the apparent intersection of any two curves using the Apparent Intersection snap option found in the Snaps tool palette. This is accessed from the Snaps item located under Window on your Menu Bar. Simply select the option and then pick two curves.

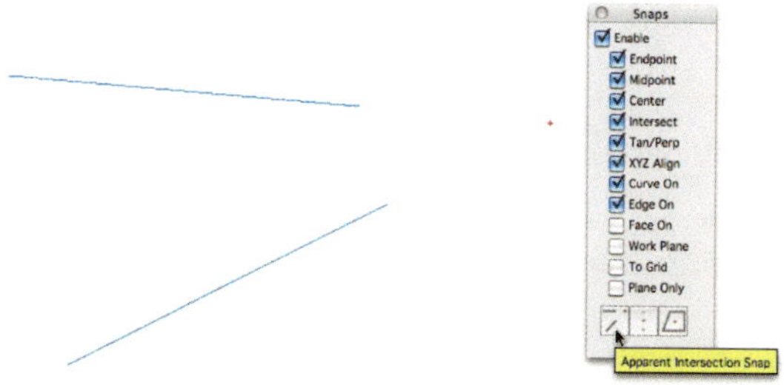

Figure 1.19 – Using the Apparent Intersection Snap feature

The curves do not need to be lines. As shown in Figure 1.20 below, you can use other curve types such as splines and arcs. The apparent intersection is the intersection of the extended tangents.

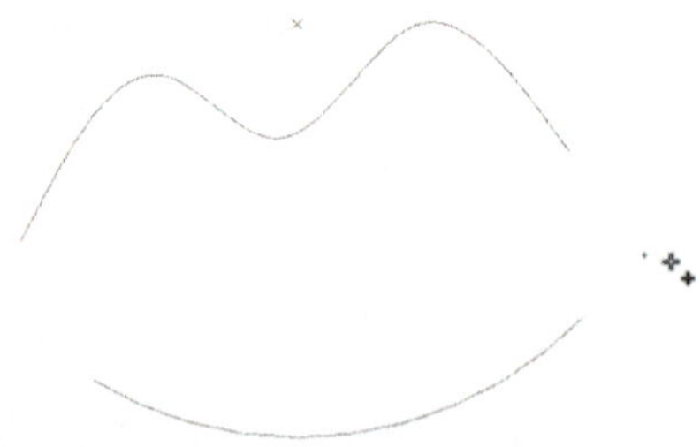

Figure 1.20 – Finding Apparent Intersection of Splines and Arcs

Can I toggle snaps using a shortcut?

Snaps can be toggled on and off using a shortcut key. To assign a key for snap toggling, select File : Shortcuts and next select the Snap category. From the Command list, select the Enable option and assign the desired shortcut.

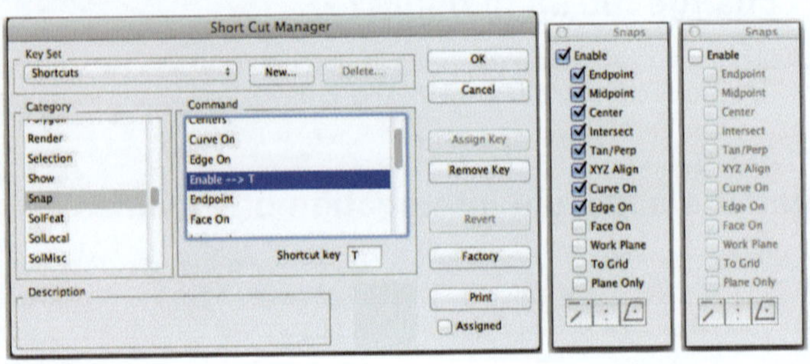

Tool Palettes

How do I tear away tool palettes?

The Main Tool Palette has tear away tool palettes indicated by icons with an arrow in the lower right corner. Press, hold, and move the mouse to tear away a tool palette.

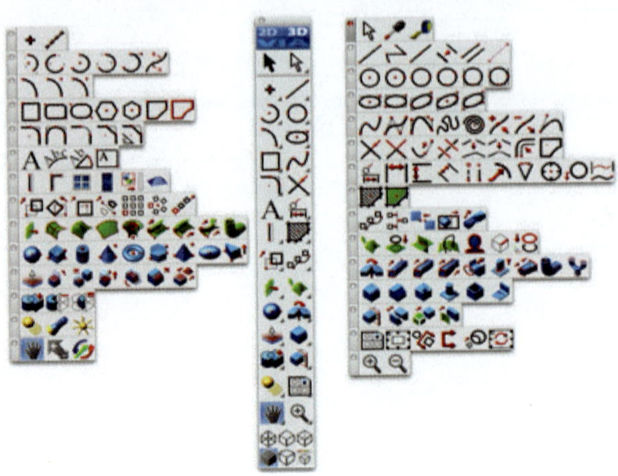

Figure 1.21 – The Main Tool Palette shown with the palette tear offs

Tool palette positions are remembered from session to session.

How do I collapse tool palettes?

In order to collapse a palette, right click on the title bar of any tool palette. You will receive a menu of options that control palette collapsing. This menu can be seen in Figure 1.23 on the following page; the options for palette collapsing have been highlighted with a red box in this figure. Figure 1.22 displays a collapsed palette.

Figure 1.22– Collapsed Palette

Palette Collapse will automatically open and close a window to its title bar as you move the mouse into the window.

How can I control the orientation of my tool palettes?

To control the horizontal or vertical orientation of the palette, you can right click on the title bar of any tool palette. You will receive a menu of options that will allow you to control the horizontal or vertical orientation of the palette. Figure 1.23 illustrates this menu and highlights the orientation options in blue.

> **Did You Know?**
>
> To assist you in quickly identifying a tool, icons in the tool palette are color-coded.
>
> Curve icons are **black**.
>
> Surface icons are **green**.
>
> Solid icons are **blue**.

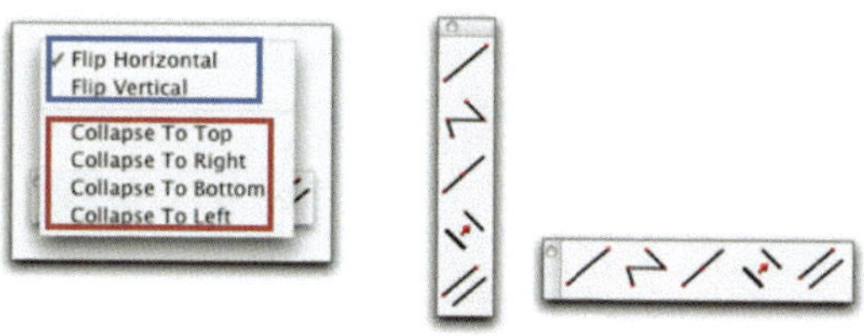

Figure 1.23

Is there a way to neatly align tool palette edges?

To improve your organization, you can drag palettes next to each other to snap them together. This can be seen below in Figure 1.24, in which the palettes for line, solid primitives, solid from profiles, and feature based solids have been snapped together.

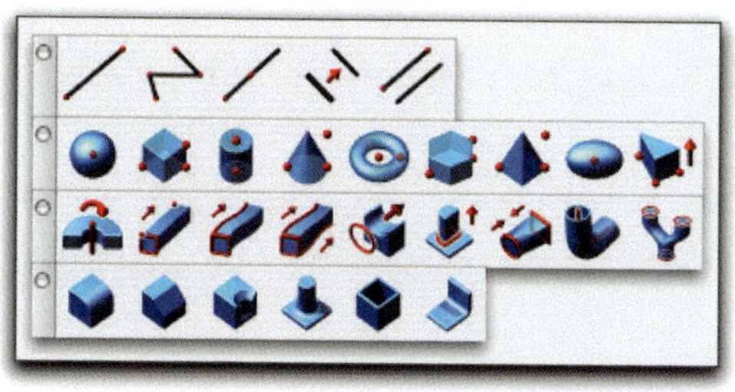

Figure 1.24 – Snapped palettes

After switching from two monitors to one, I've lost my tool palettes!

If you work on a laptop and sometimes work with an external display connected, you may lose all your palettes when you move from the two-screen setup to a one-screen setup or change the multi monitor layout. This is because the palettes are still located on the second monitor and are no longer available.

- To fix this, go to the Preferences dialog and select the General category.
- From these options, press the Factory Page button.
- This will reset all palette locations to the center of your main display.

How can I display more colors in the Pen Palette?

By hitting "More" at the bottom of the Pen Palette, you can choose from more colors. This option displays a floating palette with four-color palette size options. Clicking the expand button will change the palette to display 16, 64, 128, and 256 colors (PC Only).

You can modify the last color by double clicking on a color and specifying a new color. The colors in the palate are defined in the RGB.txt file located in the application Environ folder.

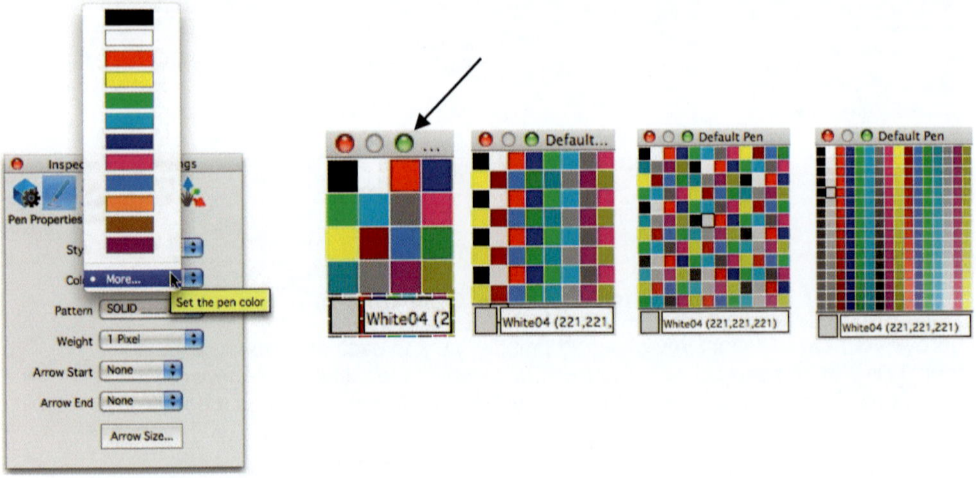

Figure 1.25 – By clicking on the green expand button, different palette sizes can be displayed

Preferences

How do I save my Preferences as Defaults?

- First, open up a new sheet with no geometry or hidden layers on it. This is very important, as these can cause the Preference file to slow-down drawings or even corrupt the file.
- Next, make the changes to the variables desired.
- Then, go to Layout.
- Select Preferences.
- Finally, choose the Save Preferences option.

The Preferences that have just been saved will **not** take effect until you restart the program.

How can I make user defined layers and views present for new drawings?

The startup.dat file is a great place to store user defined views, layers, and pen styles that you would like available in every session. When ViaCAD launches, it looks for the presence of this file and if there, ViaCAD reads its contents into the program. To create a startup.dat file, launch ViaCAD and create your designer views and layers. Save the file and rename to startup.dat. Move this file the appropriate platform specific folder listed below.

Mac: /Applications/ViaCAD 2D3D 9.app/Contents/Resources/startup.dat

PC: /Program Files (x86)/Punch! Software/ViaCAD Pro 9/exe/startup.dat

Be sure to replace the product name folder with either ViaCAD 2D, ViaCAD 2D3D, or ViaCAD Pro.

Can I transfer my keyboard shortcuts to another machine?

Yes, to quickly transfer your keyboard shortcuts from one system to another, or when you upgrade, copy the file >VC3Shortcuts.ini< to:

- On a Mac:

  ViaCAD 2D
  /Users/<yourlogin>/Library/Application Support/com.encore.viacad3dv9/VC2Shortcuts.ini
  ViaCAD 2D3D
  /Users/<yourlogin>/Library/Application Support/com.encore.viacad2dv9/VC3Shortcuts.ini
  ViaCAD Pro
  /Users/<yourlogin>/Library/Application Support/com.encore.viacadprov9/VCPShortcuts.ini

- On Windows:

  ViaCAD 2D
  c:\ Documents and Settings\<yourlogin>\Local Settings\Application Data\Punch!\ViaCAD2D

ViaCAD 2D3D
c:\ Documents and Settings\<yourlogin>\Local Settings\Application Data\Punch!\ViaCAD

ViaCAD Pro
c:\ Documents and Settings\<yourlogin>\Local Settings\Application Data\Punch!\ViaCADPro

To maintain custom palettes and the position of all your palettes, copy the file >VC3Dialogs.ini<.

How can I find out if a tool is assigned a shortcut?

To find out exactly what a tool is called so that you can find it in the Shortcut manger, hold your mouse over the tool until a tool tip comes up with the name of the tool.

It will also display any keyboard shortcut that has already been assigned to it.

For example, Figure 1.26 below demonstrates that by holding the mouse over the *Single Line* tool, you can see the tool name and shortcut key.

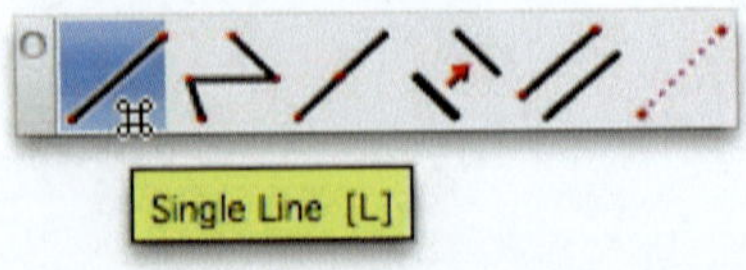

Figure 1.26 – Hitting the "L" key will activate the Single Line Tool

How do I assign a function key to a shortcut?

Function keys require some special processing to assign. Instead of hitting the function key, type in "F" then type the associated number into the Shortcut key text box.

For example, to assign the F12 to a short cut, type "F", "1", and "2".

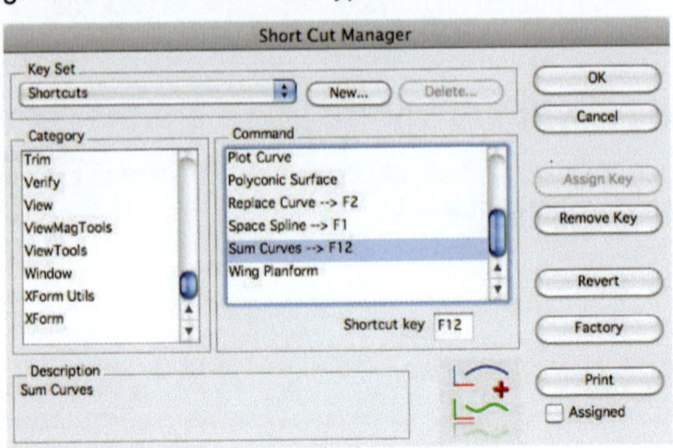

Figure 1.27

Can I make the Main Tool Palette smaller?

There are some screen resolution configurations, such as with a projector, in which the vertical resolution does not fit the Main Tool Palette. By following the below steps, you can still make the tool palette fit on the screen:

- Begin by going to Preferences.
- Next, select the User Interface category from the options listed in the Preferences dialog box.
- Check the box marked "Use Small Palette icons" and click Apply.

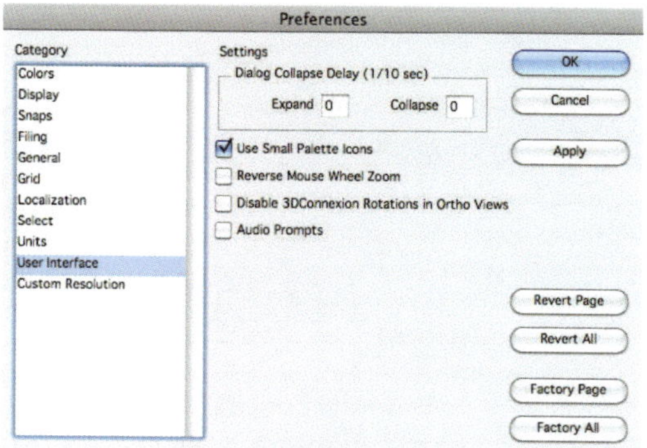

Figure 1.28

How do I show the file paths under recently opened files?

At the bottom of the File menu, after all other commands, there is a list of recently opened files. It is possible not only to show the names of these recently opened files but also their paths.

- First, if you are a PC user, go to File. If you are a Mac user, go to Application.
- Then, go to Preferences.
- Next, choose Filing from the Category list.
- Then, in the Recent Files Menu, check the Show Paths box.
- With this box checked, press OK and click on File again. You'll see that the paths of the files now appear at the bottom of the pull down.

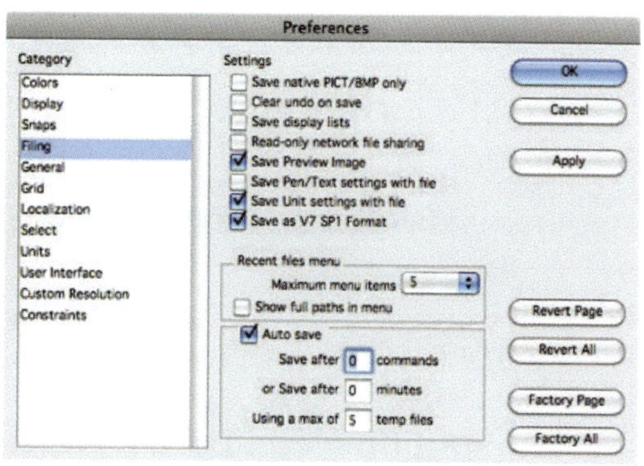

Figure 1.29 – Setting up BackUp recovery capability

You can change the maximum number of files listed from the default of 5.

How can I set up BackUp files?

ViaCAD's automatic backup can save you in situations when your current file has become damaged.

The first thing that you must do is ensure you have turned on "AutoSave". If you don't have AutoSave setting turned on, there will be nothing to recover. To turn on AutoSave:

- Go to Filing found under Preferences.
- From here, turn on Auto save. This creates a copy of your file according to your trigger option. Trigger options can be a number of commands or time.

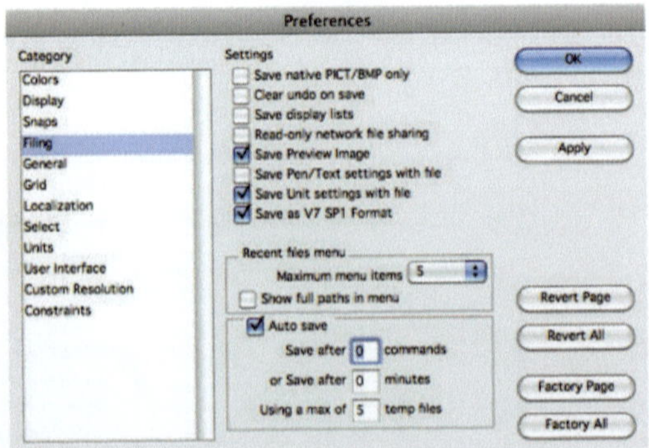

Figure 1.29 – Setting up BackUp recovery capability

After you have set up AutoSave, ViaCAD will automatically backup your files. These backup files can be located in your user documents folder in the ViaCAD folder. The back up file name is of the format: filename.bk0.v3d, filename.bk1.v3d, filename.bk2.v3d, etc.

Products purchased through the Apple App store have AutoSave disabled to meet App store requirements.

Where are the BackUp files located?

BackUp files are located in the user folders listed below.

Mac
/Users/<accountname>/Library/Application Support/com.encore.viacad3dv9/BackUp
/Users/<accountname>/Library/Application Support/com.encore.viacadprov9/BackUp

Windows
C:\Users\<accountname>\Documents\Punch!\ViaCAD Pro\Backup
C:\Users\<accountname>\Documents\Punch!\ViaCAD\Backup

Layers

When and how can I drag and drop layers?

You can drag and drop layers to re-order them but only when the layers are at the same level or in the same layer group.

To drag layers, press the Shift key. Then click and drag the layer.

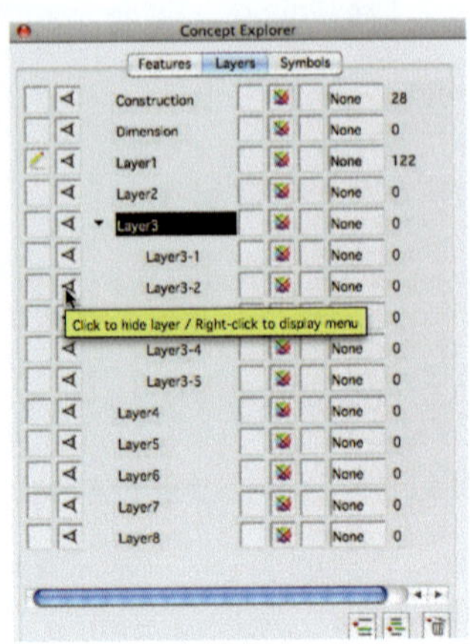

Can I suspend the repaint update when turning on/off layers?

Yes. Simply hold down the Shift key when you press on/off layer.

Is there a suggested technique for managing sketches used for solids?

If you need to create 2D sketch geometry in order to make a solid or surface, try to create the geometry and the solid/surface on two different sub layers so that you can easily hide the sketch geometry without having to select each item individually.

Ideally, use a structure such as this:

Figure 1.30 - Layers

- Item A
- Item A Solid
- Item A Sketch Geometry

If your construction layer starts to become crowded, you may need to create additional layers. The sub layer button is located in the lower right corner of the layer manager.

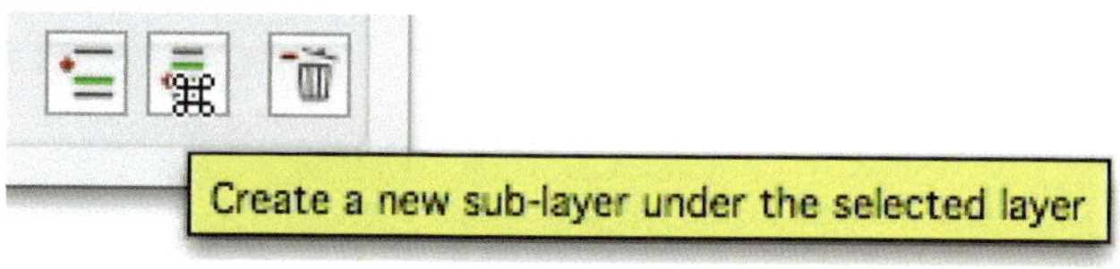

Figure 1.31 – Sub layer button

Performance

Does resolution impact performance?

For large files, the resolution you choose will impact your repaint (screen refresh) performance. Generally, your repaint performance in controlled by the number of vectors and facets (used to represent surfaces & solids) that make up the visible drawing.

If you want to know how many vector segments and facets make up the drawing:

- Go to Verify on your Menu Bar.
- Select Object Counts. This will show you the curve and facet display list sizes.

The numbers displayed represent the approximate memory and actual counts. In the image below, there are 15,535 facets composing the drawing.

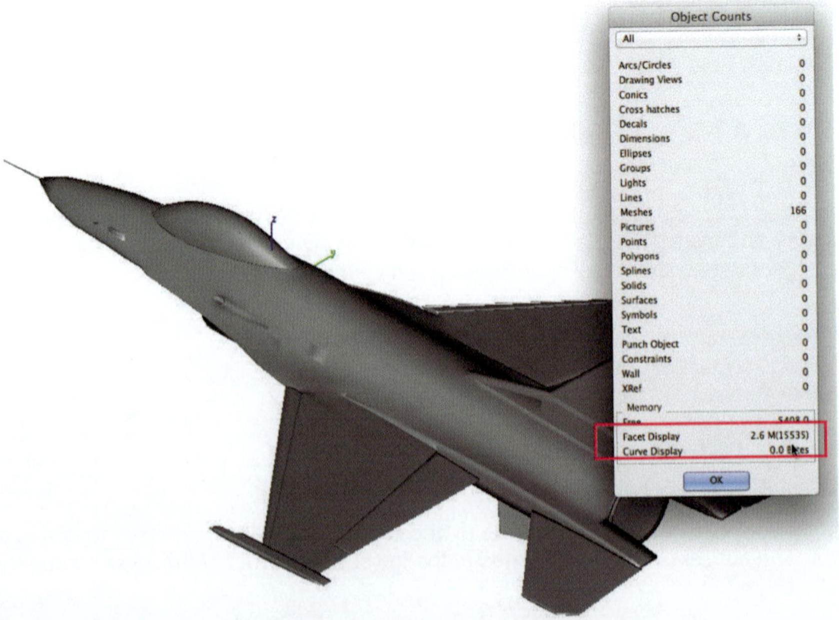

How do silhouette edges impact performance?

A silhouette edge separates the front of a face from the back of a face and is view dependent. Displaying silhouette edges improves the visual interpretation of a model. However, as the silhouette needs be updated for every view orientation change, it does impact performance.

You can turn off this calculation through the Inspector Display page for an entity. From here, you can select the Off option under Silhouette Editing.

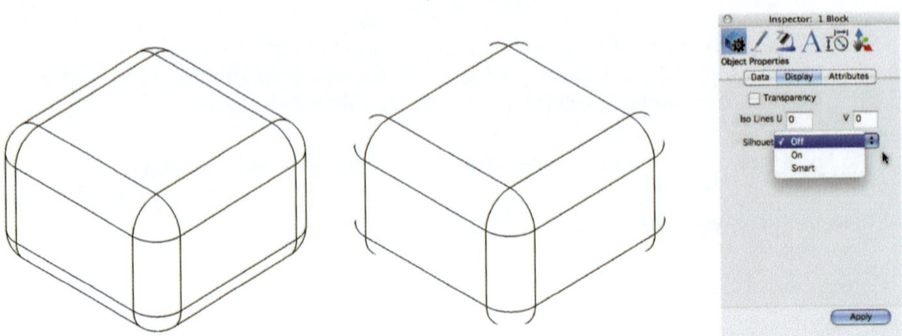

(a) On (b) Off (c) Silhouette Editing

Figure 1.32 – Silhouette Edge Display

Since the view orientation does not change in a zoom or pan operation, performance is not impacted with these viewing operations. Spline surface silhouettes are not calculated due to performance reasons.

Does anti-alias impact performance?

Anti-Aliasing is a graphic technique of blending lines drawn to the screen to reduce stair-stepping or jagged appearance. In areas of pixel transitions, the edges are blended to give a smoother appearance. While anti-alias is a great tool for reducing the jagged appearance of lines, this feature can impact your display speed performance. The amount will vary on your graphics board but could result in as high as a 15% performance penalty.

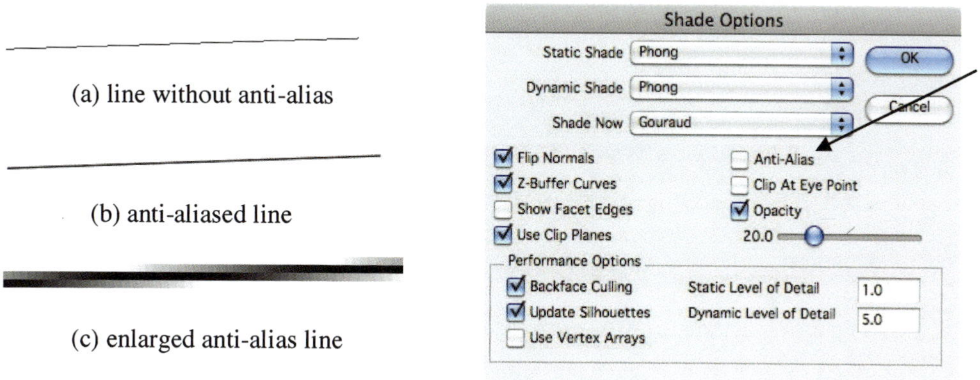

(a) line without anti-alias

(b) anti-aliased line

(c) enlarged anti-alias line

Figure 1.33 – Anti-Alias

Is it possible to reduce the disk space required by ViaCAD?

The symbol library folder takes up a great deal of disk space (approximately 1 GB). This folder contains a large collection of symbols for AEC, Electrical, Mechanical, and Process Plant & Piping categories. You can delete this folder if you have no need of these symbols to reduce the disk space required by ViaCAD.

What does the spinning rainbow cursor on Mac imply? 

The rainbow cursor is displayed by the Mac OS when an application does not acknowledge events sent by the operating system after 5 seconds. It is not a cursor displayed by the application. This typically implies an intense calculation, disk operation, or low memory situation.

Concept Explorer

What is Concept Explorer?

Concept Explorer is a dialog user interface that provides access to the Layer Manager, Feature Tree, and Symbol Manager.

Concept Explorer is turned on/off from the Menu bar under Window.

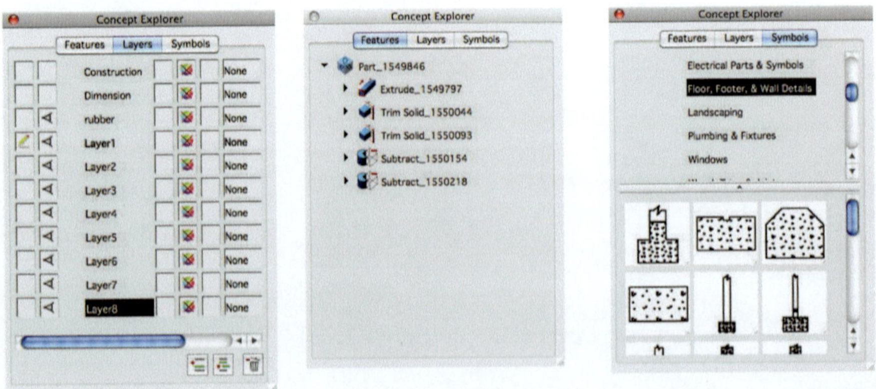

Figure 1.34 Concept Explorer

How do I filter the objects that are displayed in the Feature Tree?

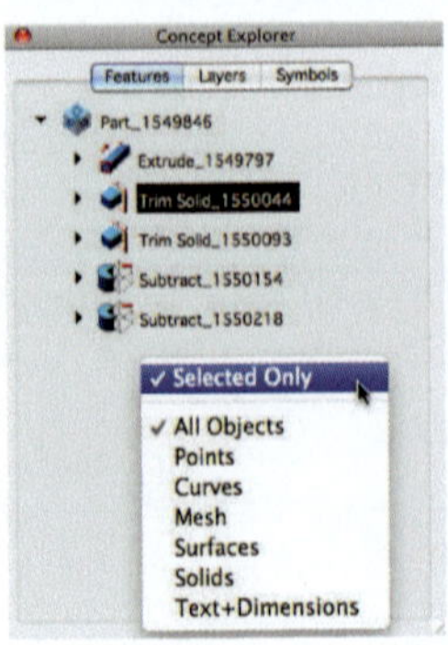

The default behavior of the Feature Tree is to display only selected objects. However by right clicking in an empty area of the dialog box you can access a menu list to filter what is displayed.

If the dialog box is full of items and there is no empty place to click, press right button along with the shift button.

Figure 1.35 – Display Filters

Can I minimize the size of Concept Explorer?

Concept Explorer displays a large amount of information that can take up valuable screen space. To minimize the screen space Concept Explorer takes up you can right click in the title bar and minimize up to the title bar.

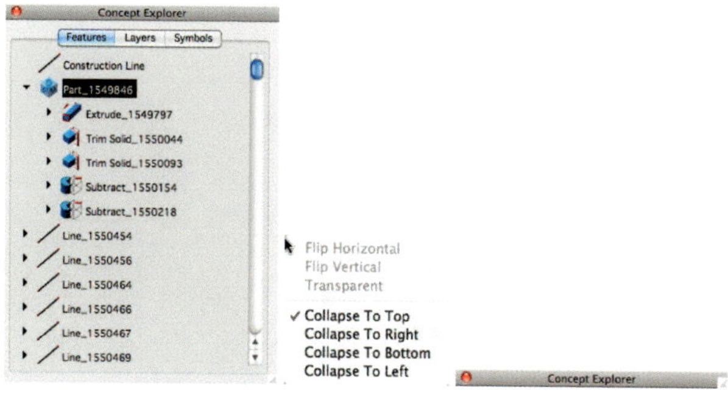

Figure 1.36 – Minimize to Title Bar

2 CHAPTER 2
DRAFTING

Overview

Drafting provides a collection of essential tools used to create and manipulate 2D objects such as curves, text, and annotations.

Text and Dimensions

How do I set text attributes such as font size, style, and color?

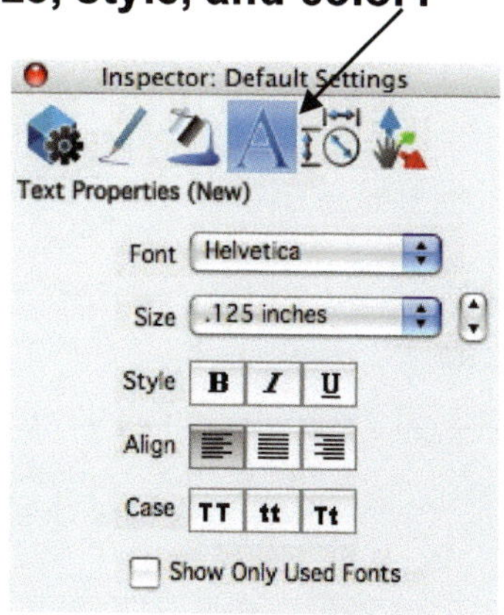

Figure 2.1 – Using Inspector to set text attributes

- To set font size, style, and color, show the Inspector.
- Select the Text tab, highlighted in Figure 2.1 to the right, to bring up the Text page.
- The Text page allows you to change the font type, size, and style attributes.
- If it says (New) after Text Properties, this means your assignments will apply to newly created Text objects.
- If it says (Selected), only the attributes of the selected Text objects will be changed.

A faster way to change your text attributes is to right click on the Text object. This will display a popup that can change the font, size, and style of the text.

How do I set the dimension font size?

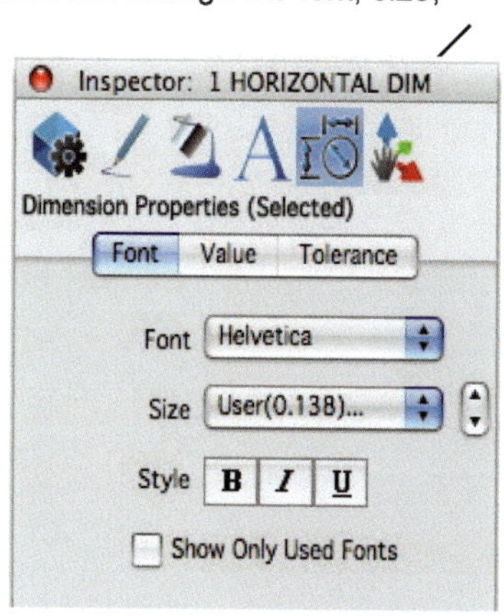

Figure 2.2 – Using Inspector to set dimension attributes

The Inspector contains a tab just for all the dimension settings including font size. This tab is highlighted in Figure 2.2 to the right.

- Select the dimension you want to change the font size for and then pick the desired size from the menu.

You can also right click on a dimension to change its font size, type, and style.

Can I copy text and dimension attributes from one object to another?

Yes, you can quickly copy text and dimension attributes from one object to another by using the *Eye Dropper* tool. This tool can be accessed from the tear away palette found in the top right corner of your main tool palette.

Attributes that can be copied include:

- Line Font
- Material
- Layer
- Photo Render
- Fonts
- Dimension Styles
- Wall Properties

Figure 2.3 – Eye Dropper tool

How can I filter which attributes get copied with the Eye Dropper tool?

- On a Mac: press the Option key with the *Eye Dropper* tool.
- On Windows: press the Control key with the *Eye Dropper* tool.
- This will display a dialog box that allows you to control the line, font, color, layer, and render material properties.

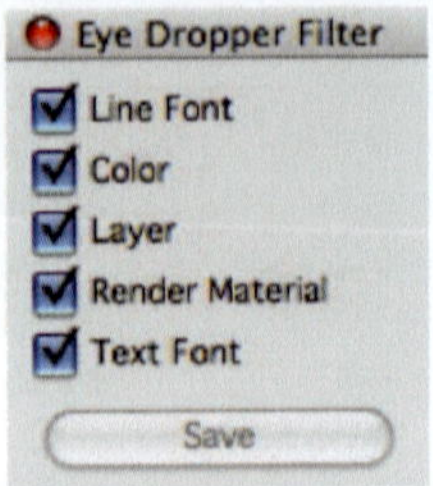

Figure 2.4 – Filtering with Eye Dropper

How can I align text of a dimension?

A quick technique for aligning dimension text is to use the *Align Tops* tools.

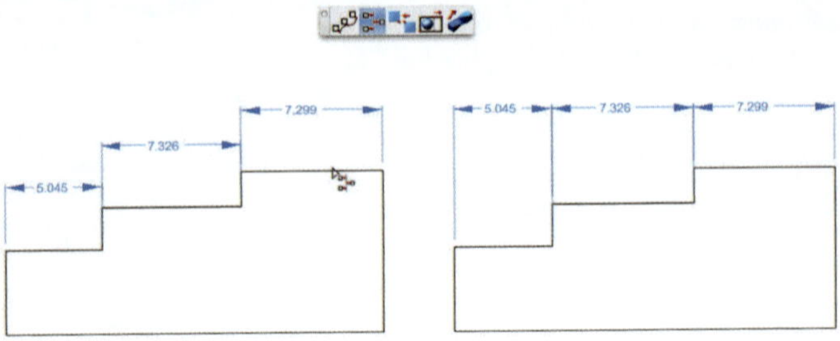

Figure 2.5 – Aligning dimension text with Align Tops tools

How can change the measured Dimension Value?

The dimension value is measured between the start and end leader points and converted into a text value based by default on your format settings.

- First, select the dimension and open up the Inspector dialog box.
- From there, select the Object Properties tabs. You will notice the text field displays the "#" symbol. The "#" symbol tells the application to use the measured value.
- Thus, to override this behavior, simply replace the # symbol with your desired text.

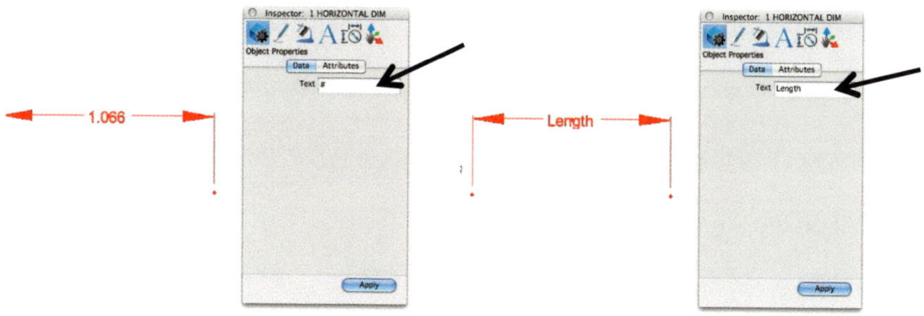

Figure 2.6 – Overriding Dimension Value

How can I insert text in front or behind the Dimension Value?

You can specify additional text to the dimension by placing it before or after the "#"symbol in the Inspector Object properties tab.

Figure 2.7- Adding Pre/Post dimension text using Inspector Object dialogue Box

How can I add multi-line text to a dimension?

You can add more lines of text just by typing " **\P** " after the " **#** " symbol in the Inspector Object Properties tab.

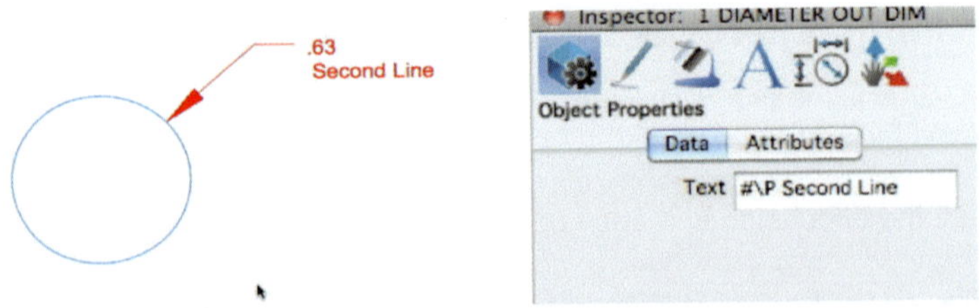

Figure 2.8- Adding Multi-Line Text using Inspector Object dialog box

How can I dimension a reflex angle?

The *Angular Dimension* tool always finds the angle less than 180 degrees. However, there are times when you may want to dimension the larger angle. After you've created your dimension, you can modify the position used to measure the angle by doing the following:

- Begin by selecting the dimension.
- Go to Edit on the Menu Bar.
- Select the Show Points command. This will show you the position used to measure the angle.
- Then move this point to the other side to change the measured angle.

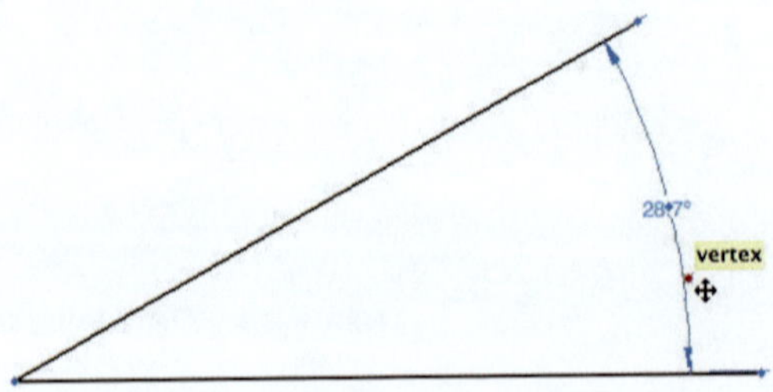

Figure 2.9 – Dimensioning a Reflex Angle

What is a stacked dimension?

Many architectural designers prefer to format their fractions as follows: ½. This version can be obtained using the fraction standard located in the Dimension Value tab of the Inspector.

Figure 2.10 – Standard Fraction

Mechanical designers prefer their fractions like this: $\frac{3}{8}$. The mechanical version is obtained by setting the standard to "Stacked Fraction" in the Dimension Value tab of the Inspector.

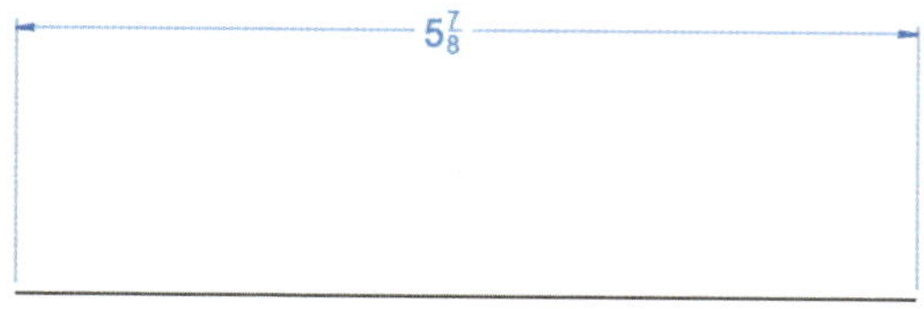

Figure 2.11 – Stacked Fraction

How can I make my text always horizontal to the screen?

By default all Text objects are displayed as 3D in isometric views by extracting the vectors from the glyphs and calculating a set of facets.

You can change this behavior to have your text always displayed perpendicular to the screen by setting the Screen Horiz check box inside the Inspector Objects properties attribute.

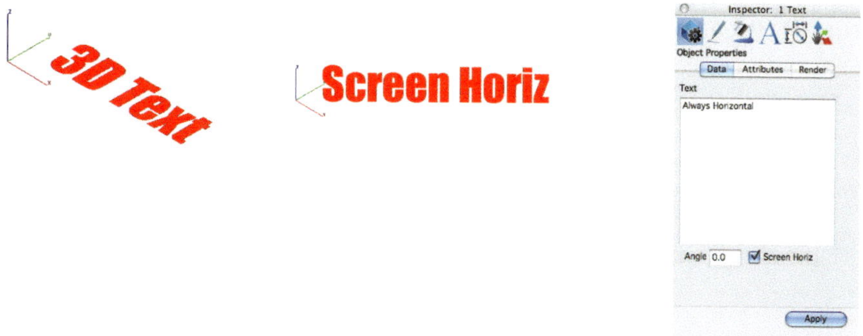

(a) Text in 3D (b) Text Always Horizontal (c) Screen Horiz Setting

Figure 2.12 – Adjusting text display

How can I control the draw order of text?

Normally objects are drawn in the order they are created. However there are times when you might like to control the order, especially with filled polygons and text.

- Select Arrange from the Edit menu
- Use the commands Send to Back and Bring to Front to arrange your objects' ordering.

Figure 2.13 – Controlling draw order

What does the "Scale value with text size" check box do?

The Scale Object with Text Size option is located in the Value Tab of the Dimension

Properties. This option will scale all dimension attributes such as arrowhead size, arrow leader, extension over, and extension gaps proportionally with the text size. For example, changing the text size from 10 to 20 will also scale up the arrowhead size by 2.

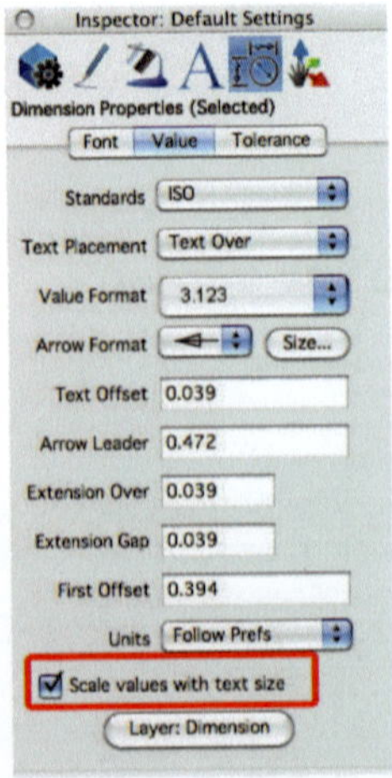

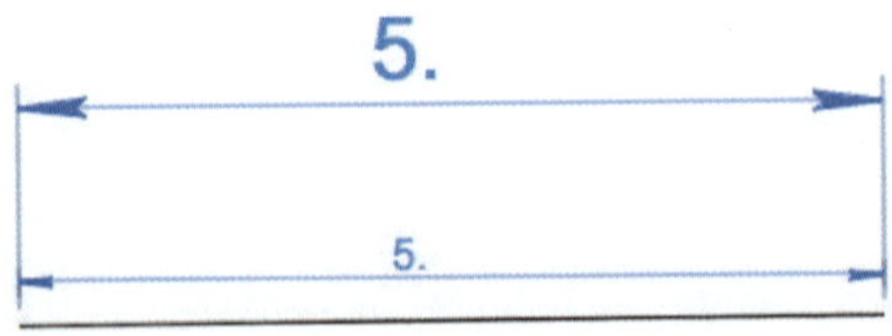

Figure 2.14 – Scaling values with text size

What objects can I use with the Smart Dimension tool?

You can select any curve, surface, or solid. What you select controls the dimension type created.

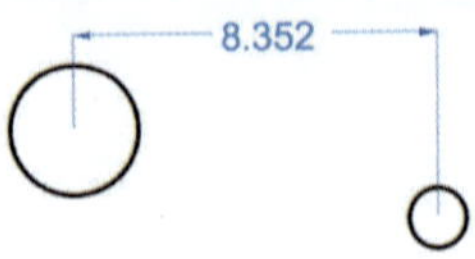

- *Center to Center* - Hold the Shift key and select two center points to measure the distance between two circle centers.

- *Minimum Distance* - Hold the Shift key and move your cursor until you see the "On" label to do a minimum distance dimension.

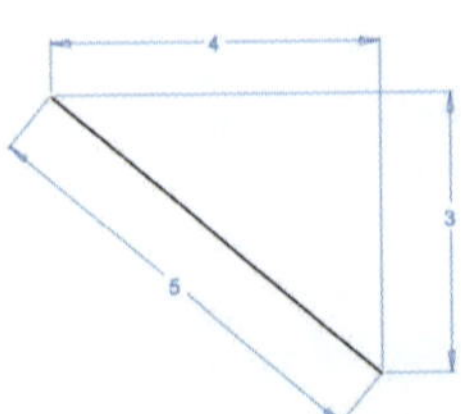

- *Line* – Click on the line and move your cursor to automatically create a horizontal, vertical, or parallel dimension based on the location of your cursor.

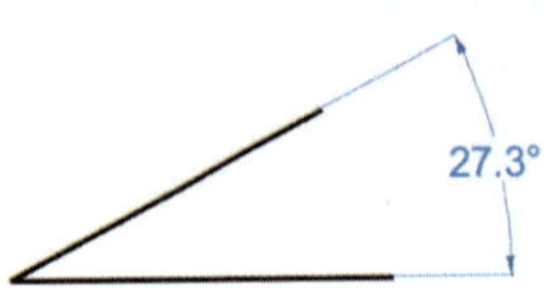

- *Angular Dimension* - Hold the Shift key and select two lines to do angular dimensions.

- *Endpoint to Endpoint* - Hold the Shift key and select two end points from any curve type to do an endpoint-to-endpoint dimension.

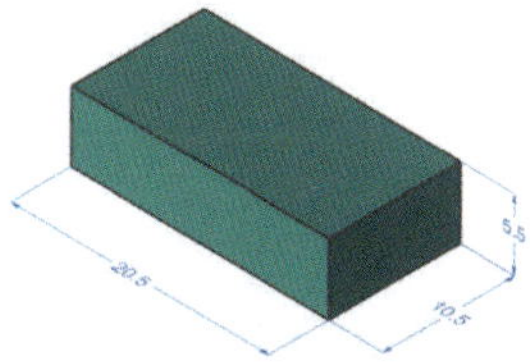

- *Vertices of a Solid* - Hold the Shift key and select two vertices of a solid to measure their distance. The work plane controls the place of the dimension.

When working with Vertices of a Solid, the dimensions will update when solid updates.

Can I set Balloon Dimensions to calculate the width automatically?

Yes, using the Inspector: Object Properties page you can set the Balloon width to "0". Hitting apply will then calculate the width based on the width of the text.

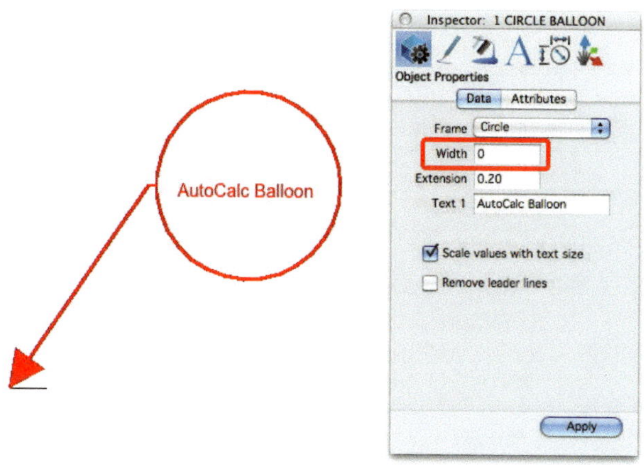

Figure 2.15 – Automatic balloon dimensioning

Curves

How do I change the color of a curve to a custom color?

There are two ways to change the color of a curve to a custom color that include using the Inspector and by right clicking on a curve.

Method 1: Using the Inspector

- Open up the Inspector and select the Pen category.
- Click on the *More…* menu item which will display the Default Pen palette.
- Next double click on any color to display the operating system color dialog box. The operating system color dialog box provides a variety of ways to create custom colors.
- Once you click out of the system dialog box, the color in the Default Pen palette will change to your custom color.

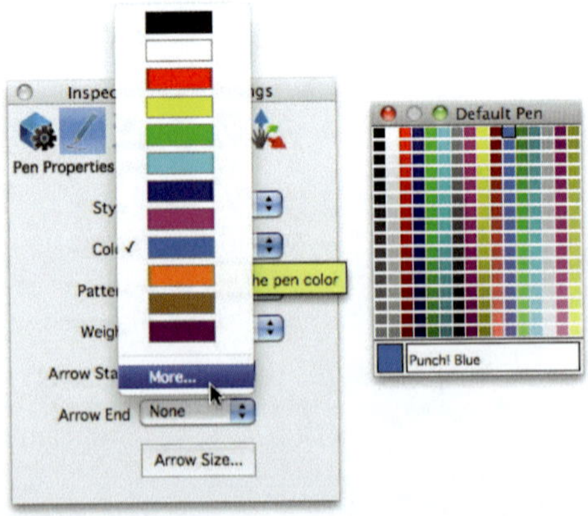

- If a curve is previously selected, this will modify the color of the selected curves. If no curve is selected, this will change the default creation color for the next objects created.

Figure 2.16 – Pen Palette

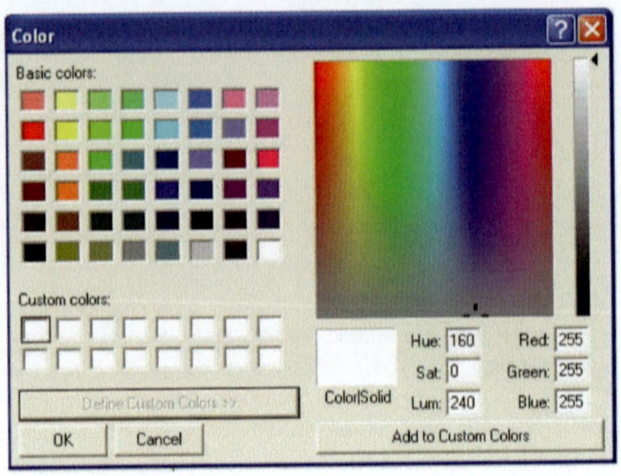

Figure 2.17 – Inspector to Custom Color

Method 2: Right Clicking on Curve

- If you right click on any object it will display a context sensitive menu that includes an option to change the color of the object.

Is there a quick way to create construction lines?

A quick technique for creating construction lines while in any tool is to press:

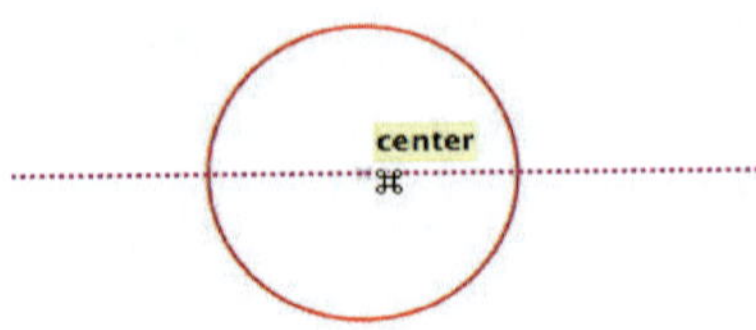

Figure 2.18 – Horizontal Construction Line

- On a Mac: Press and hold the Apple Command key (⌘) while dragging approximately horizontal/vertical to create a horizontal/vertical construction line.

- On Windows: Press and hold both the Control and Shift keys while dragging approximately horizontal/vertical to create a horizontal/vertical construction line.

Additionally, you can use the keyboard shortcuts displayed in Table 2.1 to quickly create construction lines.

Table 2.1 – Keyboard shortcuts

Construction Lines	
Shift H	Horizontal construction line at cursor
Shift V	Vertical construction line at cursor

If you start your drag with a LogiCursor marker highlighted, the construction line will precisely go through this point.

Construction lines are drawn relative to the xy axis of the work plane.

Can I create an arc tangent to 3 curves?

Yes. To create an arc tangent to 3 curves, select the *Three Points Arc* tool and then press the appropriate key below while clicking on the three curves.

- On a Mac: Option key
- On Windows: Control key

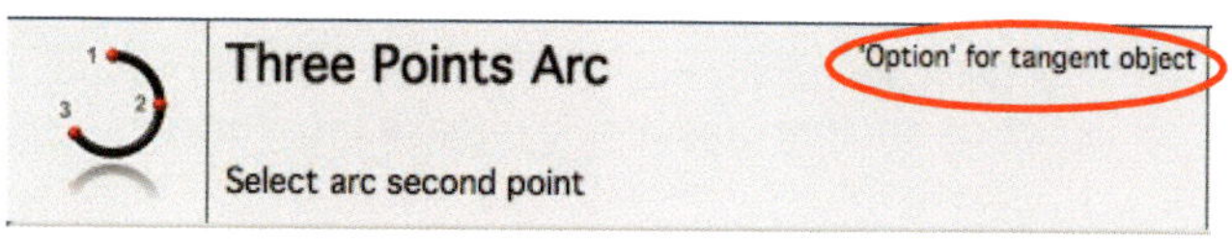

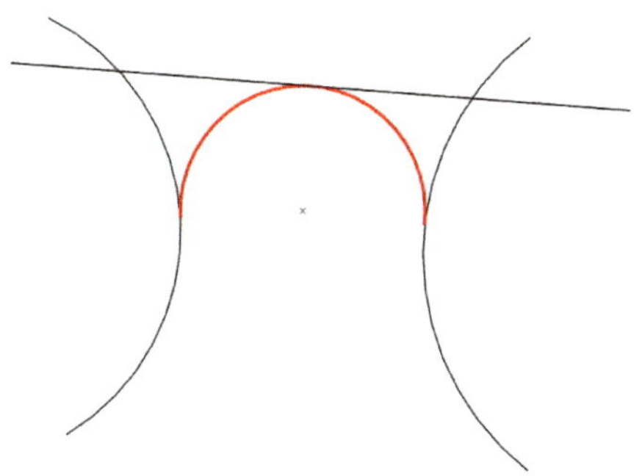

Figure 2.19 – Using Three Points Arc tool to create and arc tangent to 3 curves on a Mac

Can I create an arc at a specified length?

There is no specific length parameter with arcs to do this, however you can use the data entry window with a little math relating the starting point,length, and radius.

The angle of an arc is related to the length by the below equation:

Total Angle = Length / ((2 * Radius*PI)/360)

To apply this within the CAD application, first create an arc with the correct start point and radius using the Three Point Arc tool. After the arc has been constructed, select the arc and tab over to the Total Angle field in the data entry window. Type in the following for a desired length of 15 and radius of 5 in the Total Angle field and hit carriage return.

15.0 / ((2 * 5 * PI)/360.0)

To confirm the arc is at the desired length, select the arc and the Verify : Length command from the Menu Bar.

How can I create a tangent line?

- Select the *Single Line* tool.
- Move the pointer so that it is on the object off of which you wish to create the Tangent line, and so that the LogiCursor displays the word "On". (Keep in mind that this will not work if anything other than "On" is displayed.)
- Drag the mouse away from the object in a roughly tangent direction and pause, continuing to hold the mouse button down.
- A line appears, and the LogiCusor displays the word "tangent" near the beginning of the line. Move the mouse around, and notice that the line will stay tangent as the pointer moves.
- It is a simple matter then to locate the second endpoint of the line at another Tangent point on another object, and release the mouse.

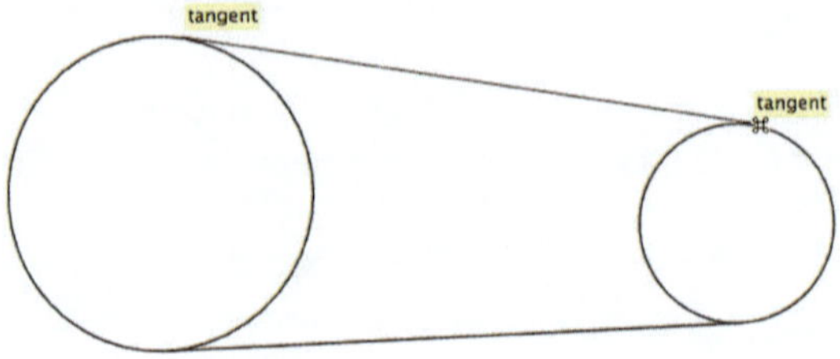

Figure 2.20 – Creating tangents

You can also use the *Multi Line* tool to achieve the same effect.

This feature works equally well on Lines, Arcs, Circles, Ellipses, and even Splines.

How can I create a circle tangent with two curves and diameter?

- Select the *Circle Three Point* tool.

- Move the pointer so that it is on the first line from which you wish to create the Tangent circle, and so that the LogiCursor displays the word “On”.
- Move the pointer so that it is on the second line from which you wish to create the Tangent circle, and so that the LogiCursor displays the word “On”.
- Click the third point between the two lines.
- Move your cursor to the data entry window and type in the desired diameter.

While the tool is still active, you can continue change the diameter and maintain tangent updates. Once you leave the tool, the circle is no longer relate to the two lines.

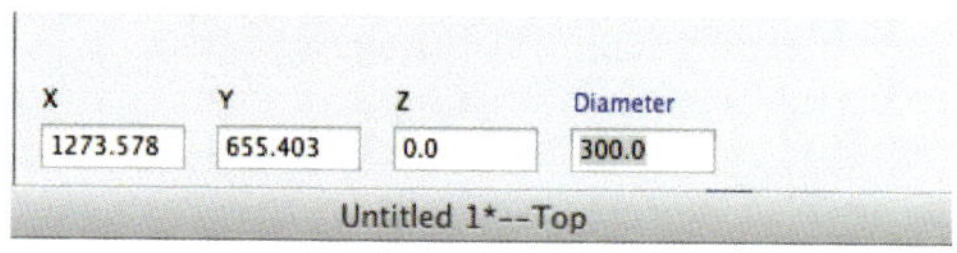

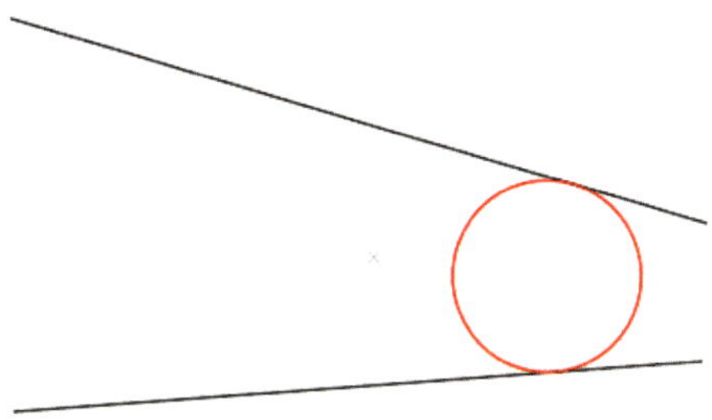

How can I make a polyline from a collection of lines?

A polyline is a single entity that contains multiple line segments. The *Join Curve* tool found on the Curve Utilities Palette can be used to make a collection of connected lines into one polyline object.

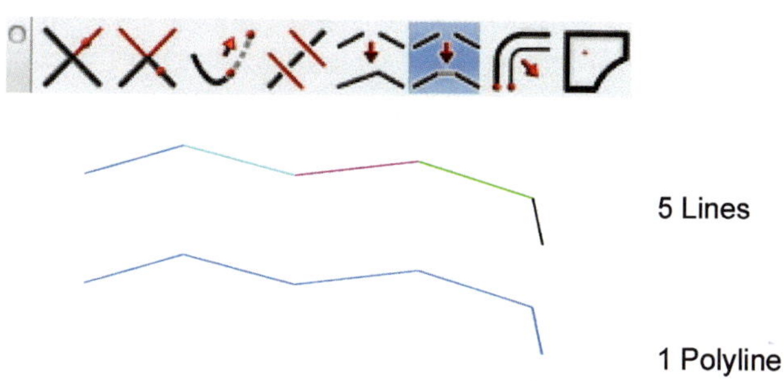

Figure 2.21 – Use Join Curve tool to make polyline from collection of lines

You can also create a polyline from the Change Object type command.

Can I delete a polyline segment?

To delete a point on a polyline, use the *Remove Spline Point* tool located in the Splines tool palette. This tool will remove not only a spline point but also a polyline point.

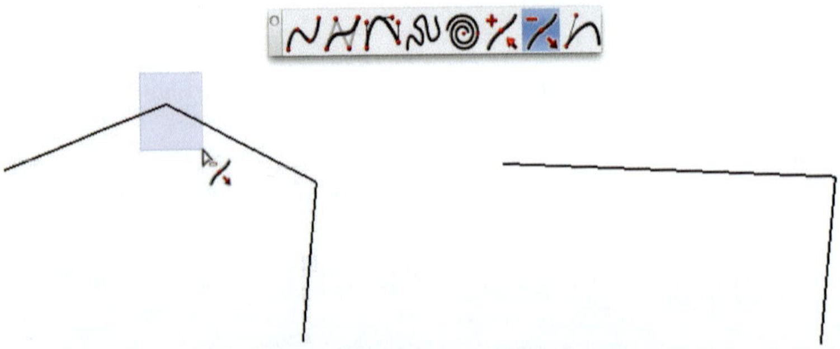

Figure 2.22 – Using Remove Spline Point to delete a polyline segment

Can I draw arcs and polylines in the same command?

It is very common when drawing something like the outline of a part to want to stop and draw an arc or two and then go right back to drawing straight lines again. In ViaCAD, you can do this without having to switch between tools multiple times.

Select the *Multi Line* tool and start digitizing points for a line. To create an arc:

- On Mac: Hold the Option key. The tool prompt will say Option = Arc.
- On Windows: Hold the Control key. The tool prompt will say Control = Arc.

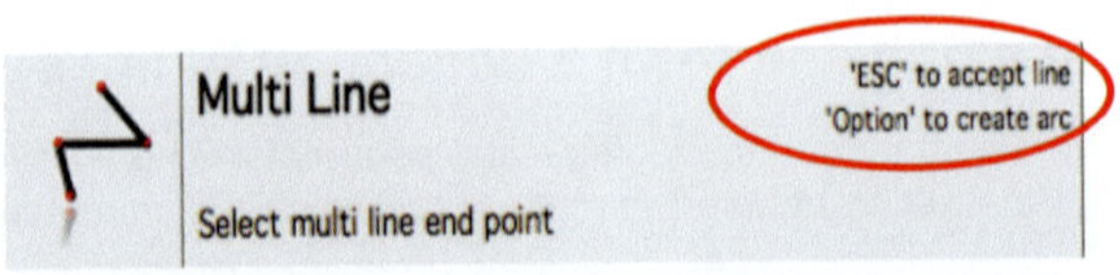

As long as you hold that key, you can draw a series of arcs, each one starting out tangent to the line or arc preceding. To return to the *Multi Line* tool, simply release the key.

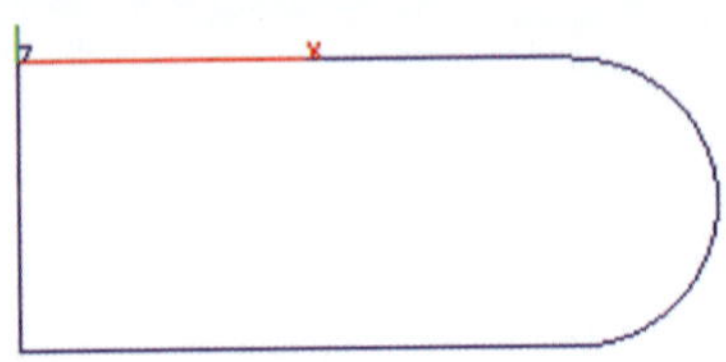

Figure 2.23

This optional behavior becomes available only after at least one straight line segment has been drawn. The program needs the first line piece so that it has geometry to which it can make the new arc tangent.

How can I find the center of a rectangle?

There are several ways to find the center of a collection of lines forming a rectangle.

Method 1: Create a point entity at the center using the Midpoint snap tool.

- First, display the Snaps filter dialog box located under the Window menu.
- Then, pick the MidPoint Snap option.
- Finally, select two diagonal points on the lines.

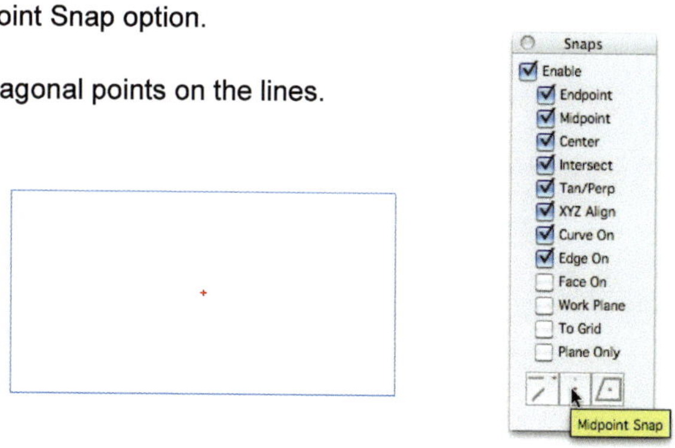

Figure 2.24 – Finding Center using MidPoint Snap tool

Method 2: Use Logicursor to find the apparent center using snap alignments.

- First, select the *Point* tool and move your cursor over the midpoint of the lines. This will "wake" them up for alignments.
- Next, move your cursor towards the middle until you see the snap "intersect" displayed. This is your midpoint of the rectangle.

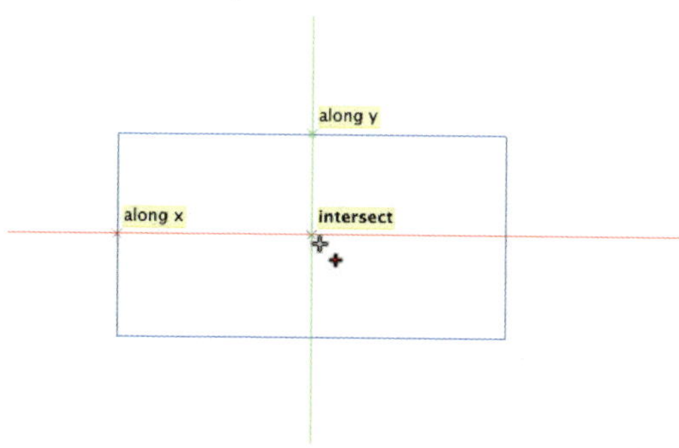

Figure 2.25 – Finding Center using Logicursor snap alignments

How can I find the center of an arbitrary shape?

- First, select the curves using the Arrow tool.

- Then, pick the Properties command located under the Verify menu bar. This displays the planar area properties of your selected curves.

- Under the Create option, check the box marked "Point at C.G." This will create a point at the center of gravity.

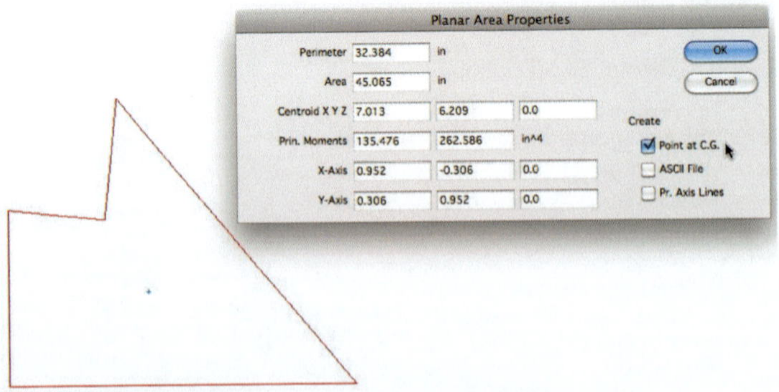

Figure 2.26 – Planar Area Properties

How can I control which curves are hatched?

The default behavior of the hatch tools is to infer the hatch curves based upon visible curve regions in the vicinity of your mouse click.

- To specify the curves explicitly, hold down the Shift key and select the curves instead of clicking the mouse in a region.

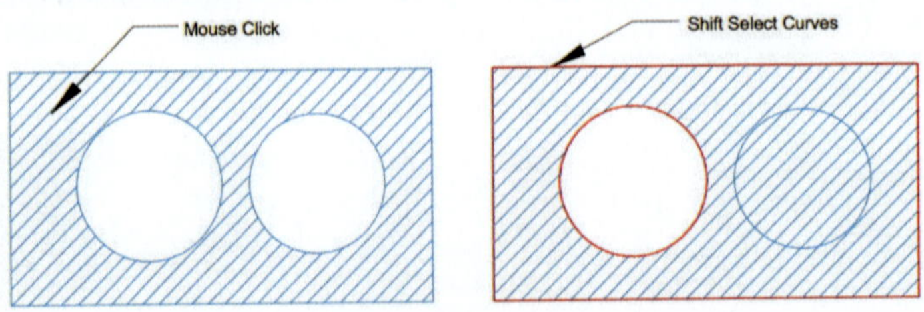

Figure 2.27- Selecting Hash Curves using Shift key

How can I find the total length of a collection of curves?

- Select the curves.

- Go to Verify on the Menu Bar.

- Select Perimeter from the drop down menu. This will add up the length of each curve selected to provide you with the total length of the collection.

If you pick a group, Verify Perimeter will total up all the curves within the group.

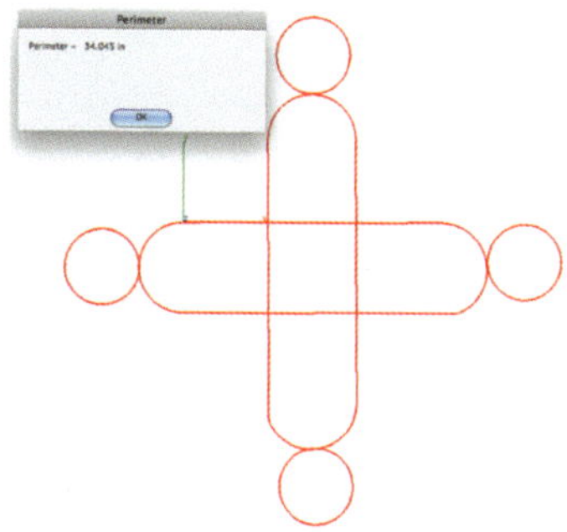

Figure 2.28 – Calculating total length with verify perimeter

How can I change the dash length of a dashed line?

We use line types such as dashdot, center, and dashed to control the line style. Sometimes you may want to increase or decrease the spacing.

- To change the dash length, go to Inspector.
- Select the Pen Properties tab.
- Under this tab, go to Pattern.
- Select the More Options dialog box. From here, you can adjust the Scale value and style of the object line pattern.

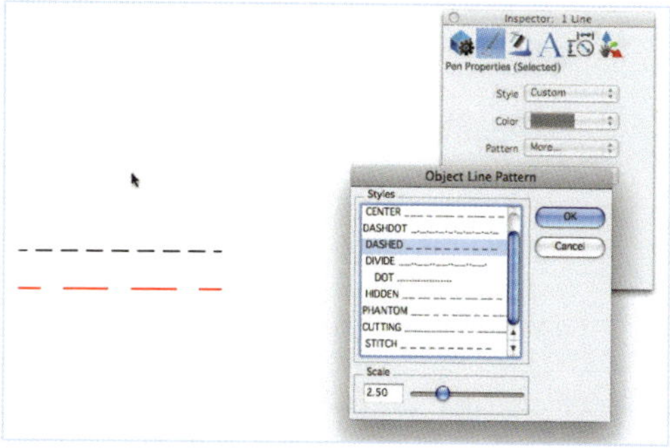

Figure 2.29 – Changing Object Line Pattern

If you have a preferred line pattern already in your drawing, you can quickly copy this to other objects using the *Eye Dropper* tool.

How can I manipulate spline points using the Arrow keys?

- Once you have constructed a spline, go to Edit on the Menu Bar.
- Select the Show Points command to display the points used to create the spline.
- Go to Preferences, which is found under File for PC users and Application for Mac users.
- Then, select General from the category options listed on the left side of the dialog box, as shown in Figure 2.30.
- Now, specify the Arrow key nudge distance by typing a non-zero value into the box. This indicates the amount your point will move when the Arrow key is pressed.

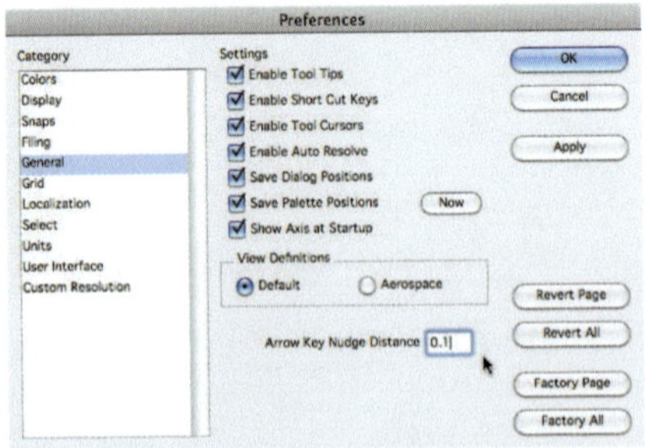

Figure 2.30 – Setting Arrow Key Nudge Distance

Holding Shift key while nudging with the Arrow key will multiply distance by 10.

How can I manipulate spline points using the Gripper?

- Once you have constructed a spline, go to Edit on the Menu Bar.
- Select the Show Points command to display the points used to create the spline.
- Display the Inspector dialog box.
- Check the Enable Gripper box.
- Now you can move points on the spline by moving the handles of the Gripper.

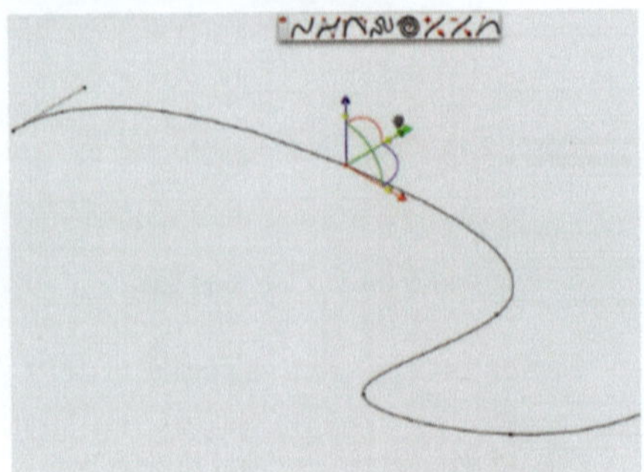

Figure 2.31 – Manipulating Points on an Interpolate Spline with Gripper

In addition to moving points, you can use the Gripper to scale and rotate points using the handle. The point of rotation and scaling will be about the Gripper's origin. Note that as you move, rotate, and scale with the Gripper, a Data Entry Window is activated that allows precise movements. This window can be found at the top of your screen.

Which spline type should I use?

ViaCAD offers six spline types, each with its own design advantages. Table 2.2 describes some of the characteristics of these splines to help you choose the best one for your particular design task.

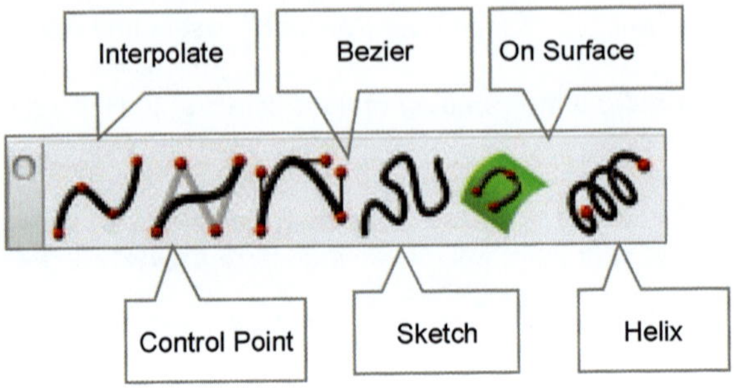

Table 2.2 – Spline Types

Spline Type	Description	When to Use It
Interpolate Spline 	This spline type is fit through the points supplied by the user. You can control the start and end tangents with the two control points not on the curve.	Use when you need your spline to go through a set of locations.
Control Point Spline 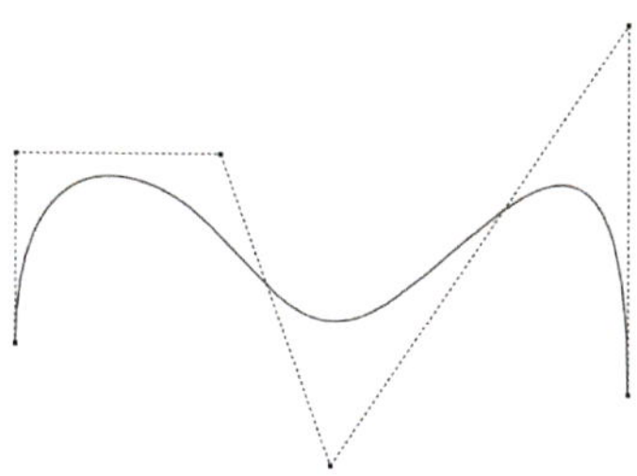	This spline type is created by providing control points. Except for the start and end points, the points may not lie on the spline.	It is easy to identify points of inflection as inflections occur when the dashed lines cross over the curve. Thus, use this when you are concerned about the smoothness of the spline.
Bezier Spline 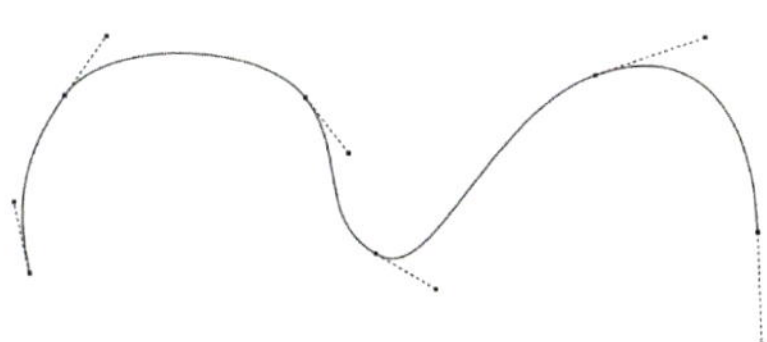	The Bezier Spline is defined by a collection of points that lie on the curve. After the spline is created, each point has an additional handle that controls the tangency at that location.	Use this when you need to control the tangency at each location.
Sketch Spline 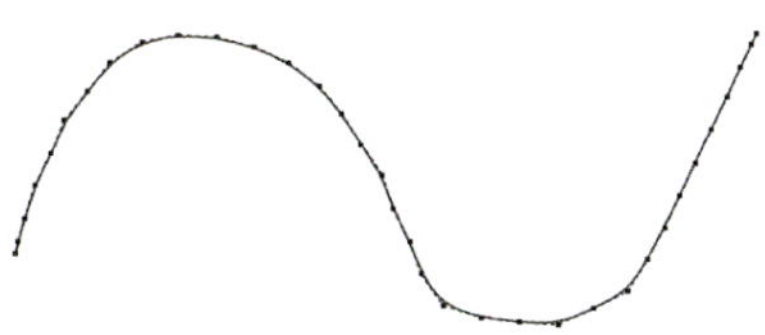	The Sketch Spline is a type of Control Point Spline in which the points are sampled as the cursor is moved across the screen.	This is good for free hand sketching shapes.

Spline on Surface 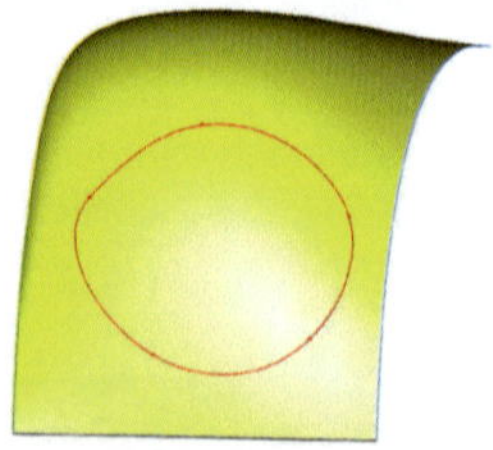	The Spline On Surface tool creates an Interpolated Spline that lies in on a surface.	This is useful for trimming out portions of a surface.
Helix Spline 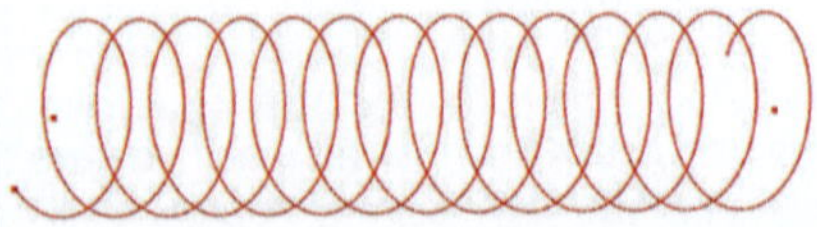	The Helix Spline is defined by two points along with pitch, diameter, length, and draft angle parameters.	An example use of a helix spline is to model a path for a bolt thread.

What are the points of interest for a Control Point spline?

The Control Point Spline is one of the more versatile splines in ViaCAD. Mathematically, the Control Point Spline is a Non-uniform Rational Basis Spline (NURB). This provides a flexible definition for producing smooth (G2) curves.

You construct this spline using control points. Except for the start and end locations, the control points do not necessary lie on the curve that is created.

An interesting feature of the control point spline is that whenever a line is drawn between two consecutive points across the curve, you have an inflection point.

The curvature comb of a spline can be displayed using the Verify Show Curvature tool.

Check List

It's important to take the time to ensure you are creating a good curve, as good curves lead to good surfaces. In turn, good surfaces lead to good solids. Here are a few things to remember when working with curves:

✔ Use the least number of points you can to describe the curve you want.

✔ Avoid inflection points in your designs, either by ensuring all control points are on the same side of the curve or starting a new curve / surface at the point.

✔ It's very easy to let your will to control a curve's curvature plot adversely impact the character or design intent of said

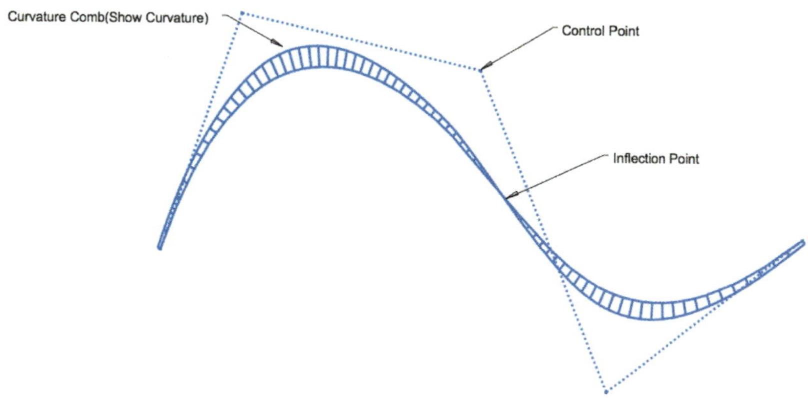

Figure 2.32 – Control Point spline

How can I identify the degree of a curve?

Curves in ViaCAD are defined by mathematical equations. The highest exponent associated with the equation is its degree. For example, a line is considered of degree 1, a circle degree 2, and a spline by default in the program is created as a degree 3 polynomial.

Table 2.3 – Example of 3 common curve types, equations, and degrees

Curve	Equation	Degree
Line	$Y = mx + b$	1
Circle	$X^2 + Y^2 = r^2$	2
Cubic Spline	$at^3 + bt^2 + ct + d$	3

To identify the degree of a curve in ViaCAD:

- Begin by selecting the curve.
- Go to Verify on the Menu Bar.
- Select the Check Object command. In addition to checking for issues with the curve, this command displays some interesting curve attributes such as degree, rational, closed, periodic, number of knots, and number of control points.

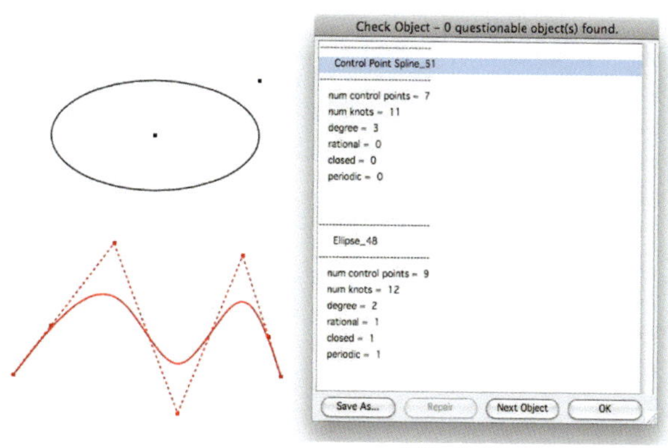

Figure 2.33 – Check Object command

What is geometric continuity?

Geometric Continuity G(n) is a measure of smoothness where the higher order (n) generally provides an increasing measure of smoothness. The three common types of continuity you will find in ViaCAD are:

- *G0 Positional Continuity* - Positional continuity exists whenever the end positions of two curves are coincidental. The curves may meet at an angle, giving rise to a sharp corner or edge.
- *G1 Tangential Continuity* - Tangential continuity requires the end vectors of the curves to be parallel, eliminating sharp edges.
- *G2 Curvature Continuity* - Curvature continuity requires that the end vectors must not only be parallel but also of the same length. All splines created in ViaCAD are G2 continuous between the start and end positions.

How can I tell if my curve is smooth?

A smooth curve has no abrupt changes or discontinuities. A useful measure of smoothness is curvature, which can help identify abrupt changes in a curve. ViaCAD has a Curvature command located under the Verify menu. The figure below shows the curvature plotted along the curve.

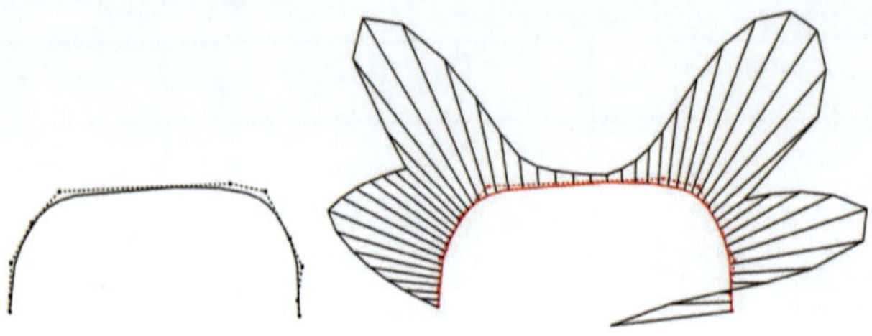

Figure 2.34 – Unsmooth spline revealed by plotting curvature along a curve

How can I smooth a curve?

The spline in Figure 2.34 above has several issues that include spiky curvature distribution and an inflection point near the end of the curve. Inflections indicate a sign change in curvature, which is typically undesirable in a smooth curve.

To remove these problematic inflections:

- First, ensure all the control points are on the same side of the curve.

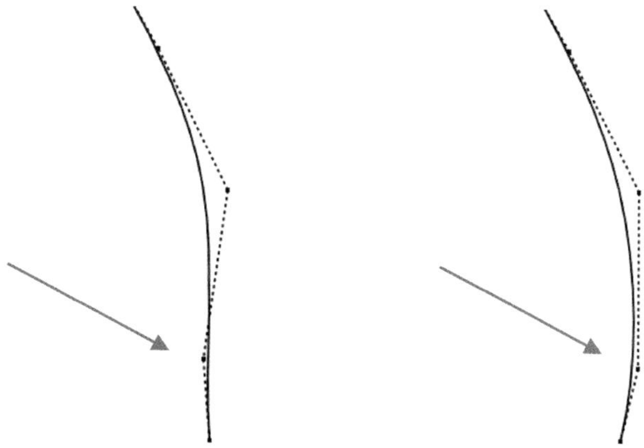

Figure 2.35 – Moving control point to other side removes the problematic inflection

- The next step to smooth this curve is to even out the curvature. To do this, you can nudge with arrow keys or use the Gripper to move points while dynamically watching the curvature graph update.

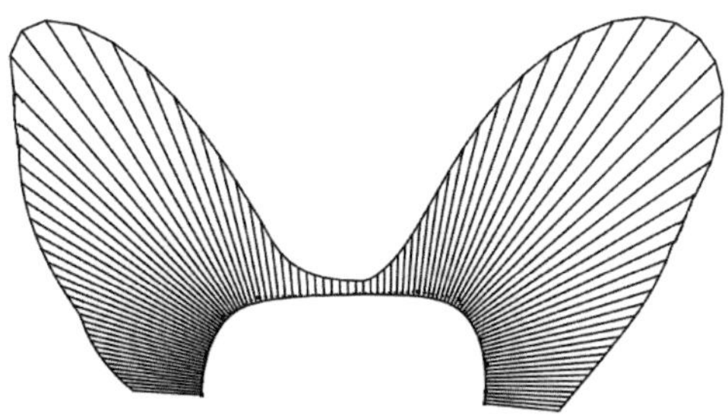

Figure 2.36 – Smooth Curve

How can I match the slope of a spline to another curve?

- Go to the Spline palette and select the *Modify Slope* tool.
- From the prompt line, select the Reference option from the pull down. This will allow you to reference a point on another curve, extract the slope, and assign it to the start of your spline.

Other useful tools for matching include the *Free Slopes, Reverse, Explicit*, and *Free Magnitude* tools.

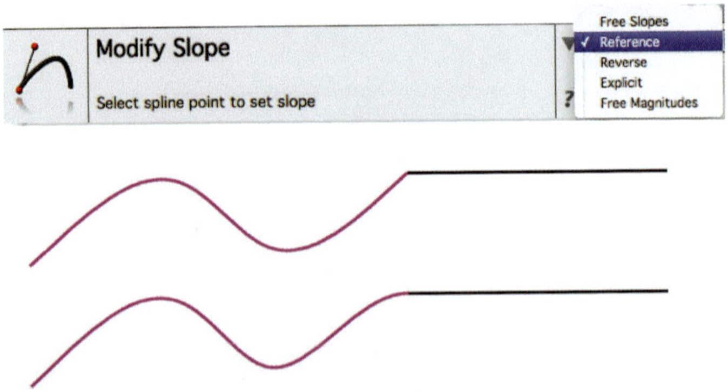

Figure 2.37 – Modify Slope

Can I match a slope with G2 continuity?

The *Spline Modify Slope* tool only matches G1 (tangent) continuity. To achieve G2 (curvature) continuity, you will need to manually modify the control points as shown in this tip. In the example below we will modify the start of an arc to be G2 continuous with a neighboring arc.

- First, turn on the curvature graph for the two curves. Be sure to adjust the scale of the graph using the Curvature Settings dialog box located under Verify on the Menu Bar. You will be using the graph to visually guide you to G2 continuity.

- Next, change the curve type to a Control Point spline. To do this, right click on the curve you want to change. This will display a pop up menu with options that include Change Object Type.

- Then, turn on the control points of the resulting spline by selecting it and picking the Show Points command from the Edit menu. You will be modifying these points later.

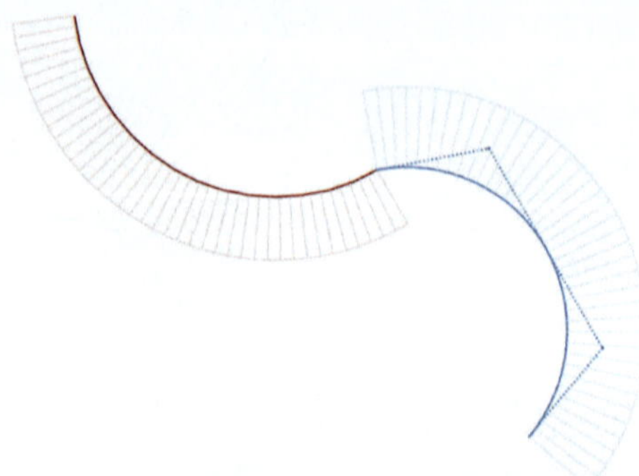

Figure 2.38 – Turn on the curvature graph, change to a Control Point spline, and display control points

- Elevate the curve to at least degree 5. By elevating the curve you will add more control points, which will help you localize the shape changes. The initial arc was a degree 2 curve and converting it to a spline did not change the degree. Thus, you will need to elevate this curve 3 times. The Elevate Curve tool is located in the Spline tool palette.

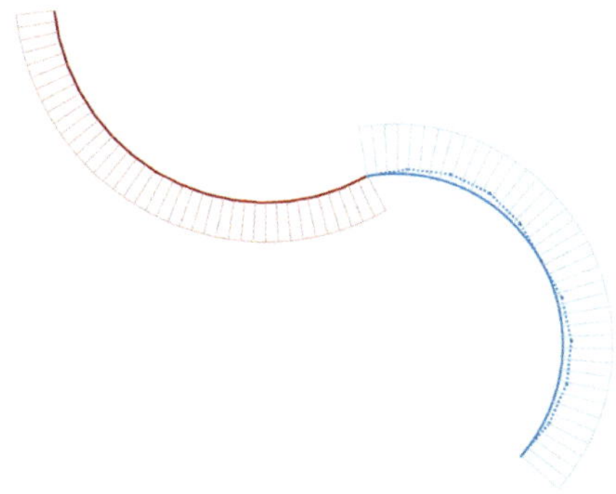

Figure 2.39 – Using the Elevate Curve tool to elevate the curve to degree 5

- Next, add a construction line off the tangent of the curve we are matching.
- Turn on the Gripper and locate the origin of the Gripper to the starting point of the curve you are about to change. Select the second control point from the start of the curve. Be sure to set the Gripper attach mode to User Positioned. Use the Gripper to rotate the control point onto the construction line. After you rotate the point, you can precisely put it on the line using LogiCursor. This will give you G1 continuity to the matching curve.

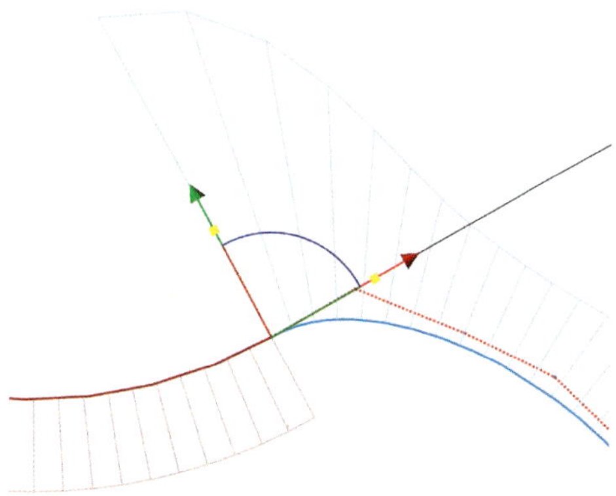

Figure 2.40 – Using the Gripper to rotate the control point to place it on the line

- The next control point movements will impact the curvature at the curve starting point. Set the Gripper origin to the point you just modified and then select the third control point from the start of the curve. Rotate this point to also lie on the construction line. Moving the third point to the line corresponds to zero curvature. If you are matching to a line, you are done. However for objects with curvature, you will need to continue on to the next step.

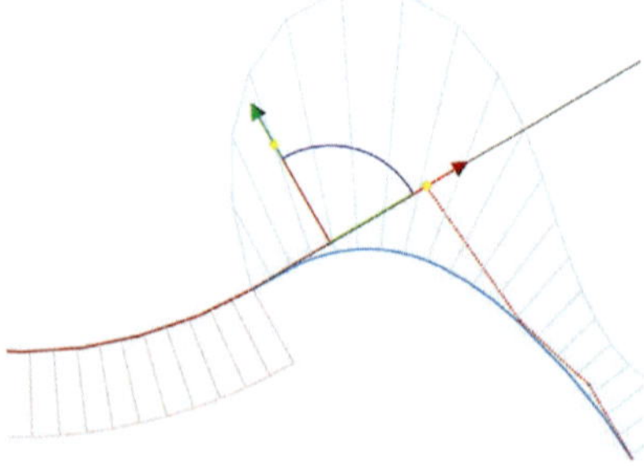

Figure 2.41 – Manipulating the third control point from the curve start

- Note that the scale and direction are still not lined up with the matching arc. Our next trick is to move the third control point perpendicular to the construction line until the curvature lengths of the two curves line up. Use the Gripper Axis to Object option to align the Gripper Axis to the construction line. Then select the third control point and move it along the line by dragging the green arrow (y-axis) of the Gripper. Move up and down until the length of the curvature graph is the same as the matching curve.

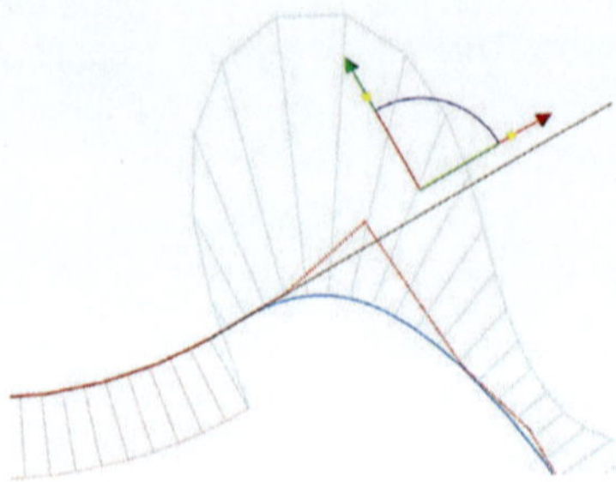

Figure 2.42 – Manipulating third control point to equalize lengths

- Lastly, to further smooth out the curvature, move the third control point along the red arrow (x-axis) of the Gripper until you have your desired results.

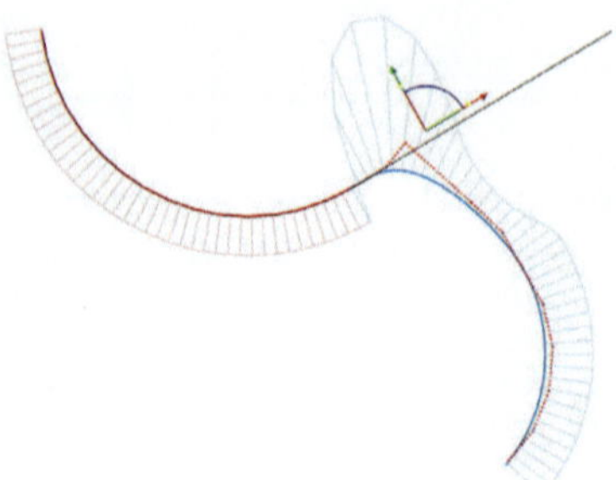

Figure 2.43 – Smoothing out curvature

What tool is used to relimit a curve?

The *Trim* tool is used to re-limit curves to other objects. Located in the Curve Utilities Palette, this tool is one of the most frequently used features to modify curve extents.

What objects can I trim a curve to?

Most users are aware that you can trim a curve to another curve. However, a hidden feature of the *Trim* tool is that you can also trim a curve to a surface or solid.

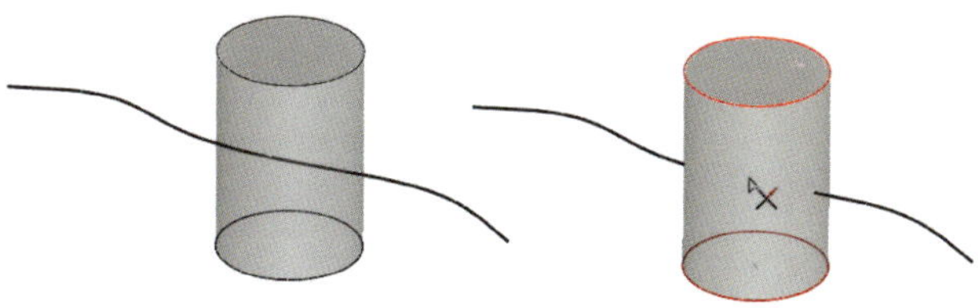

Figure 2.44 – Trimming to a Solid

Don't forget an infinite plane is a surface. This means that you can also trim a curve to an infinite plane.

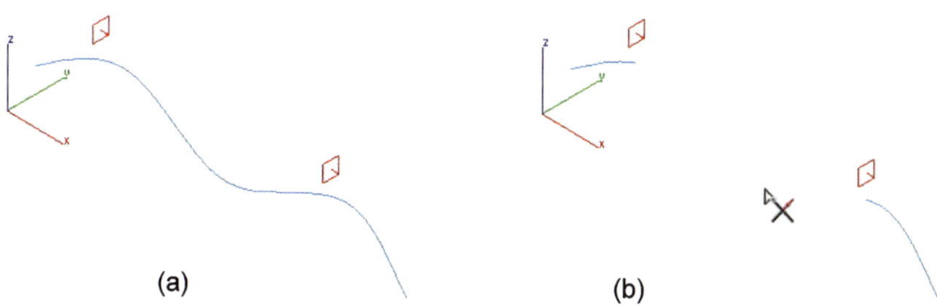

Figure 2.45 – Trimming to an infinite plane

Can I extend the number of objects selected when trimming?

Simply press the Shift key in conjunction with *Trim* tool.

Double click everything for speedy trimming.

How can I extend a curve to a selected boundary?

Although you would normally use the *Trim* tool to shorten an intersecting line to a specified boundary, you can also use it to extend a non-intersecting line to a selected boundary.

To use the *Trim* tool to extend a curve to a selected boundary:

- On a Mac: Hold the Option key with the *Trim* tool.

- On Windows: Hold the Control key in conjunction with the *Trim* tool.

If you don't hold the Option/Control key and try to use the *Trim* tool with two non-intersecting lines, you will delete the entire object. This is shown in Figure 2.44 (a).

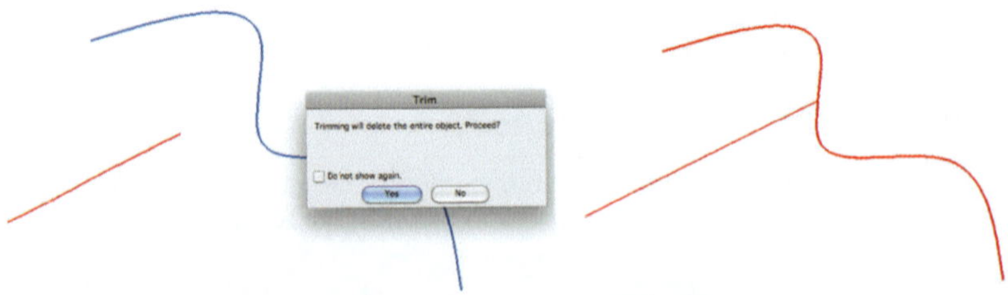

(a) (b)

Figure 2.46 - Using Trim tool to extend curve to boundary in (b)

Can I use the *Trim* tool to keep a selected curve section?

While you would normally use the *Trim* tool to delete selected objects, you can also use the tool to keep certain portions of objects while deleting the non-selected parts.

To use the *Trim* tool to **keep** selected curve sections:

- On a Mac: Hold the Option key. The tool prompt should change from saying "Select curve section to delete" to "Select curve section to keep."

- On Windows: Press the Control key. The tool prompt should change from saying "Select curve section to delete" to "Select curve section to keep."

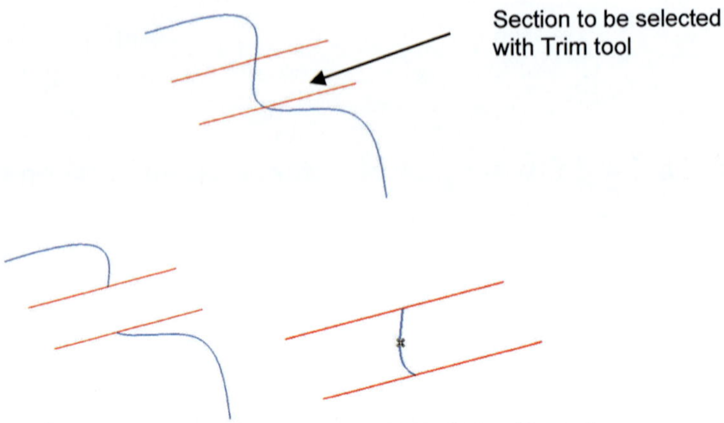

(a) Without Option/Control (b) With Option/Control

Figure 2.47 - Using Trim tool to keep selected portion (b)

By using Select All in conjunction with the *Trim* tool, selected objects not only serve as a trim boundary but also can be trimmed depending on where you click with the mouse.

> **Did You Know?**
>
> Can't figure out how to use a tool? Use the Tool help feature found at the top of your screen. This will take you to an online page with information about the tool straight from the users manual.

Symbols

How can I insert a symbol?

The ViaCAD products include thousands of pre-made CAD symbols categorized under the AEC, Electrical, Mechanical, and Process Plant & Piping headings. To insert a symbol:

- Go to Window on your Menu Bar and select Concepts Explorer from the drop down menu.
- From the Concepts Explorer dialog box, select the Symbols tab.
- Simply drag and drop and of the symbols found under this tab into your drawing.

How can I create custom symbols?

- First, create the entities associated with your symbol. A symbol may consist of curves, surfaces and/or solids.
- Then, shrink the window down to about 128 x 128 in width/height to generate a nice preview.
- Save the file to the appropriate location:
- On a Mac:

  ViaCAD 2D
  /Users/<yourlogin>/Library/Application Support/com.encore.viacad3dv9/Symbols

  ViaCAD 2D3D
  /Users/<yourlogin>/Library/Application Support/com.encore.viacad2dv9/ Symbols

  ViaCAD Pro
  /Users/<yourlogin>/Library/Application Support/com.encore.viacadprov9/ Symbols

- On Windows:

  ViaCAD 2D
  c:\ Documents and Settings\<yourlogin>\Local Settings\Application Data\Punch!\ViaCAD2D

  ViaCAD 2D3D
  c:\ Documents and Settings\<yourlogin>\Local Settings\Application Data\Punch!\ViaCAD

  ViaCAD Pro
  c:\ Documents and Settings\<yourlogin>\Local Settings\Application Data\Punch!\ViaCADPro

- Lastly, if you are using the V7 builds 966 or greater, go to the Concepts Explorer Symbols window and right click "Reload".

If you don't have a current version, you will need to exit the app and restart to rebuild the symbols contents. Later versions have a save to symbol listing.

BOMs

How can I apply custom attributes to objects?

Attributes provide a way to assign custom data to an object. Example attributes include, piece, part number, and description. Once assigned to an object, these attributes can be gathered up to make a Bill of Materials (BOM) table.

- After drawing your objects or inserting your symbols, select the object that you would like to attribute by left mouse clicking on it.
- Go to Window on your Menu Bar.
- From the Window drop down menu, select Attribute and BOM to bring up the Attribute dialog box.

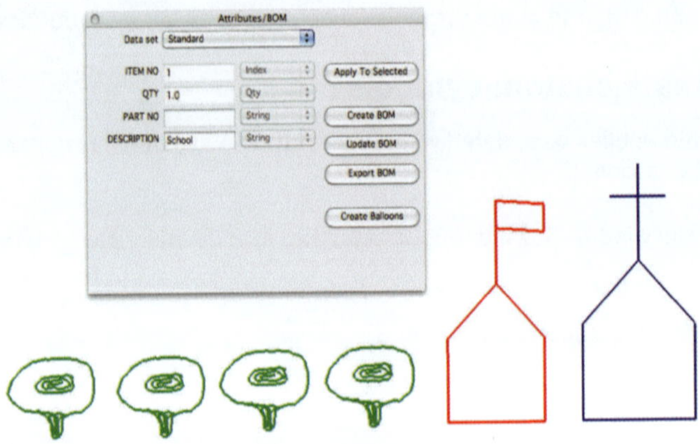

Figure 2.48 – Attribute dialog box

- Using the Attribute dialog box, add a description. For example, in Figure 2.48 above, the description "School" has been typed into the text field.
- Now, click the Apply to Selected button.
- Repeat these steps for all of your objects.
- Once you have attributed your objects, create a BOM table by clicking on the Create BOM button, which is located directly below the Apply to Selected button in the Attribute dialog box. This button can be seen in Figure 2.48.
- Now, click on screen to bring up the BOM settings dialog box. This dialog box can be seen in Figure 2.49 to the right.
- Select a text height. For example, in Figure 2.49 the text

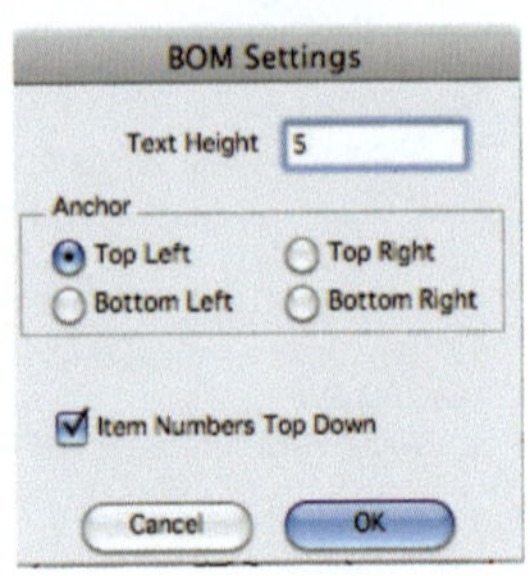

Figure 2.49 – BOM Settings dialog box

height has been set to 5 inches.

- Select OK to insert a table.
- Finally, locate the table in a desired location by left clicking on your screen. You can always move the table later using the Gripper.

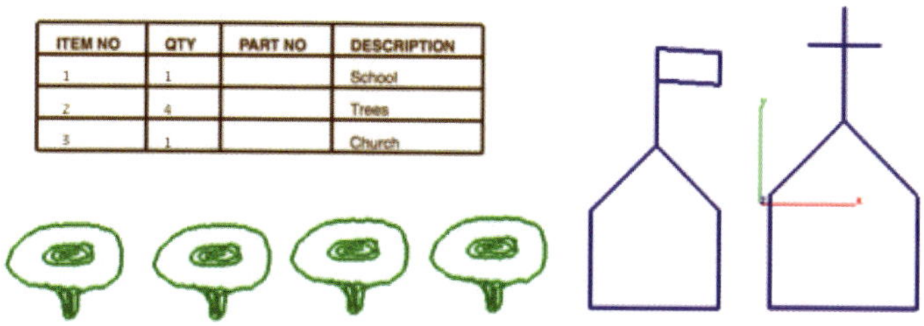

Figure 2.50 – An example BOM table

Like any other object in ViaCAD, you can adjust the color and pixel size of the BOM table by going to Pen Properties in the Inspector.

How can I delete BOM attributes that I have applied?

- First, select the object you wish to delete an attribute from
- Then, go to Window on your Menu Bar.
- Select Concepts Explorer from the drop down menu to open up the Concepts Explorer dialog box.
- Select the Features tab.
- Under this tab, you should be able to click on the object's name to bring up a scroll down menu.
- Scroll down until you see the attribute you would like to remove. Right click this attribute to bring up a menu.
- From this menu select the Remove Attribute option. The attribute has now been removed from the object.

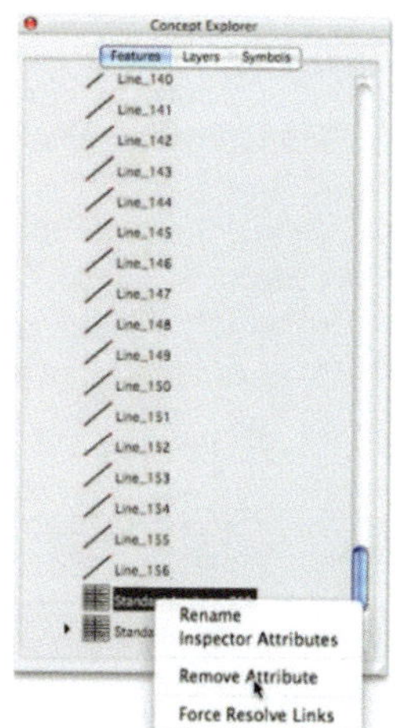

Figure 2.51 – Remove Attribute

- To regenerate your BOM table, go back to the Attribute dialog box and select the button Update BOM. Now the attribute has been removed from both the table and the object.

With the release of Version 8, you can now delete BOM attributes with a dedicated tool option.

Can I copy BOM attributes from one object to another?

The *Eye Dropper* tool will copy BOM attributes from one object to another.

Can I create a custom set of attributes?

The Attribute collection is shown in the BOM folder. Simply copy the existing one and modify it to suit your current BOM.

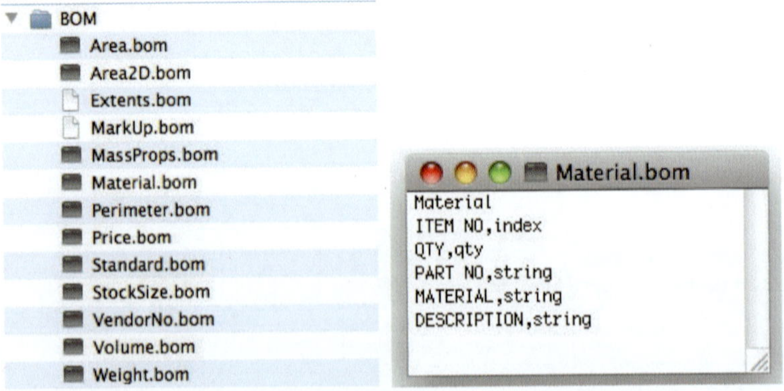

Figure 2.52 – Creating a custom BOM

Draw Views

Can I create a new Hidden Line style to be used in draw views?

- Go to the Pen Styles tab in the Inspector dialog box.
- Select the New option. This will let you define a name, color, weight, and pattern for a custom line style.
- You can then use this new pen style in a draw view.

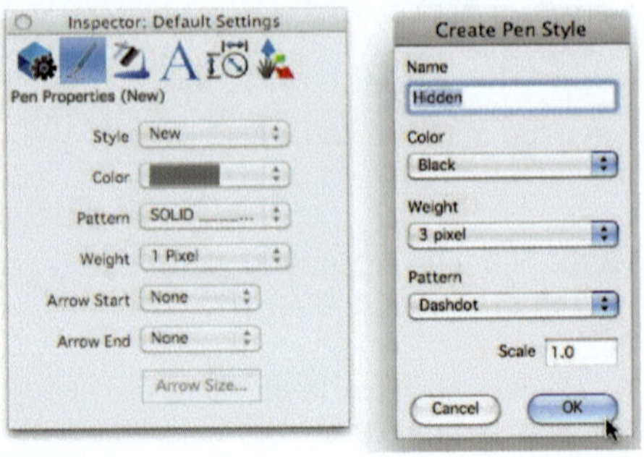

Figure 2.53 – Creating new Hidden Line Style

If you edit the pen style later, all draw views will automatically update if they use a custom pen style.

How can I add objects to a draw view?

- Select the 3D object you want to add to the draw view.

- Go to Edit and select Copy command.
- Next, click on the draw view to activate.
- Then go to Edit again and select the Paste command.

You may need to turn on and off layers between your 3D object and 2D draw view.

Can I unfold a draw view?

Holding the Control key and dragging an edge of a draw view will unfold the draw view. The edge you drag defines the orientation of the folded view.

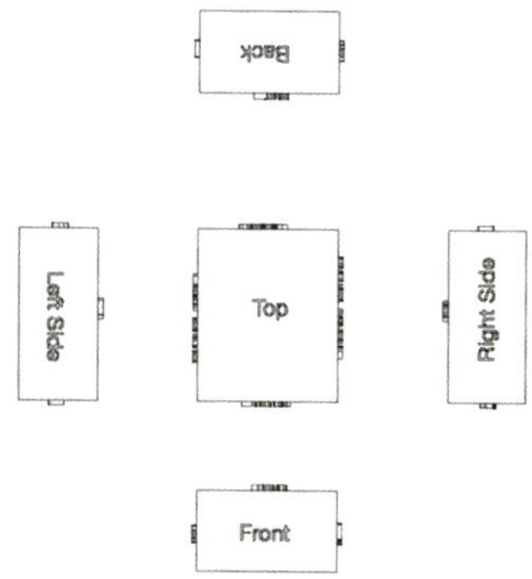

Figure 2.54 – Unfolding a draw view

Where did my model go after using the Model to Sheet tool?

The *Model to Sheet* tool creates new layers from the resultant drawing. It also changes the display layer to the new draw views.

To re-display you model:

- Go to Window on the Menu Bar.
- Access the Layer Manager.
- Turn your layer containing the model back on.

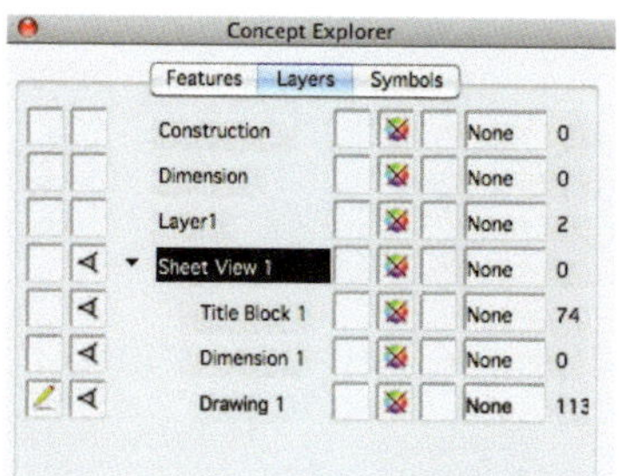

Figure 2.55 – Redisplaying Model

How do I make a custom Model to Sheet template?

The *Model to Sheet* tool provides a variety of drawing configurations through the Layout option in the dialog box. The Layouts are simply ViaCAD files with a drawing border and draw views. These files are located in the Template folder as part of the standard install. Adding a file to this folder will add the file to the Layouts drop down list.

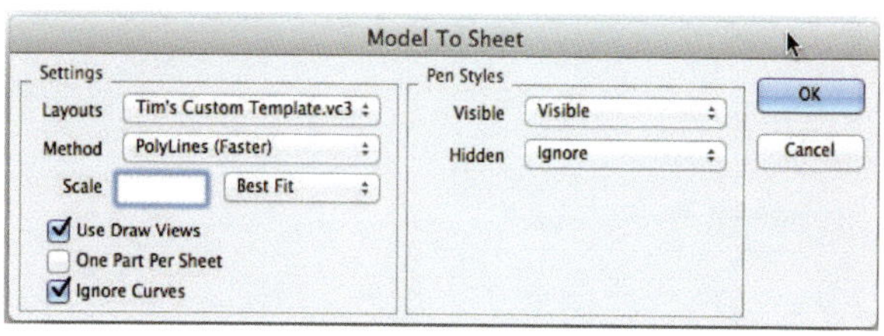

Figure 2.56 – Custom Template

Some tips to create a template:

- Templates are located in the application install folder specified below.

  Windows
  C:\Program Files (x86)\Punch! Software\ViaCAD 3D 9\Templates\ModelToSheet
  Mac
  /Applications/ViaCAD 2D3D 9.app/Contents/Resources/Templates/ModelToSheet

- Modify an existing template

  Use the file system to copy an existing template. Rename the copy as your custom template.

  Launch ViaCAD, open the custom template and add your modifications. You add and remove draw views, change view orientations within a draw view, and custom title blocks and borders.

  Save the file back into the Templates folder.

- Create new template

  If you create a new template from scratch, be sure to include at least one draw view. To create a new draw view, tear out the Model To Sheet tool palette and select the second icon from the left.

3 CHAPTER 3 SURFACE MODELING

Overview

ViaCAD supports a variety of surface construction and utility tools. Surface construction types consist of skinning and lofting, covering, nets, and sweeps. Surface utility tools provide the means to cut, intersect, project, trim, or rebuild surfaces.

- **Skinning -** Fits a surface through a series of disjoint curves (points, lines, arcs, circles, splines), creating a surface or solid body. The resulting body can be open or closed, depending on the curves used as input.
- **Lofting -** Fits a surface through a series of curves and the surface associated with each edge, creating a new surface. It provides control over the tangents of the surface using bulge factors at shared surface edges.
- **Covering -** Creates a surface from a closed loop of curves. Includes options for tangencies, guide curves, and bulge factors.
- **Nets -** Stretches a surface across a MxN "grid" of curves and supports curve directional alignment and simplification to a plane, when appropriate.
- **Sweeping** - Sweeps a curve along a vector, one rail, or two rails.
- **Surface Utilities** – A collection of tools that will modify or extract additional information for a surface.

Skinning and Lofting

What is skinning?

Skinning is a modeling technique that fits a surface through a collection of curves. The skinned surface is a two-variable parametric function S(u,v) in which the curves define the u parameter of the surface and the skin surface algorithm defines the v parameter. In ViaCAD, this is represented as a procedural surface that does not permit C1 or G1 discontinuities.

Ruled, Skin, and Skin with Guide are three construction methods for creating skinned surfaces. These tools are located in the Surface from Curves tool palette.

An example of a skinned surface can be seen in FIgure 3.1 on the following page.

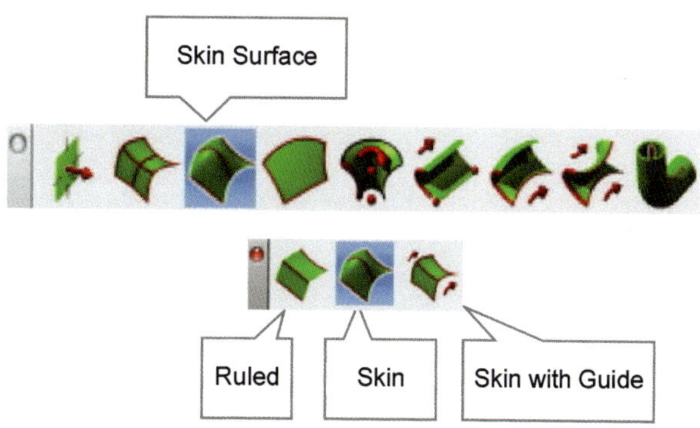

Figure 3.1 – Examples of Skinned (left) and Lofted Surfaces (right)

What is lofting?

Before the days of computer aided design, large shapes such as aircraft fuselages were typically designed by drawing parallel cross-sections. These cross-sections were then connected together with mechanical splines. Because of the large sizes associated with fuselages, designers would work in the loft, which inspired the term lofting.

Today, lofting is accomplished by mathematical procedures inside the CAD system that are somewhat based on the methods of these early designers. Lofting is generally different from Skinning in that it extracts the direction of a reference surface to create the new surface. This powerful lofting tool within ViaCAD is located under the Surface from Surface tool palette.

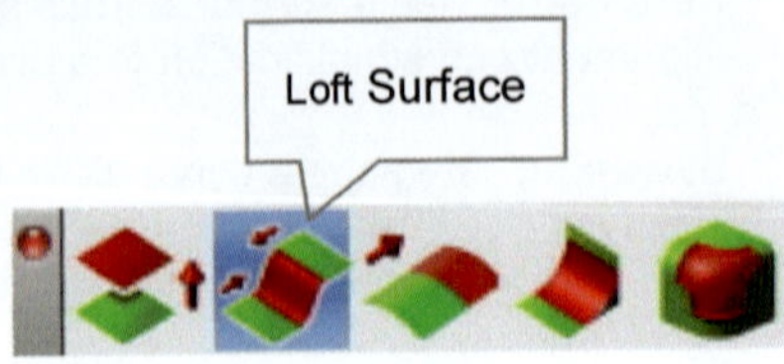

What curve types can be used for skinning and lofting?

The input curves can be lines, arcs, circles, splines, ellipses and conics.

Skinning can be used to create closed surfaces as well as open surfaces depending on the curve sections used as input.

What is a ruled surface?

A ruled surface is a special case of a skin surface in which a straight line is swept continuously between the two rails. One of the interesting properties of a ruled surface is that it is considered a developable surface. A developable surface is a surface that can be unrolled onto a flat plane without tearing or stretching it.

Figure 3.2 – Ruled Surface

What are guide curves for a skinned surface?

One option with skinning is to specify guide curves between the sections. A guide curve controls the shape between the sections. The guide curves must precisely touch the sections. Any number of guide curves can be used.

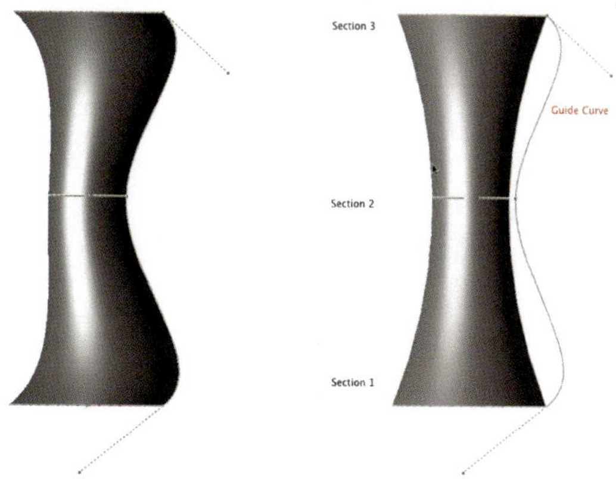

Figure 3.3 – Guide curves with a skinned surface

Can I use more than one curve as a section in a Skin Surface?

Yes, you can use more than one curve if you use the group command on your curves that lie in one section.

The curves do not need to be tangent continuous, but they must be connected end to end.

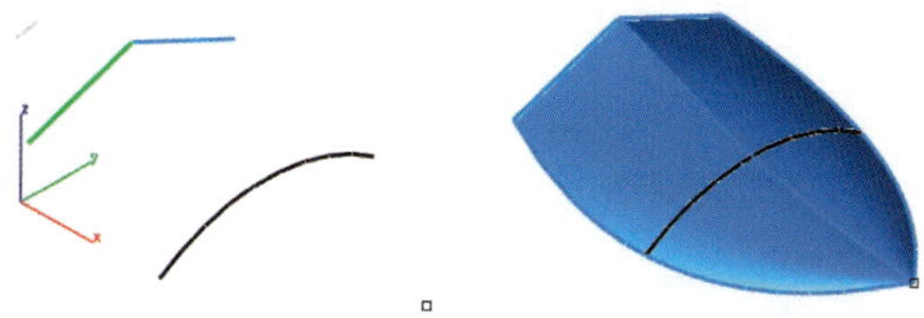

Figure 3.4

Is it possible to make a Skin Surface go to a point?

Yes, you can use a point entity in your skin surface to make it go to a point. However, the point must be at either the first and/or last section.

You cannot control the tangency or draft angles of a skin surface if the section uses a point object.

Figure 3.5

How can I control the tangency of a Skin Surface?

You can specify perpendicular slopes at each section or specify the angle and magnitude at the start and end sections.

- Method 1: After you create the surface, display the Inspector and select the Data tab under Object Properties. Select the Perpendicular Skin option to change the slope to 90° at each section.

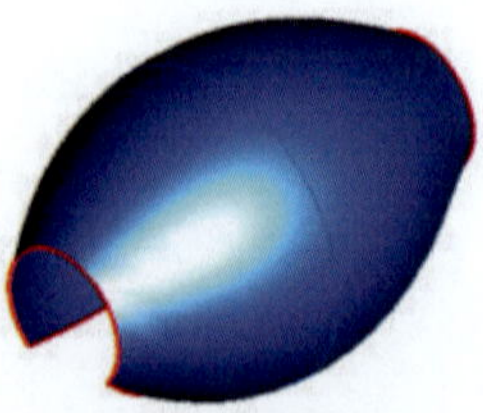

(a) Original

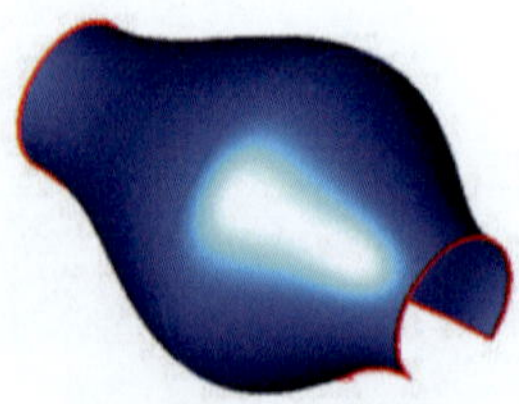

(b) Perpendicular Skin

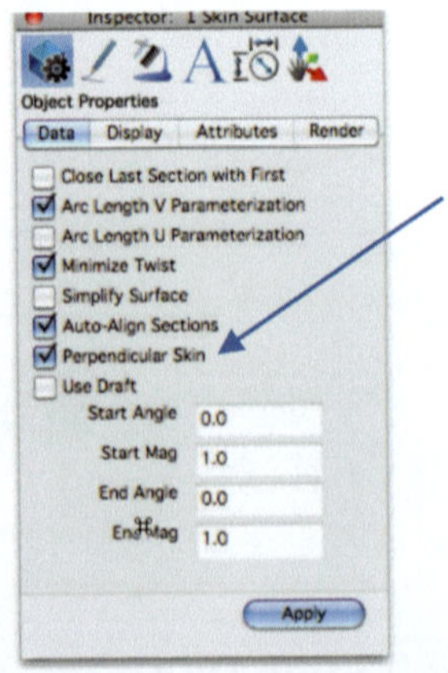

Figure 3.6

- Method 2: Another option is to specify the angle and magnitude at the start and end section to 90°. However, you cannot control the slope of the intermediate section with this method.

(a) Original

(b) Use Draft

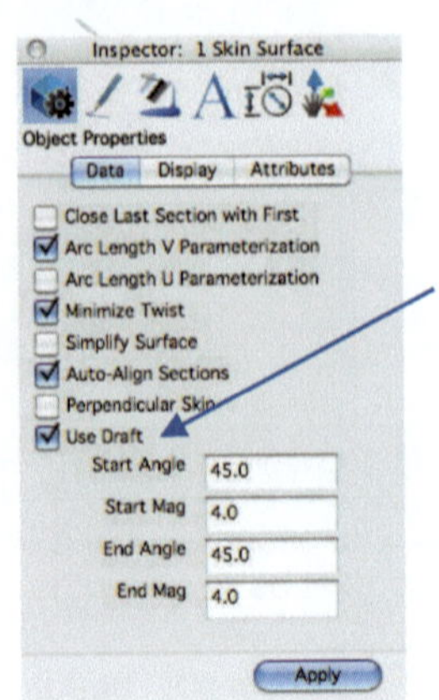

Figure 3.7

Can I remove a curve from a Skin Surface?

Yes, Concepts Explorer has an option to remove a curve from a Skin surface. To remove the curve:

- Select the surface and display Concepts Explorer.

- Go to the Features tab and click the arrow to the left of the Skin surface to see the construction history of the surface.
- Right click on the curve that you want to remove from the surface construction to bring up a popup menu.
- From the popup menu select Remove Curve.

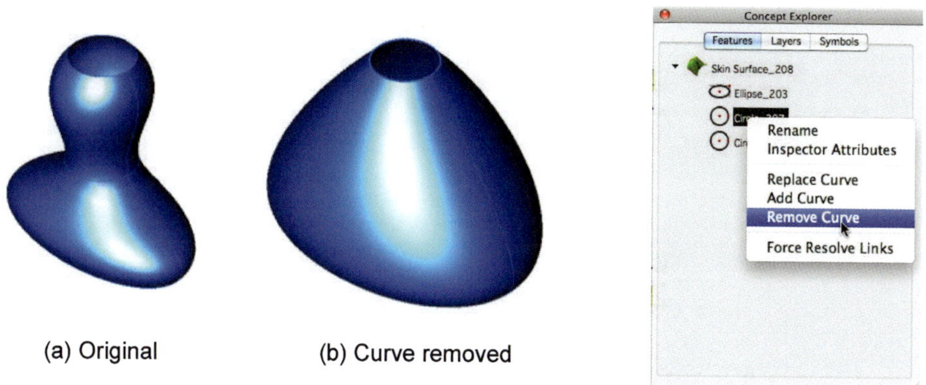

Figure 3.8 – Using Concept Explorer to remove curves

What does the "Arc length V" Option do to a Skin Surface?

The Arc Length V Parameterization option is used to control the v-direction parameterization of the skinned surface. With this, you can choose between arc length parameterization and isoparametric parameterization of the destination surface.

- With isoparametric parameterization, the surface parameter in the *v* direction follows the cross section curves.
- With arc length parameterization, the surface parameter follows uniformly parameterized lines.

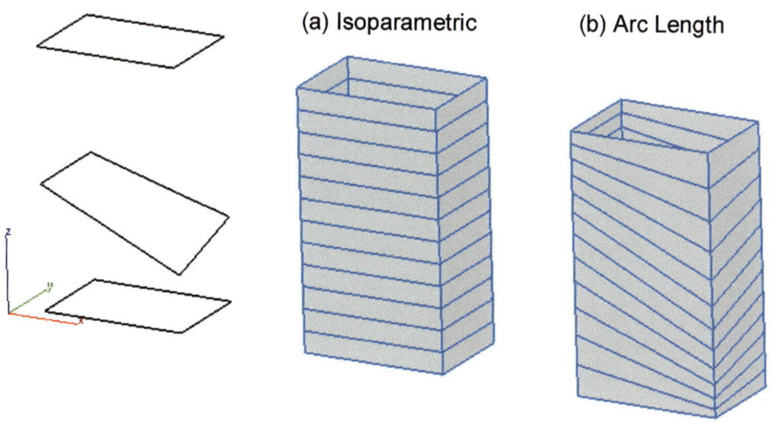

Figure 3.9 – V-direction Parameterization

What does the "Arc length U" Option do to a Skin Surface?

The Arc Length U Parameterization option is used to control the u-direction parameterization of the skinned surface. This controls re-parameterization of the profile curves so as to have arc length parameterization.

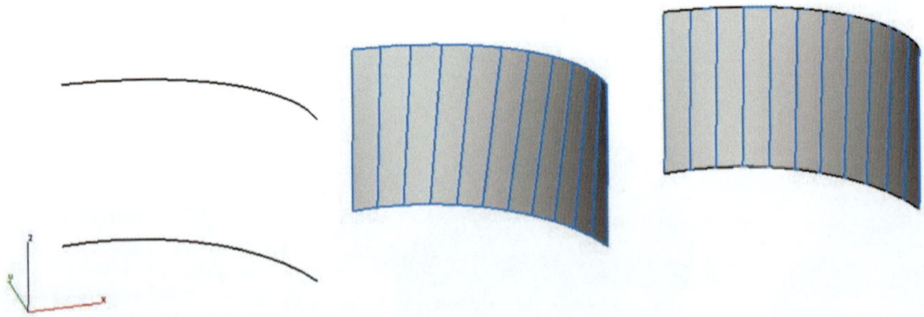

Figure 3.10 – U-direction Parameterization

The re-parameterization does not apply to circular, helical and straight profile curves, because they are uniformly parameterized already.

What does the "Closed Last Section" option do to a Skin Surface?

Selecting this option will automatically close the last section with the first section. This also makes the surface periodic creating a smooth connection.

Figure 3.11 – Using the "Closed Last Section" option

What does the "Auto-Align Sections" option do to a Skin Surface?

The default option when creating skin surfaces is to automatically align curves. This means you do not need to be concerned about the direction of the curves. If you turn this option off, you will need to manually check the curve directions or you may get a twisted surface.

Figure 3.12 – Auto-Align Sections

What does the "Minimize Twist" Option do to a Skin Surface?

This option will attempt to minimize the twisting between consecutive skin profiles. The default option when creating skin surfaces is to minimize twist.

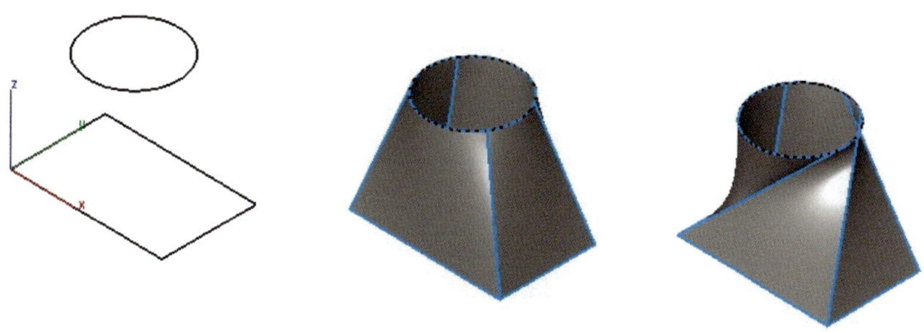

Figure 3.13 – Minimize Twist

Can I loft between a surface and a curve?

The *Loft Surface* tool additionally accepts a curve as one the two sections to loft between. However, when you loft to a curve, the initial tangent is derived from the plane of the curve and the surface.

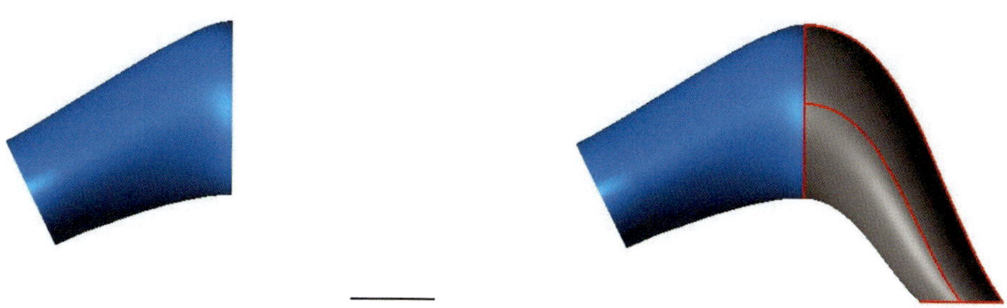

Figure 3.14 – Surface to curve lofting

For better control over the tangent, you can construct a reference surface from the curve. This allows you to control the slope. In the example below, an extruded surface was made from the curve.

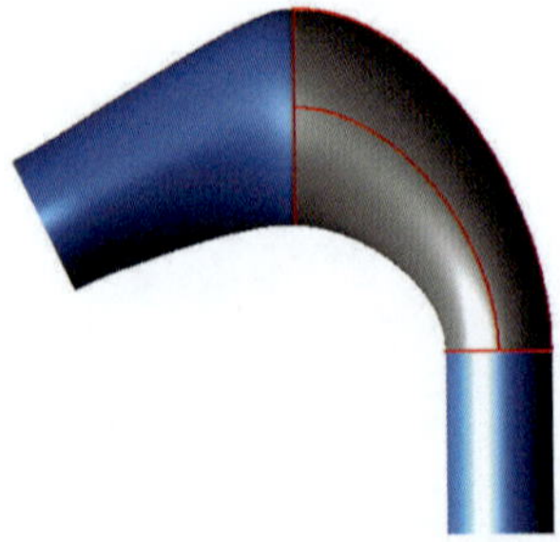

Figure 3.15 – Lofting with reference surface

What does the bulge factor control in a loft surface?

The bulge factor controls the magnitude of the tangent on each end of the lofted surface. You can control each tangent using the Bulge 1 and Bulge 2 entry fields in the Inspector Properties tab.

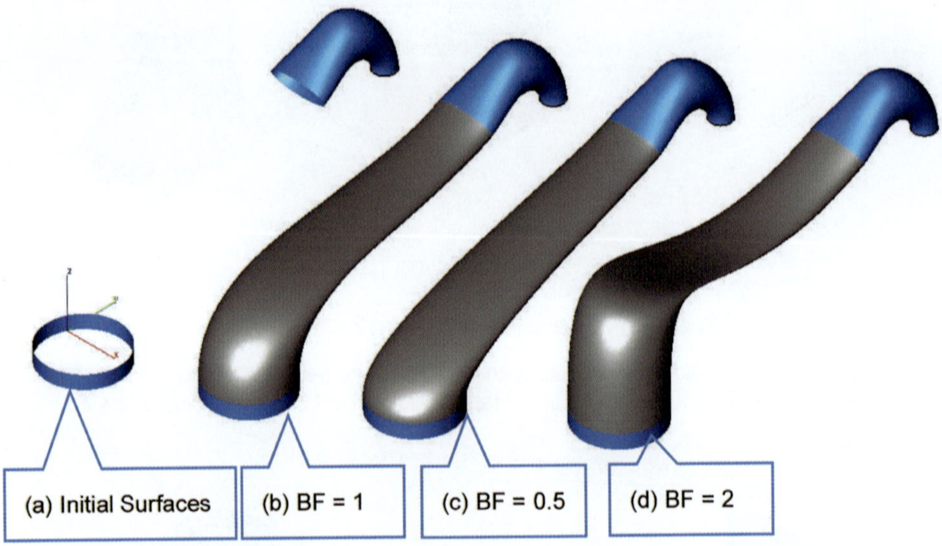

Figure 3.16 –Bulge Factor

Covering

What is covering?

Covering creates a surface from a closed loop of curves. In some cases, covering includes options for tangencies, guide curves, and bulge factors. Covering is unique from the other surface methods in that the interior shape is not defined. It is left to the covering algorithm to determine how to blend between the outer boundaries. Covering is typically categorized into two types (planar and N-sided) depending on whether the curves are planar or 3D.

What is planar covering?

Simple covering algorithms are employed for surfaces that are defined by a set of closed planar curve boundaries. Internally, they are represented as planar analytic surfaces, which are very compact and computationally efficient. Planar covers are useful (but not required) when combined with the *Sweep, Lathe,* and *Extrude Profiles Into Solid* tools. They are also suitable for use with the 2D *Boolean* tools.

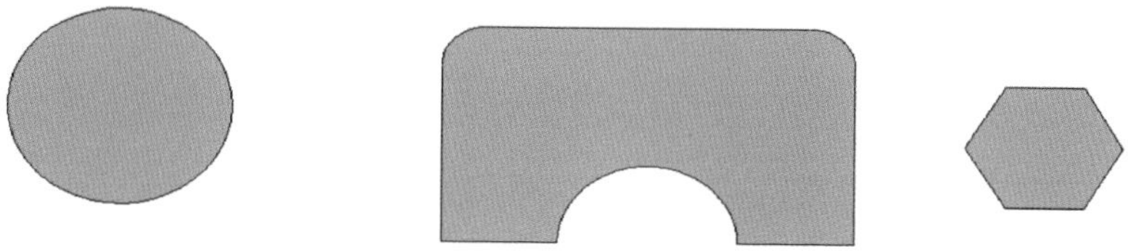

Figure 3.17 – Planar covering

What is N-sided covering?

The surface modeling kernel uses a N-Sided covering algorithm for non-planar curves. With this algorithm, any number of bounding curves can be used to define the outside shape. Internally, a smooth four-sided surface is created that uses the boundary curves as trimming curves.

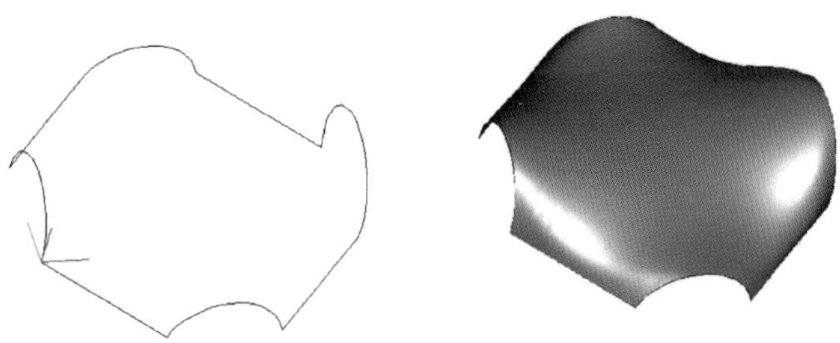

Figure 3.18 – N-Sided covering

When working with N-Sided coverings, you cannot use curves that are tangent end to end and curves that project into a plane that intersect.

How flexible is covering with Guide Curves?

ViaCAD's big brother Shark has an additional option for specifying guide curves with cover surfaces. The guide curve options are rather flexible: you can use any curve type including points, lines, arcs, circles, ellipses, and splines. Additionally, the curves need not touch the boundaries and may cross over each other. However, there is a requirement that the guide curves fall within the projected outline of the cover boundaries.

In the first example, the guide curves cross over each other.

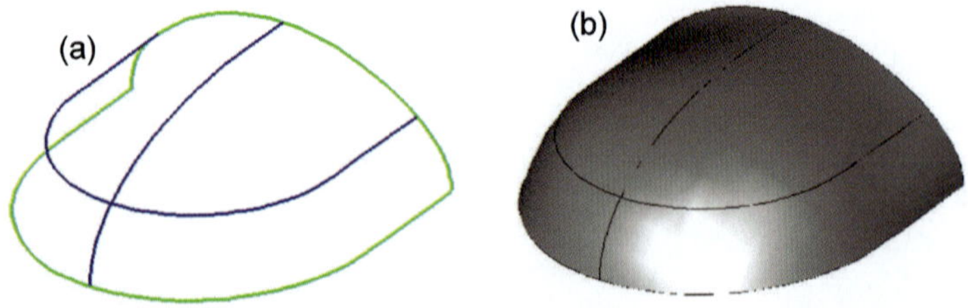

Figure 3.19 - (a) Cover and Guide Curves beside the (b) Cover Surface

In this example, the guide curves do not touch the cover boundaries.

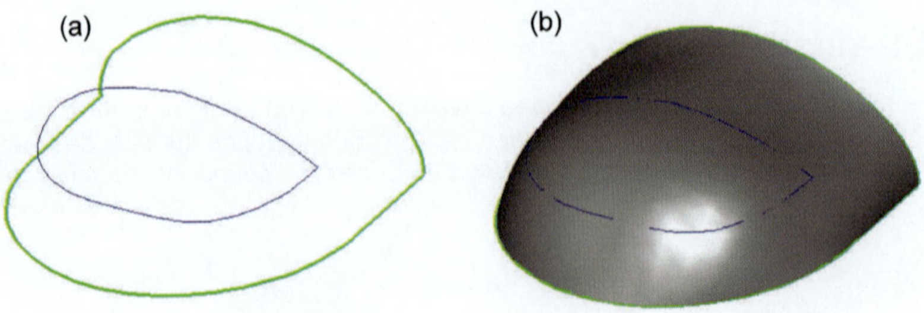

Figure 3.20 – (a) Cover and Guide Curves beside the (b) Cover Surface

In this final example, the guide curve tool is accepting point objects as guide constraints. The three squares in the image below are point objects.

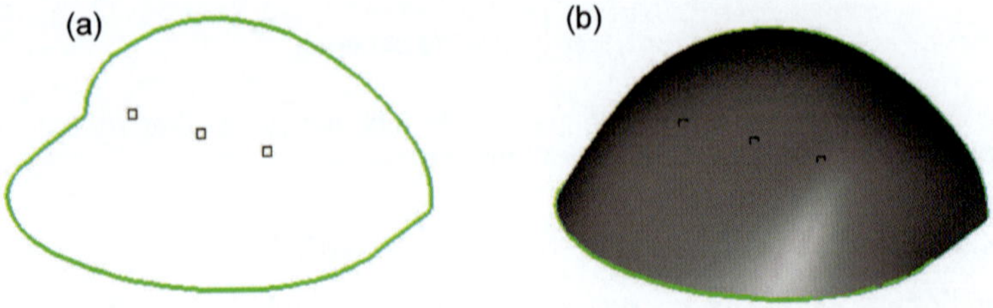

Figure 3.21 – (a) Cover and Guide Curves beside the (b) Cover Surface

Can I use internal regions for a cover surface?

If the curves are all planar, the *Cover Surface* tool supports internal regions as holes or cutouts.

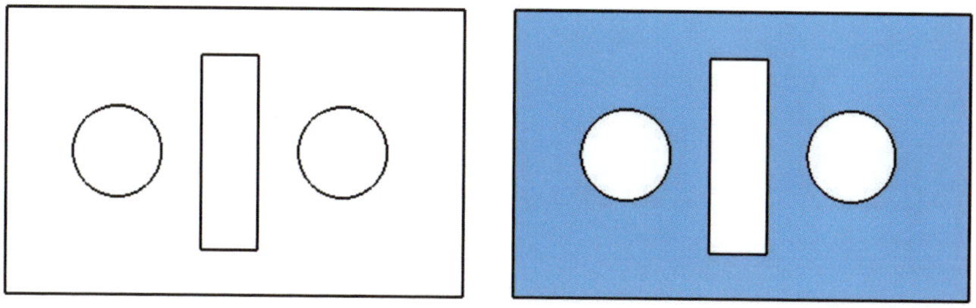

Figure 3.22

3D Covers do not support interior regions. The curves must connect end to end.

What is tangent covering?

The *Tangent Cover Surface* tool will create a surface that is G1 tangent to the neighboring surfaces. The magnitude of the tangents are controlled by the bugle factor, which ranges from 0.001 to 1.0.

Figure 3.23 – Tangent Cover Surface tool

What does it mean to fill with a tangent cover?

The example below creates a tangent cover surface between a closed loop of 12 surface edges, filling in the void with a smooth surface.

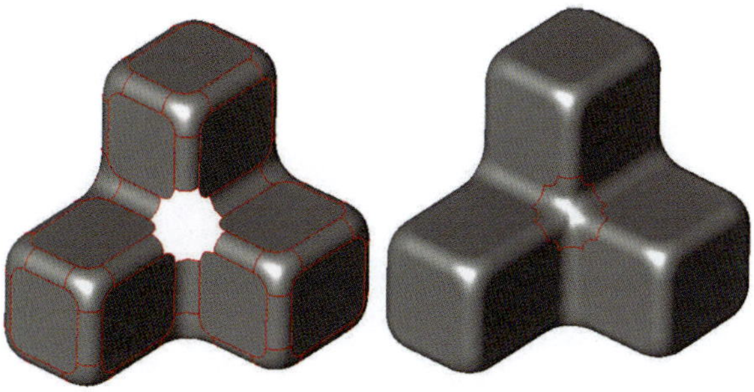

Figure 3.24 – Filling example

What does it mean to cap with a tangent cover?

The example below creates a tangent cover surface between a closed loop of 8 surface edges, capping between the edges with a smooth surface. In this case, the cap height is controlled by the bulge factor.

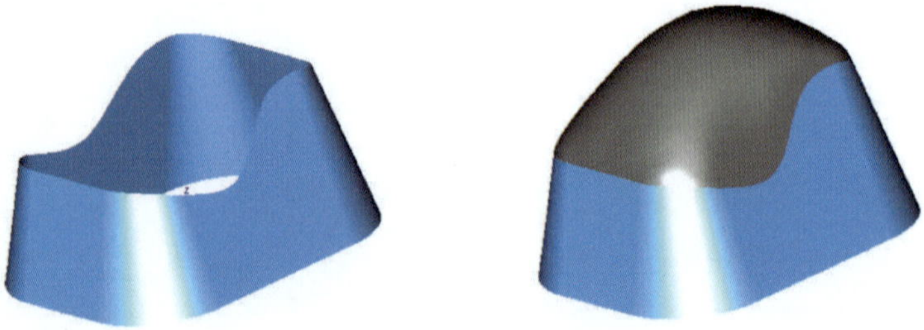

Figure 3.25 – Capping example

What is the Bulge Factor In a Cover Surface?

The bulge parameter is used to control how G1 constraints affect the shape of the covering surface.

As an example, consider slicing off the top of a cone and then performing a G1 cover to make a smooth "nosecone". When the bulge parameter is zero, the cross-sectional shape of the "nosecone" will be roughly parabolic. When the bulge is large (.4 to .7) the cross-section will be flat in the center, with sharp "shoulders" near the outside to accommodate the tangency constraints.

Typical bugle factors should range between 0.001 and 1.0. Bulge factors can be modified at any time using the data entry window or Object Info dialog box through associativity.

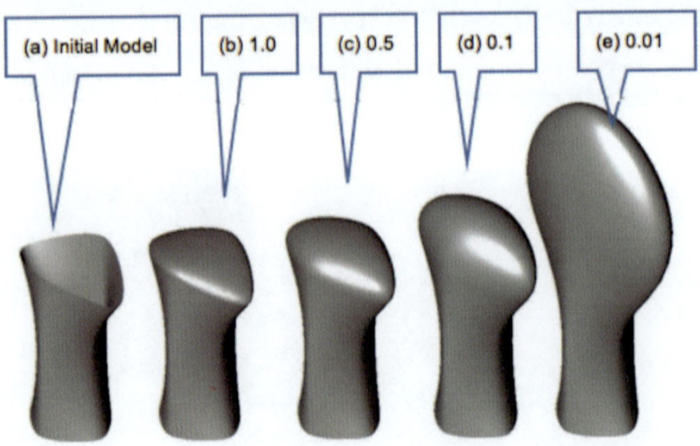

Figure 3.26 – Bulge factor examples

How can I repair curves for covering?

The two most frequent problems that prevent successful covering are curves that are slightly out of plane and curves that do not connect cleanly. This is especially noticeable when working with geometry that was imported from other software applications. Two tools that are very helpful for repairing these situations are the *Project Curve to Plane* and *Connect Curve* tools pictured below.

Tools to Repair Cover Edges

- ***Project Curve to Plane* tool** - One of the uses of *Project Curve to Plane* tool is to repair profiles that are slightly out of plane. This may happen from profiles imported from other CAD systems or accidentally placing a curve point out of plane.

  After you use the project curve to plane tool, you should check your curves for connectivity. A useful tool for quickly checking connectivity is the *Select Chain* command found under Edit on the menu. If the curves are not connected, use the *Connect Curve* tool below.

- ***Connect Curve* tool** - The *Connect Curve* tool is used to move one end point of a curve to another. The tool is great for repairing small gaps in curves or as a profile for generating a solid via sweeping, lathing, or extrude.

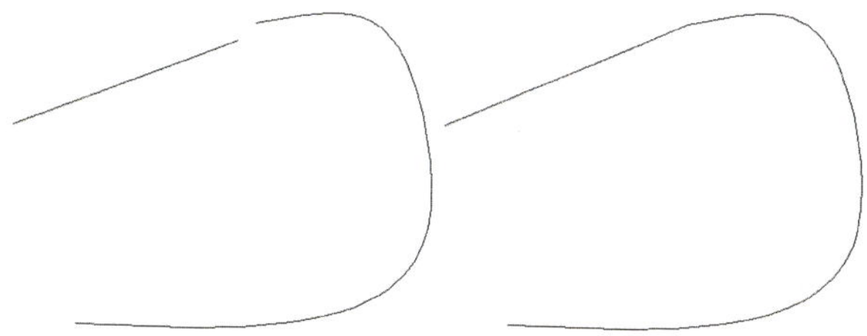

Figure 3.27 – Connecting Curves using Connect Curve tool

You can also use the *Connect Curve* tool to fix an entire profile or collection of curves. The gap tolerance in the data entry window is used to identify candidate curves to automatically close.

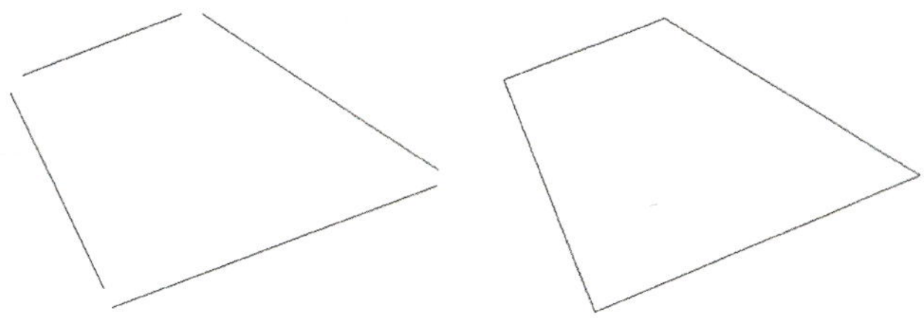

Figure 3.28 - Using the Connect Curve tool to fix an entire profile

Net Surface

What is a Net Surface?

A Net Surface is a created by a surfacing technique that uses a network of curves defining both the u and v surface parameter directions. This is different than skinning and lofting which generally takes curves defining the u parameter direction.

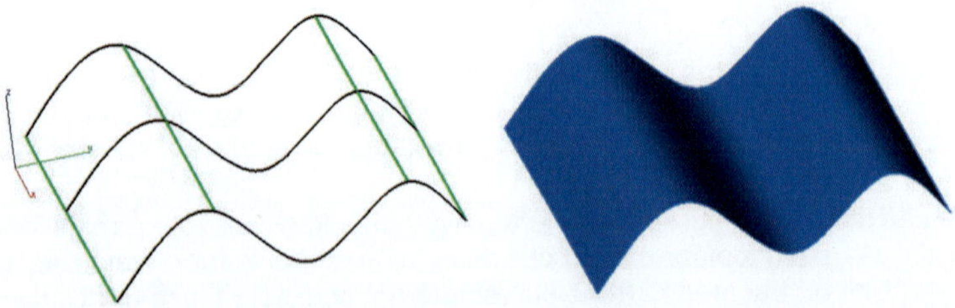

Figure 3.29 - Net Surface from 4x3 curve network

What curve types can be used for a Net Surface?

You can use all curve types except for a point entity to create a net surface. However each curve network must only consist of one curve. Additionally, you cannot use groups (which may contain curves) to define a network.

Are the direction of the curves important in a Net Surface?

You do not need to worry about the direction of the curve networks, as the algorithm will attempt to automatically align the curves.

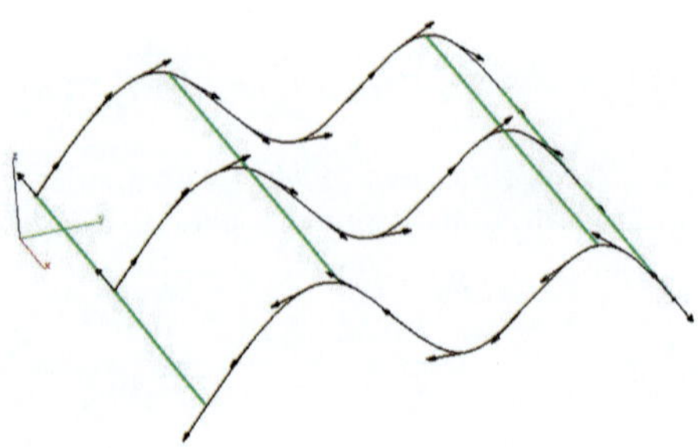

Figure 3.30- Network using curves of different directions

Do the curves in a Net Surface need to touch?

No, the curves do not need to touch in order for a net surface to function. For non-touching curves the intersection is interpolated.

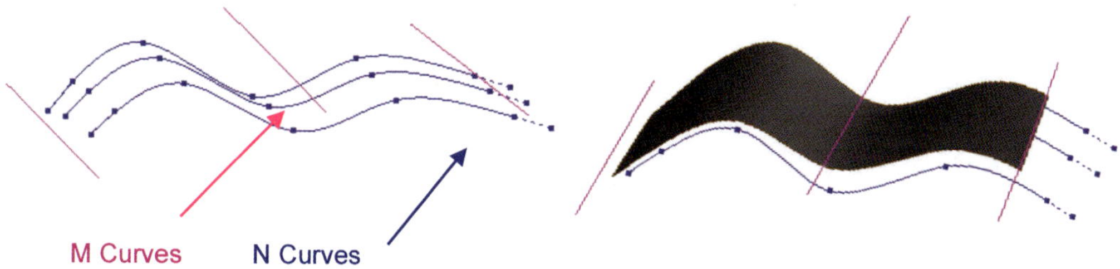

Figure 3.31 – Non-touching net surfacing

The maximum amount the curves can be apart is specified in the Data Entry Window. Additionally, the curves do not need to be planar. However, they must be curvature continuous curves. For example, some curves from Adobe Illustrator are not curvature continuous and will not work.

Swept Surface

What is a Swept Surface?

The swept surface moves an open or closed profile along a vector, one rail, or two rails to create a NURB surface. The figure below illustrates the three types of sweeping in ViaCAD.

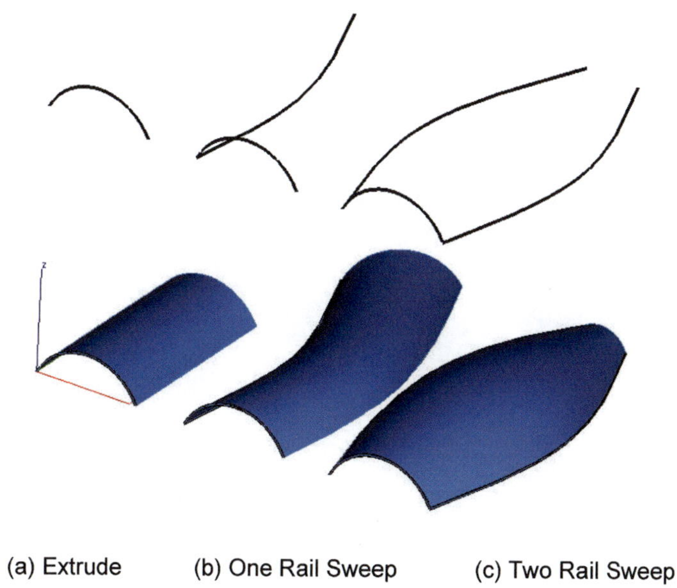

Figure 3.32 – Sweeping

What is the difference between Sweep in Place and Sweep Perp?

The one rail swept surface sweeps offers three types of sweeping:

- **Sweep In Place** - The start of the surface uses the give orientation of the profile.
- **Sweep Perp** - The profile is transformed to be perpendicular along the entire rail.
- **Sweep Rigid** - The profile is translated along the rail.

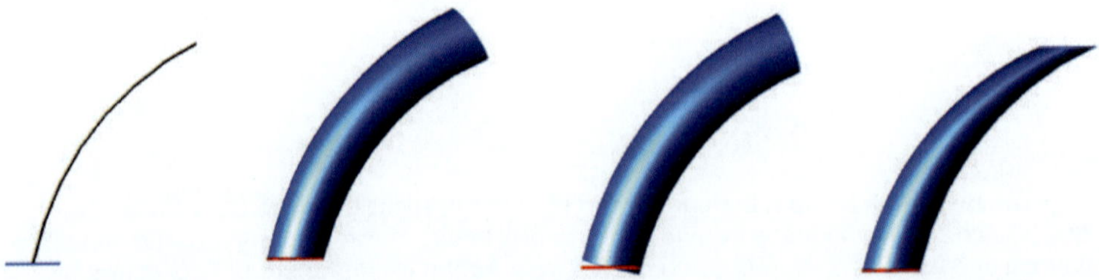

(a) Original Curves (b) Sweep In Place (c) Sweep Perpendicular (d) Sweep Rigid

Figure 3.33 – One Rail Sweep Options

What does the "Maintain Height" option do in a Two Rail Sweep?

After you create a two rail sweep, there is a check box in the Inspector Data tab to Maintain Height. This option will keep the original profile height as it sweeps across the two rails as seen in the figure below.

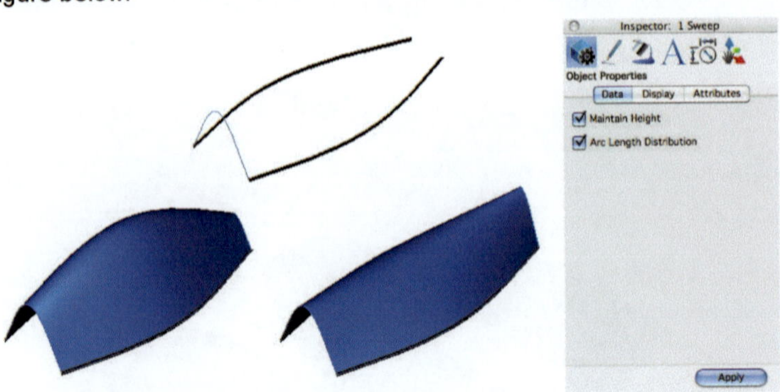

Figure 3.34 – Maintain Height

Surface Utilities

How can I tell the direction or orientation of a surface?

- Select the surface.
- Go to Verify on the Menu Bar.

- From the pull down, pick the Show Direction command.

The arrows displayed point in a direction normal to the surface.

You can use the Change Direction command under the Edit menu to flip the orientation.

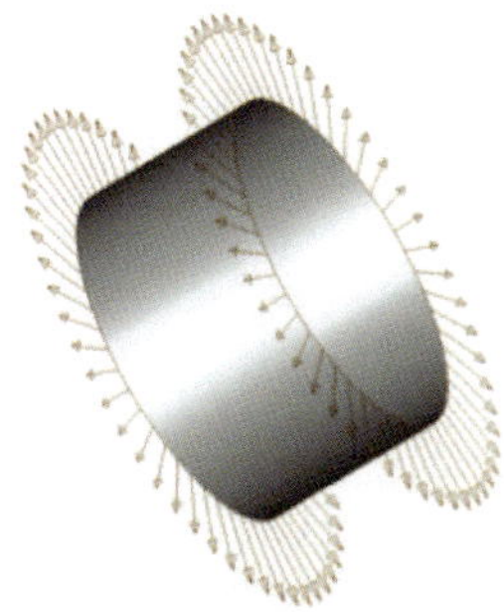

Figure 3.35 – Show Direction command

Is it possible to repair a bad surface?

If your surface has undesirable characteristics, it is possible to repair or rebuild your surface. There are several options for potentially repairing a questionable surface.

- Method 1: If you are using ViaCAD Pro or Shark, you can use the Rebuild command.

- Method 2: Change the surface resolution to include isolines. Specify enough U, V to capture the inside shape. Then, use the next surface to recreate a new surface.

How can I visualize a degenerative surface?

Some design practices try to avoid creating degenerative surfaces. A degenerative surface is a surface that goes to a point that typically occurs with three sided surfaces. A common problem with a degenerate surface is the normal is ill defined at the degenerative point. To identify a degenerative surface:

- Go to Edit on your Menu Bar.

- Open up the Object Resolution dialog box.

- Turn on isolines.

- If the isolines all share a common point, the surface is considered degenerative.

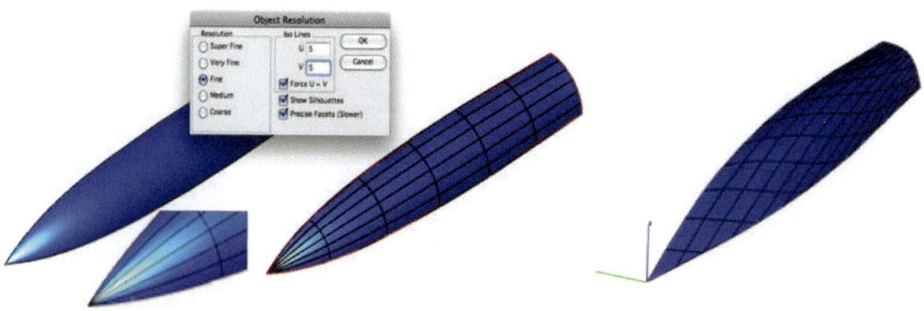

(a) Degenerative Surface (b) Normal Surface

Figure 3.36 - Surface Isolines

Turning on the isolines is also very useful for identifying surface waves or other anomalies.

How can I repair a degenerative surface?

One very useful tool for repairing degenerative surfaces is the *Rebuild Surface* tool.

The *Rebuild Surface* tool will recreate an underlying surface larger than the original and reapply the edges as trim surfaces. As a result, any degenerative edges are removed. Additionally, it samples isolines of the original surfaces to maintain the shape in the resulting surface.

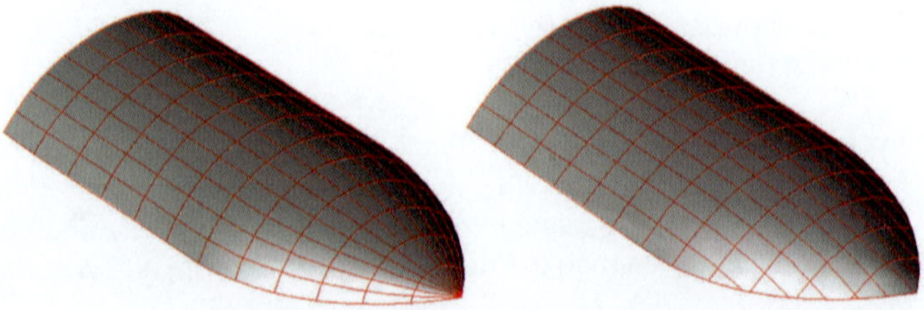

Figure 3.37 - Rebuilt Degenerate Surface

The other option regarding degenerative surfaces is to consider constructing the surface from the beginning using a surface type that would minimize a degenerative point. The example below shows the difference between using a Skin Surface and a Cover Surface for the same three curves. The Cover Surface used the right most circle and the point as guides.

(a) Original Curves (b) Skin Curves (c) Cover with Guides

Figure 3.38 – Cover vs. Skin Surface

What is surface associativity?

All surface types, including Covers, are associative to the curves originally used to create the surface. This associativity is transparently created as you construct the surface and includes not only the curves but also the parameters. Moving the curve boundaries or changing a surface parameter definition (such as revolve angle) will automatically update the surface.

When working with cover surfaces that require the boundary curves to be connected, be sure to move the curves in such a manner that they do not become disjoint or turn off the auto regen functionality in the Preferences panel.

Use Concepts Explorer to display graphical representations of associativity between objects. Additionally, clicking on the object in Concepts Explorer will display context sensitive operations. For example, to replace a curve, right click on the Replace Curve menu item in Concepts Explorer.

How can I flip the rotation direction of a Surface of Revolution?

Select the Surface of Revolution and display the Inspector data parameter tab. Change the sign of the rotation angle. In the example below the angle was changed from 180 to -180 degrees.

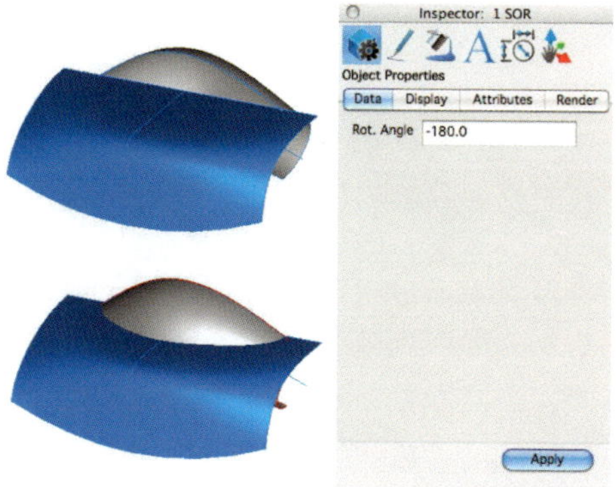

Figure 3.39

What controls the portion of a surface removed in a boolean operation?

The *Surface Boolean* tools provide a means to add, remove, and intersect portions of a surface with another surface. However, what gets removed or added may not always be clear unless you understand how surface direction impacts this tool's operation.

Typically a boolean operation involves a water tight shape in which the material is asociated with an enclosed volume. The boolean operation then adds, subtracts, or interects the two material volumes.

For a surface which lacks a closed volume, the boolean operation will identify material as everything on one side of the surface. The side of material is defined by the surface direction.

To see a surface direction:

- Select the surface and pick the *Show Direction* tool from Verify on the Menu bar. The arrows displayed indicate the direction away from the surface material.
- Use the Change Direction tool from the Edit menu bar to flip the surface direction.

Figure 3.40 below shows how the surface direction creates different results for a surface Boolean subtract. The darker surface is being subtracted from the lighter surface.

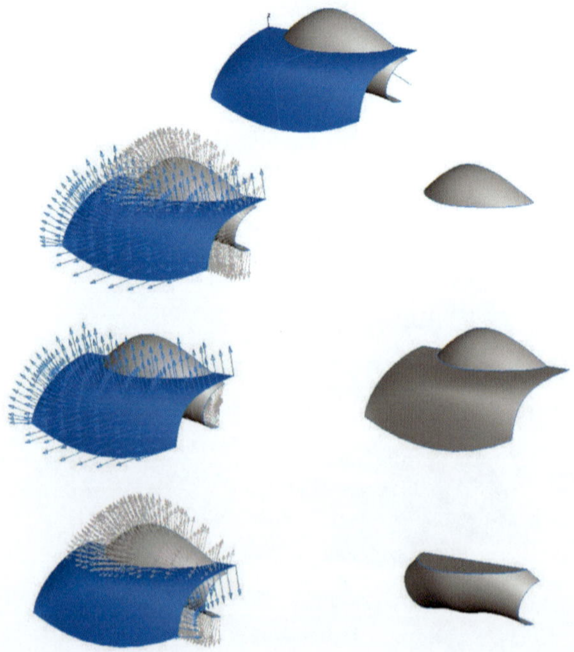

Figure 3.40

Can I do a boolean operation between a surface and a solid?

The *Surface Boolean* tool not only allows you to select a surface, but it also allows you to select a solid. When picking a surface, keep in mind that the surface direction plays an important role in determining which portion of the solid is removed.

Remember, to display the surface direction you use the Show Direction command located in the Verify menu. The arrows will point away from the side of the surface with material.

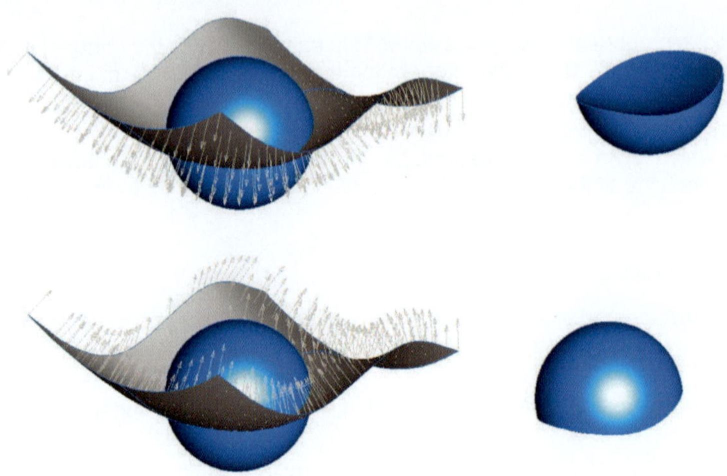

Figure 3.41

Can I fix a gap between two surfaces?

The *Match Surface* tool has an option to Match Position. This tool will move the two surfaces edges such that no gap is present.

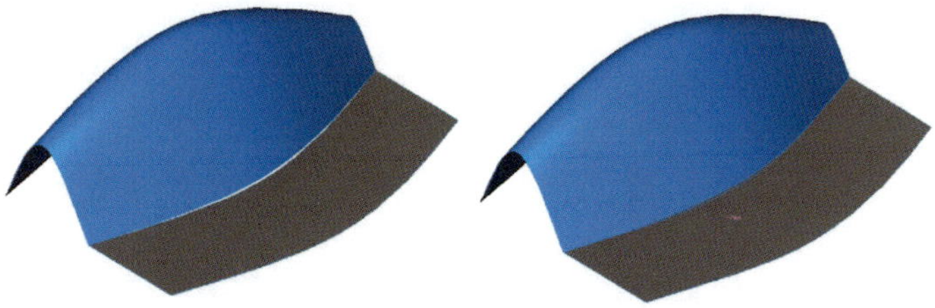

(a) Before Match (b) After Match

Figure 3.42- Match Position of Two Surface Edges

How does a Zebra Plot indicate surface smoothness?

The *Zebra Plot* tool is located under the Verify Surface Analysis located in the Menu bar. This tool provides a graphical indication of surface continuity. The conditions are identified by how the stripes flow between the two surfaces. With G0 continuity, the stripes do not line up from one surface to another whereas G1 continuity the strips line up with each other.

Figure 3.43 below shows three continuity conditions of G0 (position), G1(tangent), and G2(curvature) with zebra plots.

(a) G0 Continuity (b) G1 Continuity (c) G2 Continuity

Figure 3.43 - Zebra Plot

The Zebra Plot is based on display resolution. Be sure to increase the display resolution to get an accurate representation of the surface.

Can I project a curve by miniumum distance to a surface?

A hidden feature of the *Project Curves* tool is that you can project by the minimum distance between the curve and body. This condition is triggered if the project start and end points are the same.

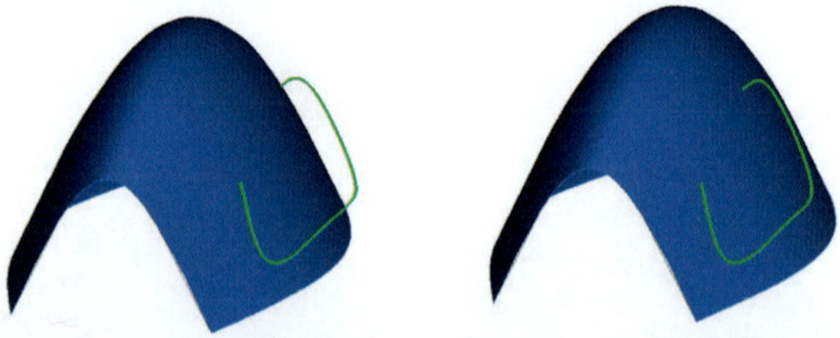

Figure 3.44

How can I create equally spaced section cuts?

- First, create a line spanning the length of the section cuts.
- Next, select the *Infinite Plane* tool command from the surface tool palette.
- Pick the Along Curve option from the Data Entry Window. Type in the number of planes that you want spaced along the curve. Note that the normal of the plane is aligned with the tangent of the curve at the location.
- Lastly, select the *Cut Section* tool and pick the planes and surface to cut.

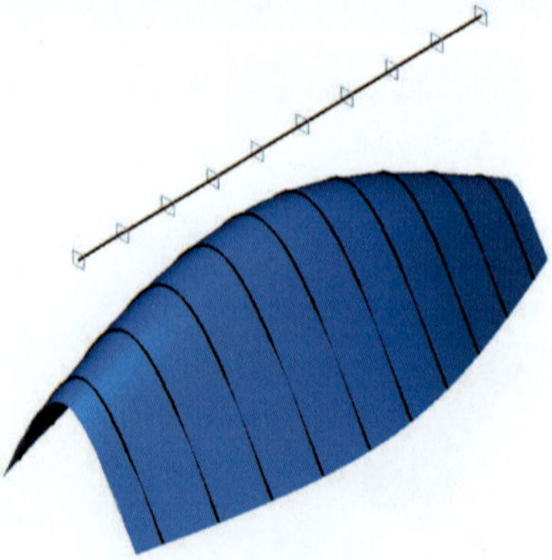

Figure 3.45

An interesting feature of this tool is that you can have each section cut placed in its own layer in which the name is related to the type of plane and location. Once each section cut is placed in a layer, you can quickly step through each layer by assigning a short cut key to the Inc Layer and Dec Layer commands located. These are located in the Layers Short Cut Manager.

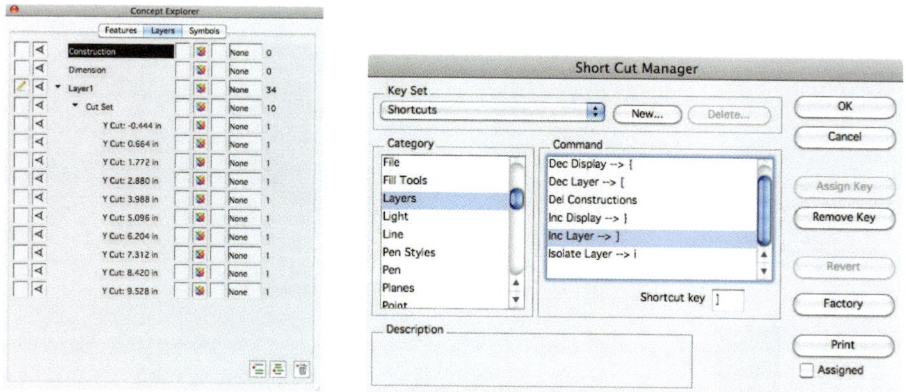

Figure 3.46

Subdivision Mesh

What is a Subdivision Mesh?

A Subdivision mesh is a method of representing a smooth surface by recursively subdividing a polygon using a smoothing algorithm. This application uses the popular Catmull-Clark algorithm based on a spline smoothing method.

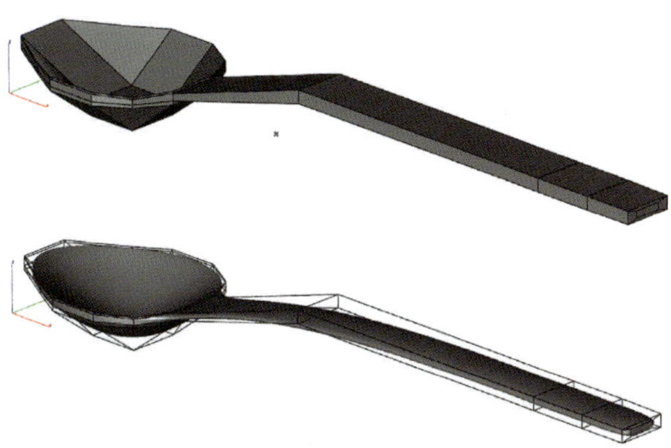

Figure 3.47 – Subdivision

How do I Subdivide a Mesh?

Any mesh can be subdivided, however quad meshes produce the best results. To add subdivision to a mesh, find the Subdivision icon located in the mesh tool palette.

Next select the mesh you want to subdivide. You can subdivide a mesh up to four times. Each time you subdivide, the mesh will appear smoother.

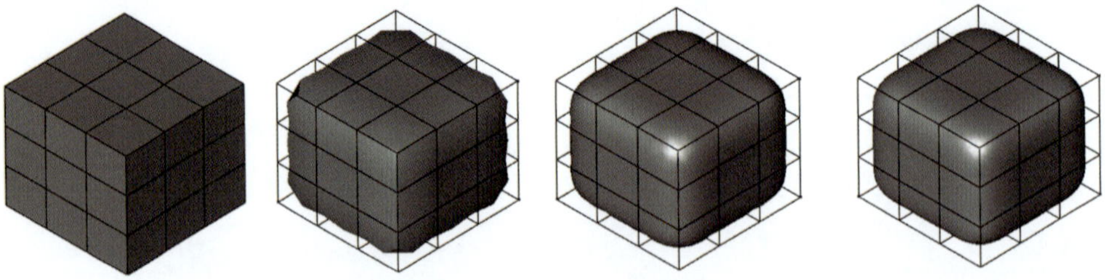

Figure 3.48 – Block with three Subdivisions

Can I reduce the number of Subdivisions?

You can manually edit the number of subdivisions associated with a mesh using the Inspector. Select the mesh, display the Inspector, and pick the Data tab. Enter the number of desired subdivisions using the "SubD Level" field. Use this to also remove a subdivision from a mesh by setting this value to zero.

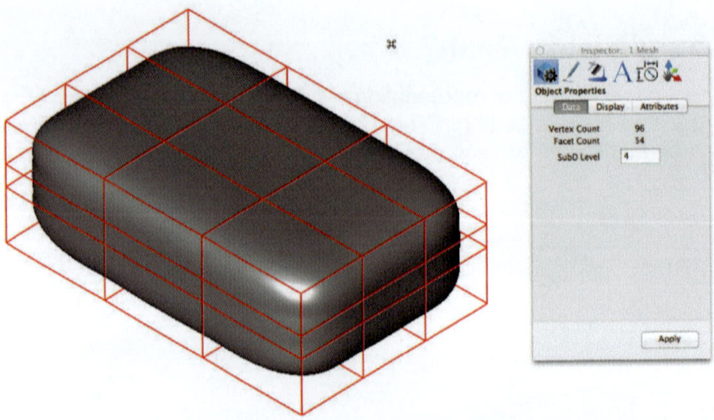

Figure 3.49 – Edit Subdivision

How do I hide the control polgyon of a Subdivision Mesh?

The control polygon of subdivided mesh is turned on and off using the Edit: Show Points command.

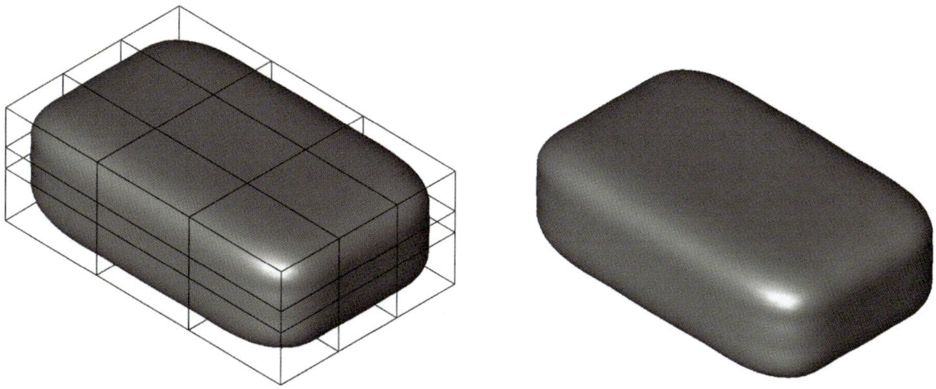

Figure 3.50 – Hide Control Polygon

Tip: Press the "t" key to toggle all meshes on the display screen between showing and hiding the control polygon of subdivided mesh.

Can I add facets without smoothing a mesh?

The default algorithm for subdivision is Catmull-Clark which produces a smooth mesh. Select the "Facetted" option from the prompt region to only add density to a selected mesh.

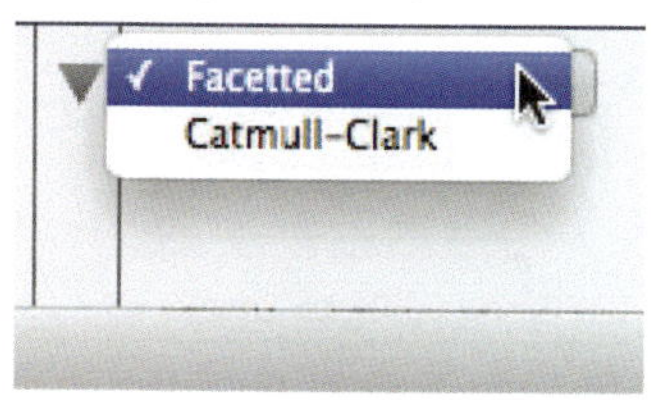

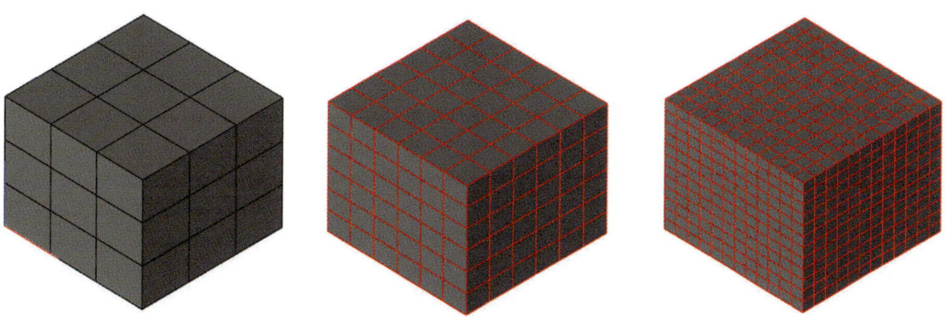

Figure 3.51 – Facetted Subdivision

How do I extrude a mesh face?

Extruding a face is possible using the Deep Select tool combined with a control key. Follow the steps below to extrude a single facet of a mesh.

1. Select the Deep Select tool. 

2. Be sure to enable the Gripper.
3. Select the Face(s) you want to extrude.

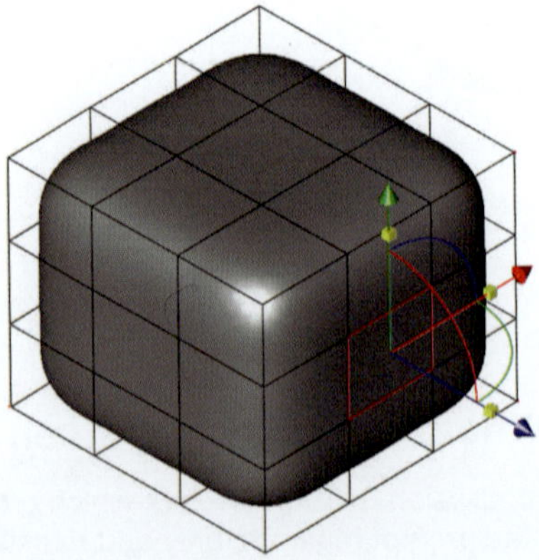

4. Hold down the Option Key (Mac) or Control Key (PC) and drag out the face.

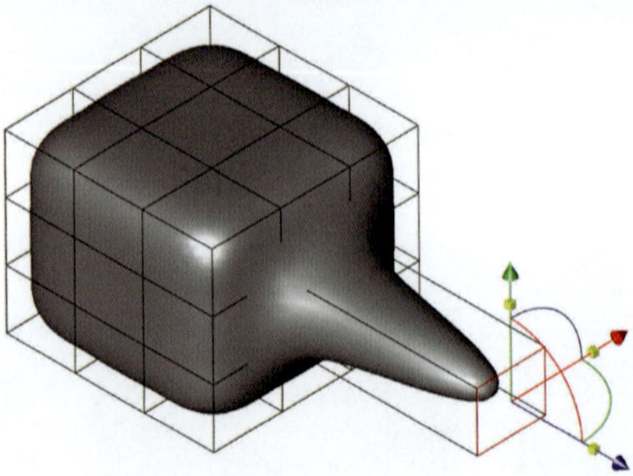

5. Continue to hold and release the copy key until you have the desired number of segments.

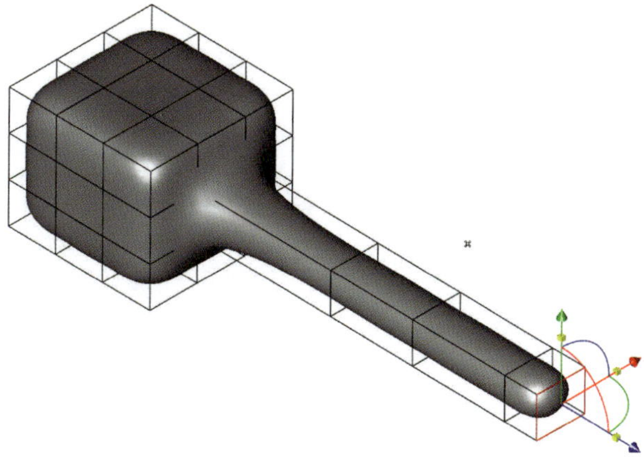

Is it possible to scale/copy a facet?

You can scale copy a single face using the Gripper while holding the Option Key (Mac) or Control Key(PC) and dragging the Scale graphical item (yellow box on Gripper axis).

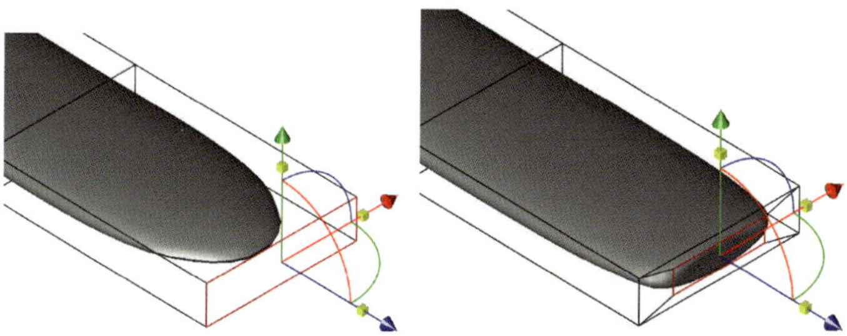

Figure 3.52 – Scale/Copy a Facet

Is it possible to delete a facet?

You can delete one or more facets by using the Deep Select tool and the Edit:Cut command. First select the desired facets to delete with Deep Select, then either hit the Delete key or Cut command from the menu bar.

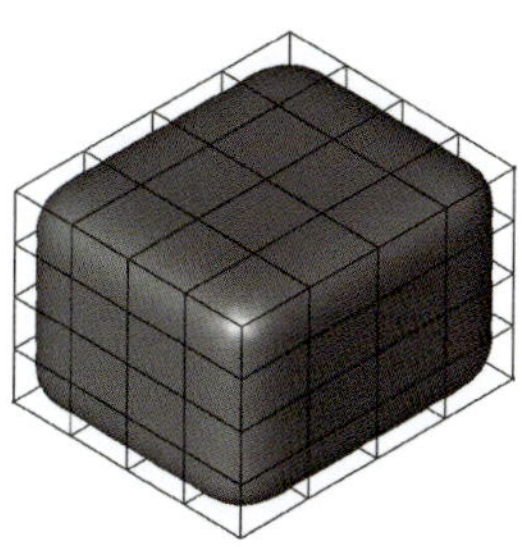

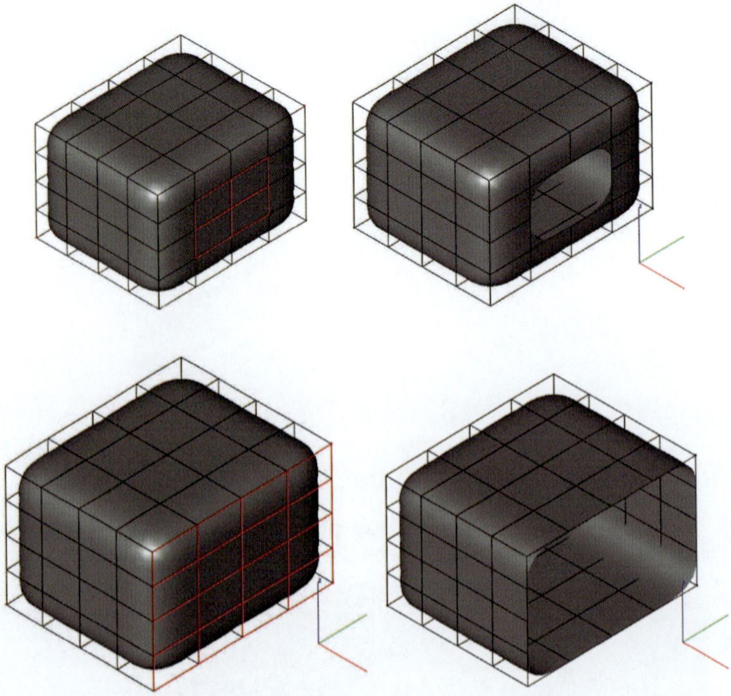

Figure 3.53 Delete Facet(s)

Is it possible to add a loop?

The Add Loop feature was added late in the first release and consequently not documented. You can add a loop to a control polygon by right clicking on a mesh to display the Object Contextual popup menu. Select the Add Loop option. The loop is added along the edge you pick.

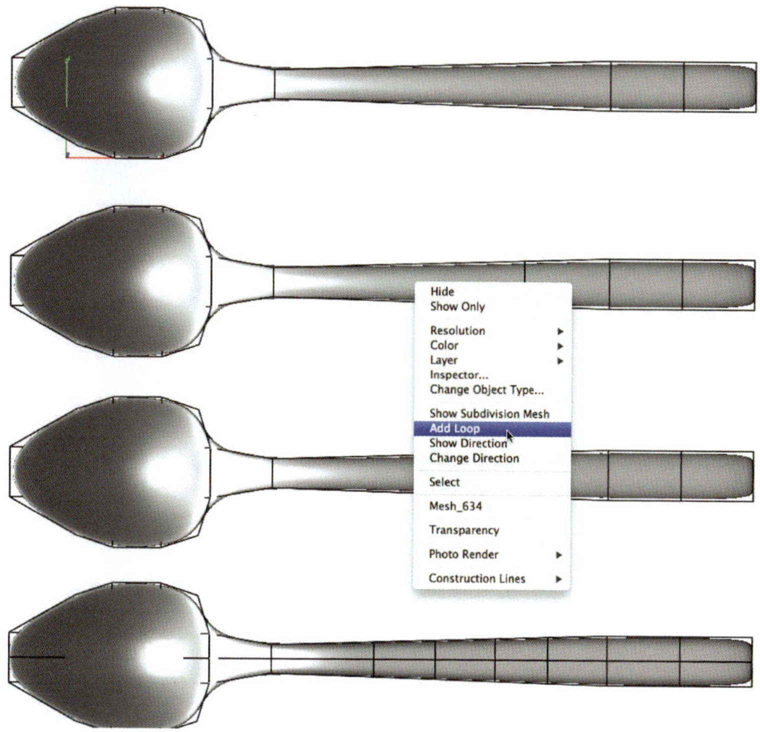

Figure 3.54 Add Loop

Does a Cover Mesh support holes?

The Cover Mesh supports inner holes as long as the collection of curves are planar. The Cover Mesh also supports non planar curves. Note that the Cover Mesh creates triangles along the curve boundary and quad meshes at the interior. The Edge Length parameter is an overall target and does not necessarily apply to areas of high curvature.

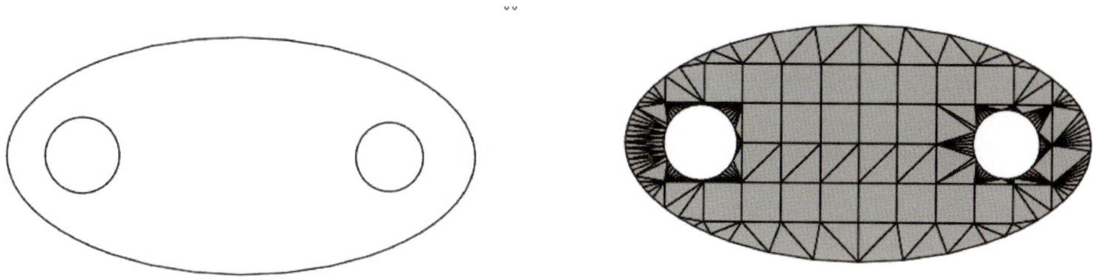

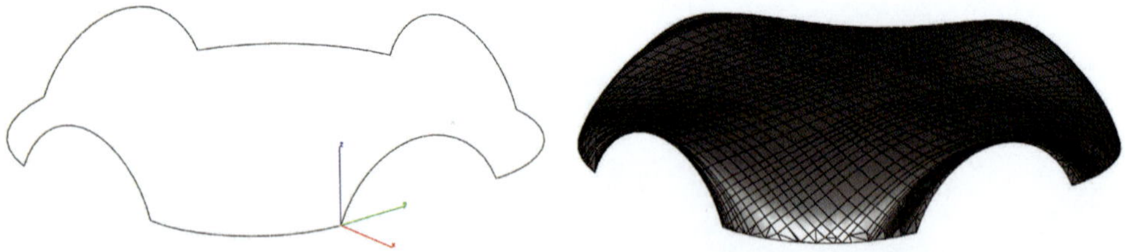

Figure 3.55 Cover Curve with Facets

Can I create an OBJ file of the control polygons?

When exporting an OBJ file, the application will always export the subdivision mesh if present. To export the control polygon mesh, you must remove the subdivision. This is accomplished through setting the “SubD Level” to Zero, located in the Data Tab of Inspector for a mesh.

Can I convert a subdivision mesh to a solid?

To convert a mesh to a solid, select the mesh and pick the Edit: Change Object Type : To Solid command from the menu bar. This feature is limited to stitching up to 2000 planar facets with no simplification into NURBs. The resulting solid is a facetted solid.

The PowerPack addon has additional features for converting large numbers of facets to analytical or NURB based solids.

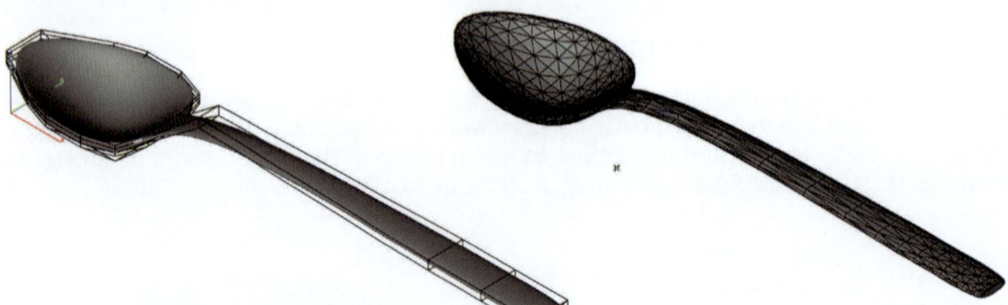

Figure 3.56 Facets to Solid

CHAPTER 4
SOLID MODELING

Overview

Solid modeling tools in ViaCAD allow you to create objects that are closed bodies with well-defined mass properties. You have access to a variety of solid modeling tools such as:

- **Primitives** – Tools that enable you to create spheres, blocks, and prisms using digitized locations.

- **Solid From Profiles** – Tools that enable you to extrude, sweep, or lathe a solid from a closed collection of curves.

- **Feature Based Solids** – Tools that enable you to add or remove material to a part using fillet, chamfer, hole boss, and shell feature operations.

- **Direct Face Editing** – Tools that enable you to modify one or more faces of an existing solid independent of previous feature tree construction.

- **Solid Modeling Utilities** – Tools that enable you to add, subtract, thicken, slice, and trim solids.

Primitives

How can I make a truncated cone?

By default the cone primitive creates a cone with a top radius of zero. However, you can truncate the cone by completing the following steps:

- Begin by selecting the cone.

- Display the Object Properties from the Inspector.
- Under the Data tab, adjust the Top Diameter parameter. By changing this value to a non-zero, you can make a truncated cone.

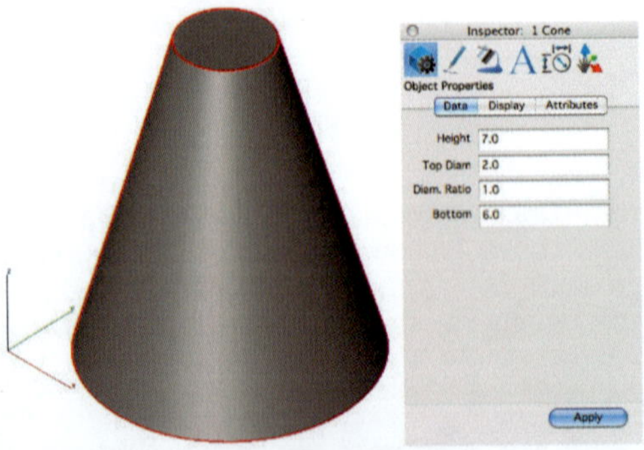

Figure 4.1 – Truncated Cone

How can I make an elliptical cylinder?

By default the cylinder primitive creates a cylinder with a circle as a cross section. However, you can make an elliptical cylinder by doing the following:

- Begin by selecting the cylinder.
- Display the Object Properties from the Inspector.
- Under the Data tab, adjust the Diameter Ratio parameter. By changing this value to anything other then one, you can make an elliptical cylinder.

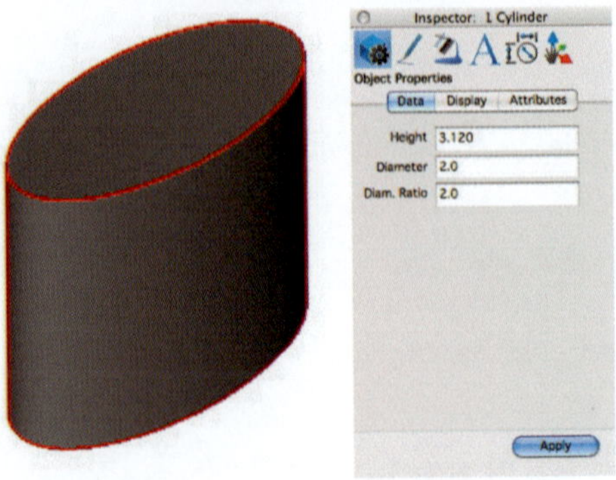

Figure 4.2 – Elliptical Cylinder

How can I access the primitive control points?

Selecting a primitive solid and picking the Edit: Show Points command will show the original points used to create a solid primitive. Moving these points will update the primitive.

However, once you perform a feature operation, these control points will be removed. You can still access the parameters through the feature tree using Concept Explorer.

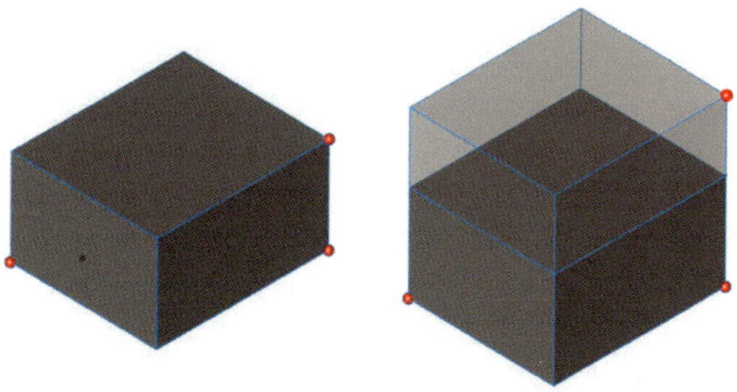

Figure 4.3 – Primitive Edit Control Points

Solid From Profiles

What can does the "Curves are not Planar" dialog box mean?

This error appears for all solid from profile tools when it encounters a profile that is not planar. To correct this problem, you need to make sure all curves in your profile are in the same plane. Because of the modeling tolerances, a curve that is out of plane by 0.001 inches can trigger this error. A tool that can assist you in fixing this issue is the Project Curve to Plane tool located in the surface utilities palette.

Projecting a group of curves into a plane may not retain connectivity. You may have to follow up the projection with the Connect Curve tool command.

How can I repair gaps in a profile?

A profile used to create a solid must connect end to end within a 0.00001 inches. Anything larger is considered a gap.

To correct this problem, you need to make sure all curves are precisely connected end to end. A convenient tool to connect close ends in a profile is the *Connect Curve* tool located in with the trimming tools. Be sure to adjust your acceptable gap size tolerance to meet the gap sizes in your profile.

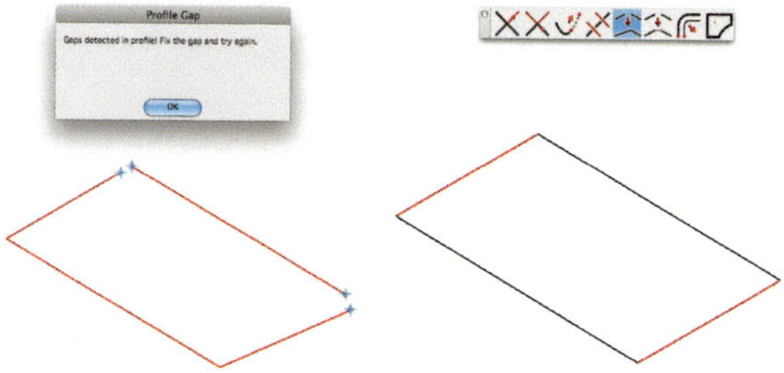

Figure 4.4 – Fix profile gaps with Connect Curve tool

How do I find overlapping curves?

Creating solids from profiles with overlapping curves will fail with an alert dialog box. To find the culprit curves, select the Arrow tool. Then select one of the curves in the profile and from the Edit menu pick Select Chain. The selection will stop at any location where there is a gap or overlapping curves.

Can I extrude a non-planar shape?

An undocumented feature of the *Extrude Solid* tool is that you can select planar or non-planar faces to extrude.

You cannot apply a draft angle to a non-planar extrusion.

(a) Non-Planar Face Extruded (b) Non-Planar Surface Extruded

Figure 4.5 – Non-Planar extrusion

How can I sweep a 3D non-planar path?

Sweeping is a powerful modeling technique for moving a section along a path to create either a surface or solid. It is similar to an extruded solid except instead of using an extrusion vector, you specify a sweep path composed of curves. The resulting surface/solid is associative to both the path and sweep curve.

You can sweep a 3D non-planar path by using the *One-Rail Sweep* tool, which sweeps along non-planar path in addition to planar ones.

To use the *One-Rail Sweep* tool to sweep a non-planar path:

- Pick one or more curves to sweep (line, spline, arc, circle, ellipse, or groups).
- Pick one or more curves for the rail path.
- From the prompt line pull down, select Sweep In Place for your profile orientation. This will preserve the starting orientation of the profile with respect to the path.
- From the second prompt line pull down, select Curve Extents. This controls how the sweep is terminated. By selecting Curve Extents, the profile will sweep across the entire curve extents.

- You can also adjust the twist and draft angles in the Data Entry Window.

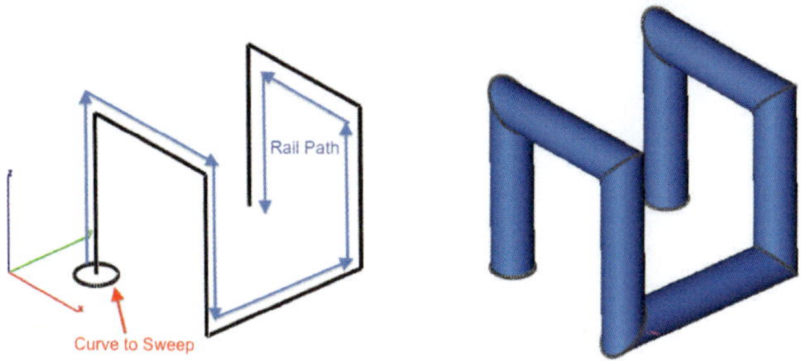

Figure 4.6 - Sweeping

When working with multiple paths, you may also select an option to define the shared ends. There are three choices you can select from the Option pull down from the tool prompt line.

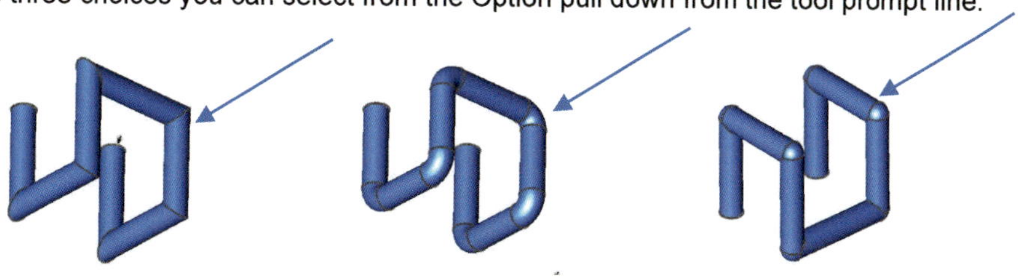

Mitered Bend Crimped

Figure 4.7 – Options for defining shared ends

How can I create multiple cutouts going the same direction in a single solid?

- Begin by drawing the holes as circles in the locations you want them.
- Then, use the *CutOut Solid* tool in the Extrude tools to select the solid.
- Next, select the outline of all your holes.
- Then, drag your cursor in the direction you want the holes to go.
- If you later decide you would like to change the location of a hole, simply drag the 2D geometry that you used to make that hole to its new location. The hole will follow.

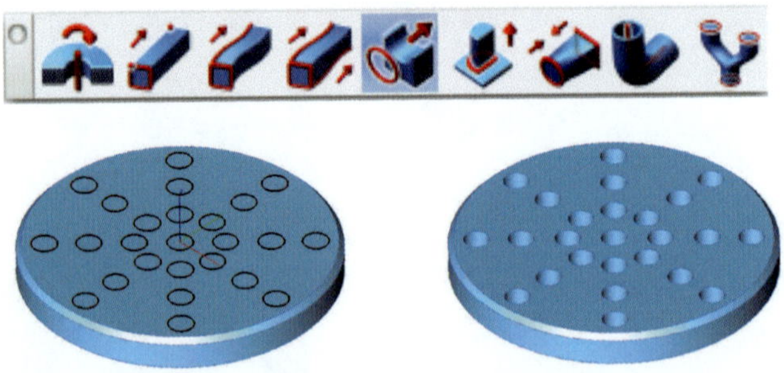

Figure 4.8 – Using Cutout Solid tool

Once you have created your holes, you can change their sizes by selecting the drawn object(s) that relate to the holes you want to change and editing them individually in the inspector. If they are all the same size, you can collectively edit the holes as one.

How can I make a pipe that overlaps?

If you are modeling a shape such as a chord, you may want to use a path that crosses back and forth. The default behavior of the *Pipe* tool is to disallow self-intersections. However, if you press the Options button you can set the behavior to allow self-intersections.

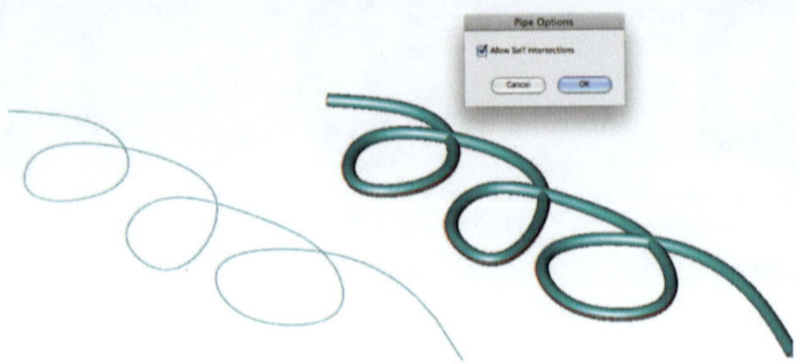

Figure 4.9

Feature Based Solids

What is a feature based solid?

A feature-based solid is a part in which the information used to create and recreate the operation is stored along with the solid. This information may include parameters and reference geometry such as edges and faces. When the edges or faces are moved because of a parameter change, the feature operation moves along with it, keeping the original relationships.

Example feature operations include holes, fillets, chamfers, shells, and bosses. In ViaCAD, you can examine the feature operations used to create a solid using Concept Explorer.

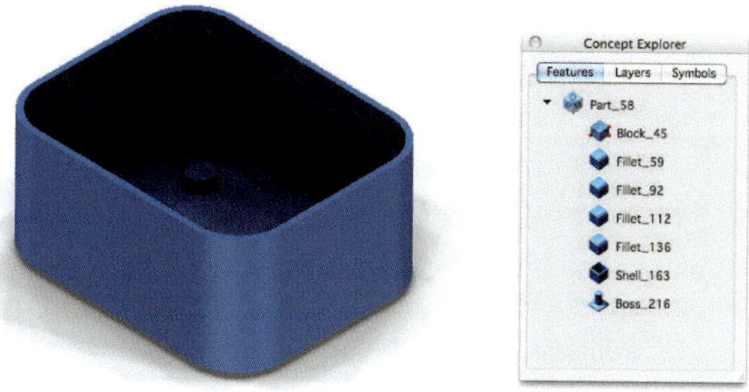

Figure 4.10

Is it possible to keep the core when shelling?

The core refers to the portion of the solid removed as part of the shelling operation. It is possible to keep the core when shelling by following the below step:

- On Windows: Press the Control key while shelling.
- On Mac: Press the Option key while shelling.

In Figure 4.11 below, the kept core has been colored and moved outside the shelled solid in (b). Before such changes, it may be hard to visualize that your solid was in fact shelled if the offset is very small (a). However, by clicking on the object, you will see an ambiguity pop up menu appear listing both the core and newly shelled solid ensuring that the object was indeed shelled. From the pop up, you can select the core and edit it appropriately.

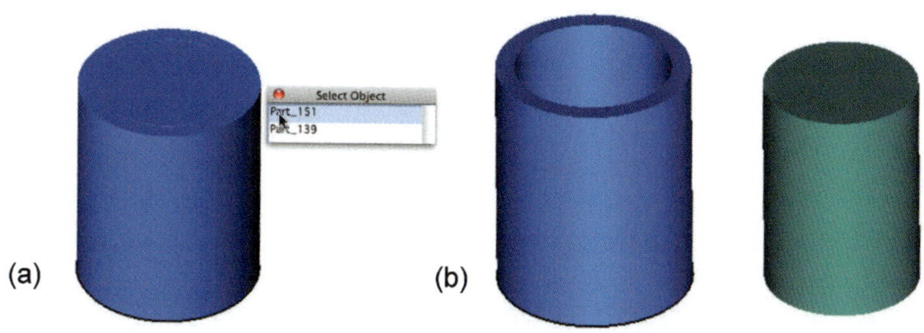

Figure 4.11– Keeping the core while shelling

Is it possible to shell a model using multiple thicknesses?

When you initially create a shell feature, all faces use the same thickness. However, you can use the Inspector to modify individual faces to have different thicknesses. In the image below the bottom face has been given a different thickness of 3.

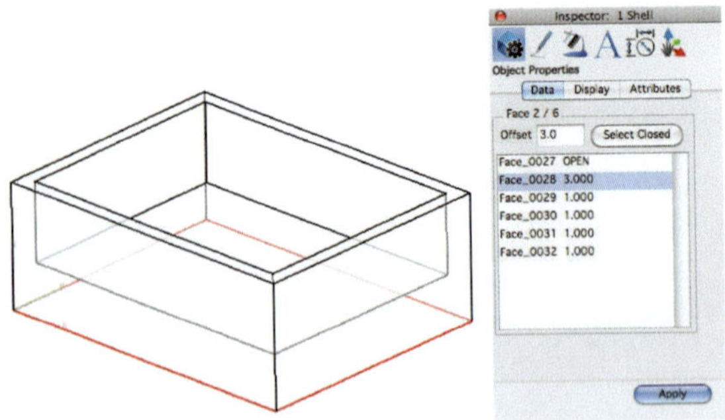

Figure 4.12– Keeping the core while shelling

How can I completely hollow a model?

The *Shell* tool will hollow out a part, leaving the faces you select open. If you do not select any face on the model, you can create a completely closed hollow model.

- To create a hollow model, use the *Shell* tool and click into an empty drawing region at the point where you are prompted to "Select open faces".

Figure 4.13 – Hollow Model

Can I associate a hole center with a point entity?

The default behavior of a hole feature is to tie the hole center to a parametric location on the face containing the hole. This is a geometric characteristic that is independent of transformations of the parent feature. However, there are times when you may want to have the hole center driven by the xyz location given by a point entity.

- To tie a hole center to a point entity, create the hole while pressing the option key. This will create a point entity at the hole center and associate the center with this point. As you move the point entity, the hole will update accordingly.

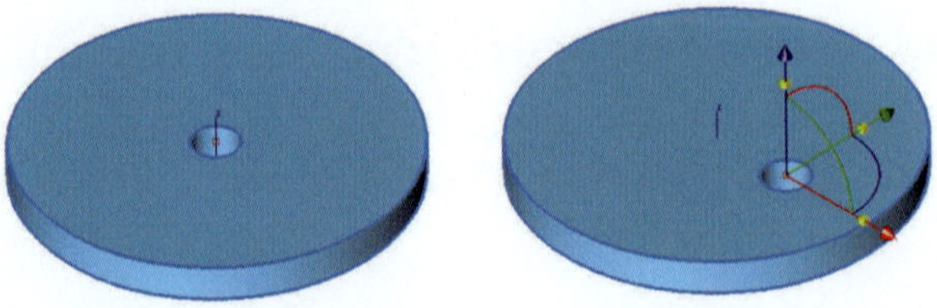

(a) Original Hole and Point Entity (b) Point Entity Moved

Figure 4.14 - Hole Associated to Point Entity

What is the "Project from Referenced Snap" dialog box for holes?

If the center location that you specify is not on the selected face, you will get a dialog box that asks, "Project from referenced snap along hole/boss axis?"

- If you select yes, the referenced snap point is projected along the hole axis to the selected face.
- If you say no, the referenced point is projected along a minimum distance to the face, which may result into a projection along the face edge.

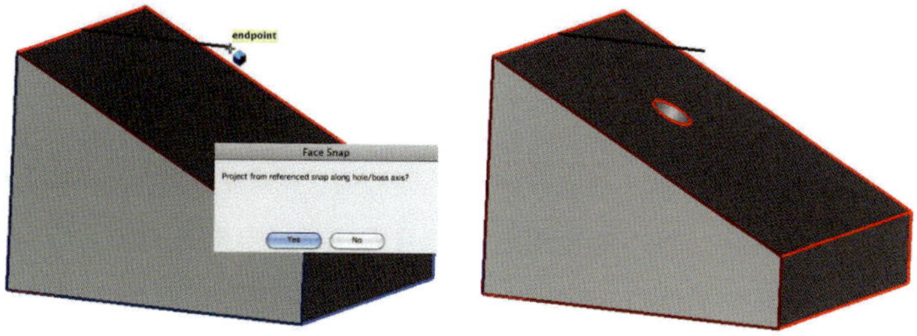

Figure 4.15 - Project Hole Snap

What are the key definitions in entity bending?

Entity bending wares a solid model around a given axis. In any bending operation, some material is stretched while other material is compressed, but the topology of the model is maintained.

ViaCAD uses the concept of a neutral plane for bending. The neutral plane is defined by a neutral root, a bending axis, and a bending direction, and defines the location along which the material is neither stretched nor compressed during bending. The material above the neutral plane is compressed and the material below the neutral plane is stretched. The location of a neutral plane varies with the type of material to be bent.

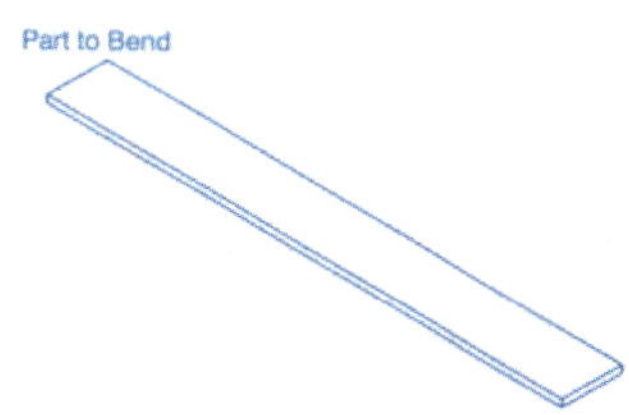

Figure 4.16 - Entity Bending

The bending axis and the bending direction define the vector normal of the bending plane. The bending axis and bending direction should be perpendicular to each other. The cross product of these two vectors also defines the positive and negative sides of the entity to be bent.

Table 4.1 – Entity Bending Terms

Entity Bending Definitions	
Neutral root	A position that, in conjunction with the bending axis and the bending direction, defines the location of neutral plane.
Bending axis	A vector that defines the rotational axis of the bending action. The two points supplied by the user define this axis.
Bending direction	An auxiliary vector used to define a bending plane. This is extracted from the selected face of the part to bend.
Bend radius	A real number that specifies the radius from the center of the bend to the neutral plane.
Bend angle	The angle in degrees that specifies the amount to bend.

How do you control which part of an entity gets bent?

The direction of the bend axis determines how the material is bent. A trick you can use to determine which portion will bend is to close your right hand around the bend axis defined by the first and second point. Have your thumb point towards the first point. Your fingers curl in the direction the material is bent. If you create a bend and it bends the wrong direction, just hit the Option key to flip the bend.

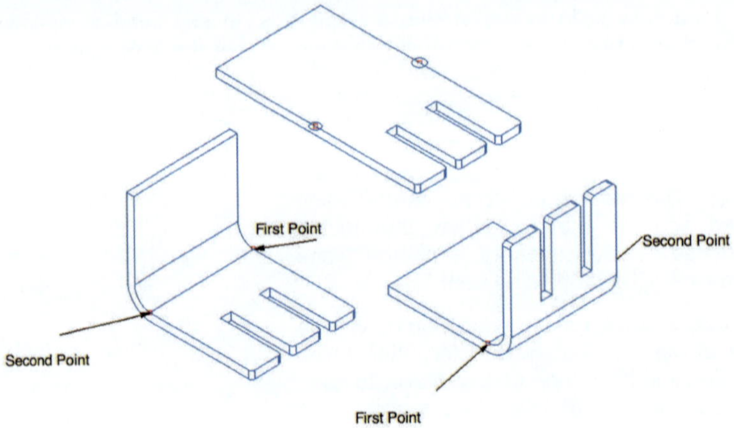

Figure 4.17 - Bend Direction

Can I bend parts that are not flat?

You can bend any part created in ViaCAD including those created using NURBS, analytics, or law based geometry. However, proper placement of the bend axis for a given set of parameters becomes more critical with parts that are not flat, as the tool will fail to create a part that self intersects.

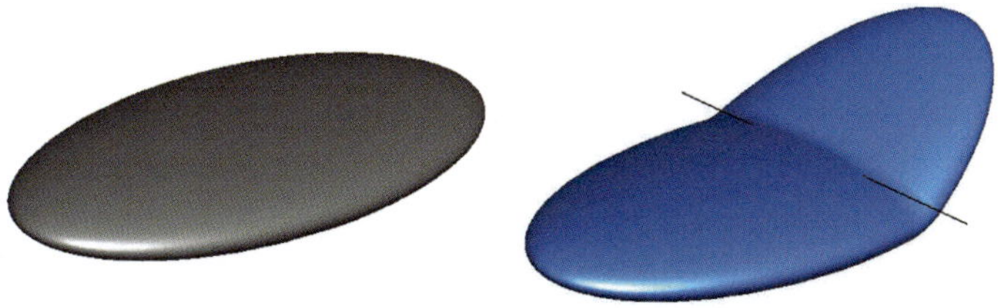

Figure 4.18 - Bend Direction

How does K-factor relate to the neutral plane?

The K-factor is a sheet metal term that defines a ratio of the location of the neutral line to the material thickness (t/T) where t = location of the neutral line and T = material thickness. The K-factor is a geometric calculation regarding the location of the neutral line after all forces are applied and is considered to take into account all unknown factors for a given setup. The K-factor is typically between 0.3 to 0.5.

With the ViaCAD entity bending tools, the depth of the two points you specify for the bend axis defines the k-factor of a bend.

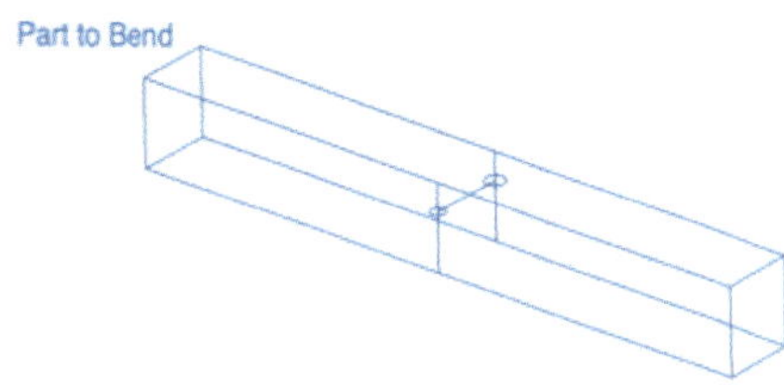

Figure 4.19 – Neutral Line

How do control the orientation of a part bent along a curve?

The bend along curve tool maps a user specified line segment to a user specified curve. The line segment is defined by the two points for the bend height axis. Any curve type may be used to map the original part. The image below shows how the line segment is used to map the part to the curve.

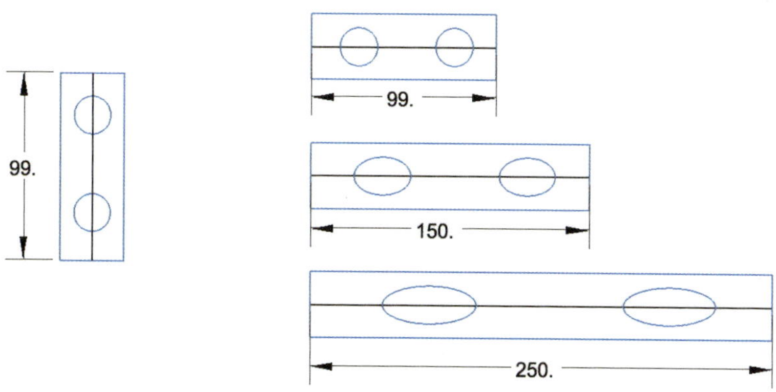

Figure 4.20 – Line Segment Mapping to Bend Curve

How can I minimize streching in the bend along curve tool?

The bend along a curve tool may stretch or compress a part based on several factors. First the part may be distorted due to different lengths between the height axis and the length of the curve you are bending too. If the bend to curve is longer, then the distance between your two points defining the height axis, the resulting part will be stretched. Therefore, to minimize stretching along the curve, try to make the length of the bend to curve the same distance as the height axis.

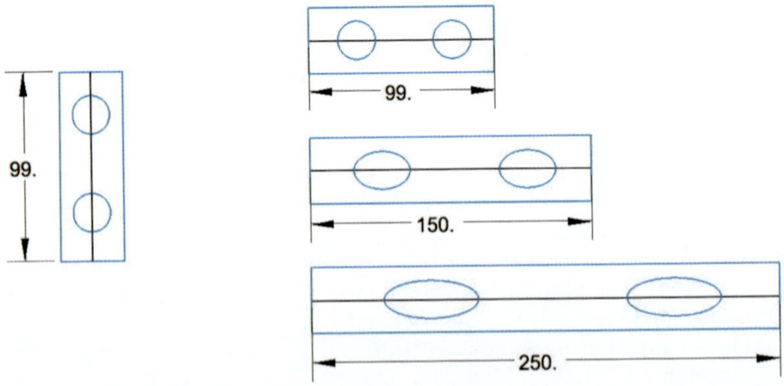

Figure 4.21 – Bend Curve Stretching

The second factor impacting distortion is the curvature of the curve of the bend to curve. In areas of higher curvature you will see higher distortion.

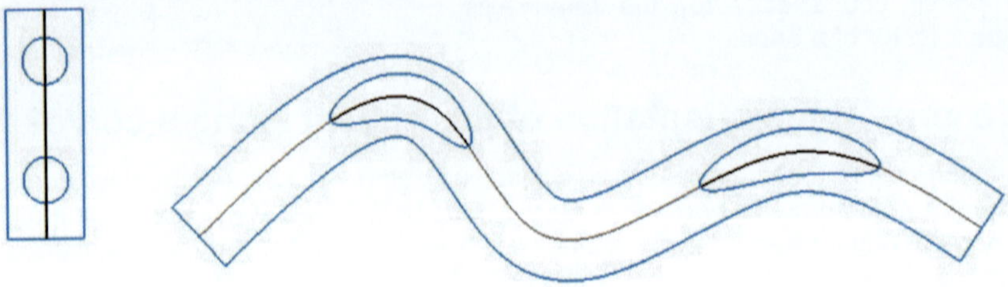

Figure 4.22 – Bend Curve Curvature

What is edge based blending?

Blending is the process of replacing sharp edges or vertices in a model with smoother tangent continuous faces of transition. These changes may be needed to make a part more photorealistic, more aesthetically pleasing, safer, stronger, or manufacturable.

ViaCAD supports a variety of user interface options for creating blends. These options are classified into constant cross section and variable cross sections blends.

Table 4.2 – Blend Options

Constant Cross Section	Variable Cross Section
Radial	Linear
Elliptical	By Position
Vertex Blend	Law Curves
Vertex Corner	Fixed Width
	Hold Line

Each of the blend options has attributes for blending neighboring tangent edges as well as allowing feature interaction.

- The **Neighboring Tangents** option will automatically add all tangent continuous edges to the selected edge.
- **Feature interaction** will search and account for additional intersections such as protrusions and cutouts within the blend region. The feature interaction option results in longer blending time.

Blending edges also support a user-defined setback. The setback is the distance measured back from a vertex common to the blended edges. Typically the setback only has meaning when three or more edges are involved with the blend operation.

The table below lists several blend types and includes illustrations of the different blending options.

Table 4.3 – Blend Examples

Blend Type	Sample Blend	Notes
Constant/Radius	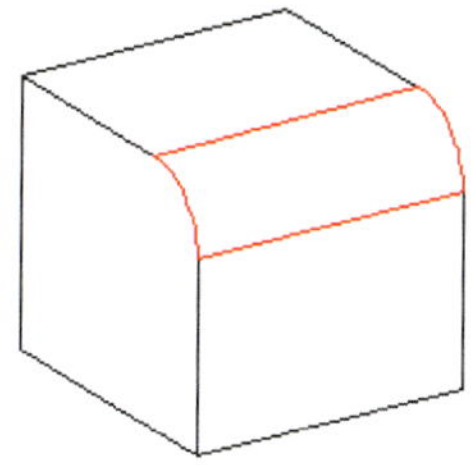	Circular cross sections
Constant/Elliptical	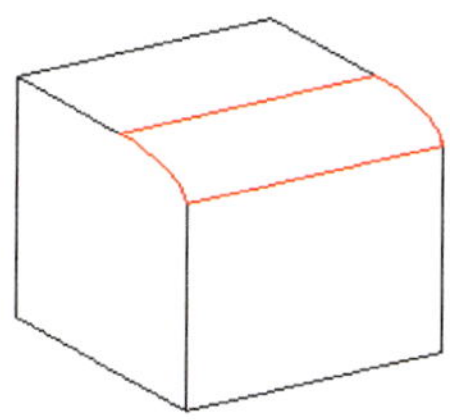	Ellipical cross sections

Constant/Vertex Blend	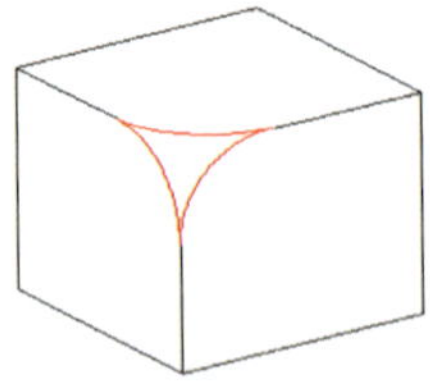	A setback is applied from the shared vertex in the amount of the radius value
Variable/Linear	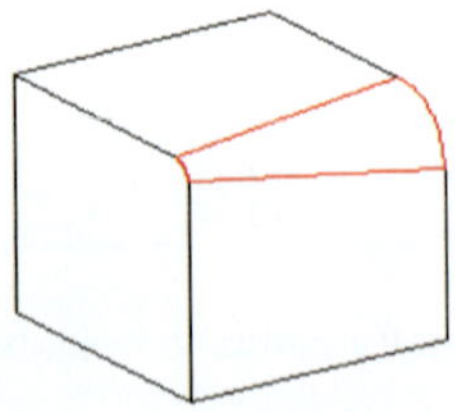	Two different radius values applied to the start and end of the edge being blended
Variable/By Position	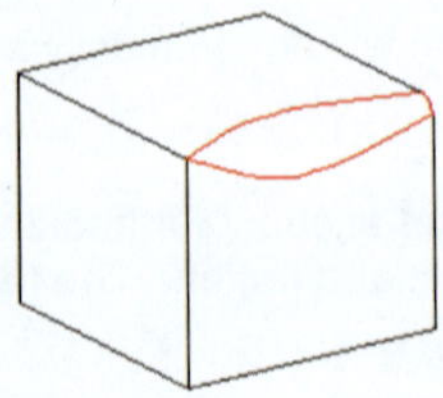	The user defines the radius value at various positions along the blended edge
Variable/ Law Curve	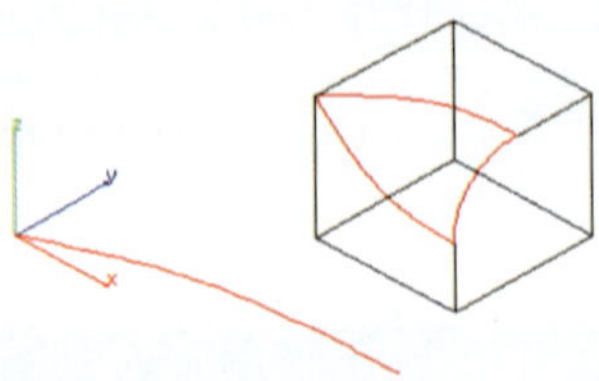	Law Curve must lie in positive xy quadrant. Great for controlling slopes of fillet tangent lines.
Variable/Fixed Width	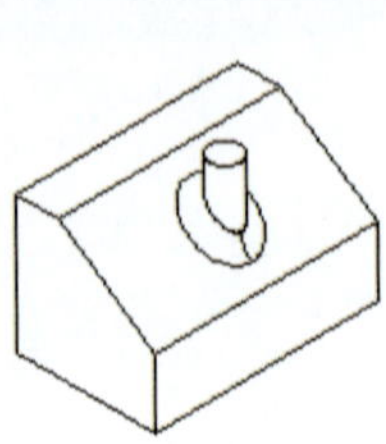	Radius changes to maintain constant width between tangent lines.
Variable/Hold Line	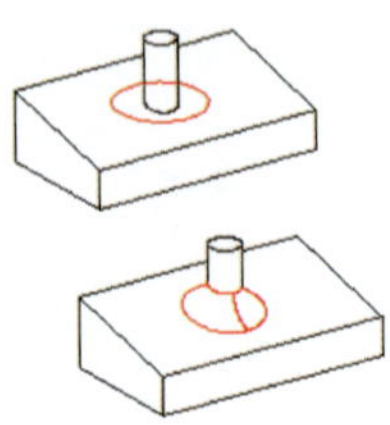	The user provides a curve that lies on the face which becomes the fillet edge line.

Multi-edge, multi-radius blend with vertex setback	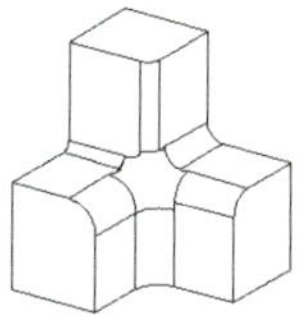	Six edges, each with a different radius, meeting at a common vertex.
Variable radius by position with zero radius start/end and tangent edge neighbors	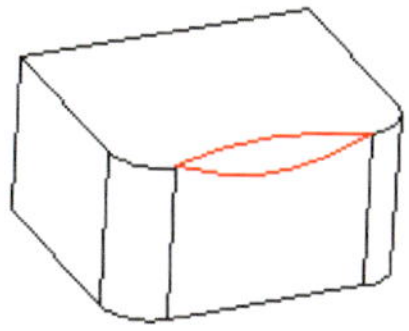	
Self-intersecting radial blends	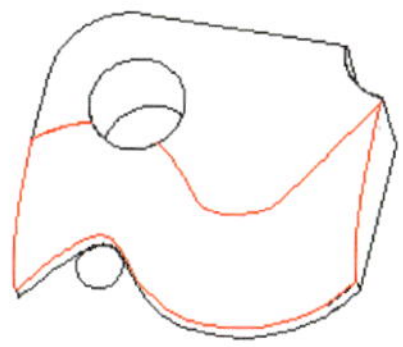	In this example, the blend radius is twice the size of the minimum radius of curvature.
Vertex Roll Blend	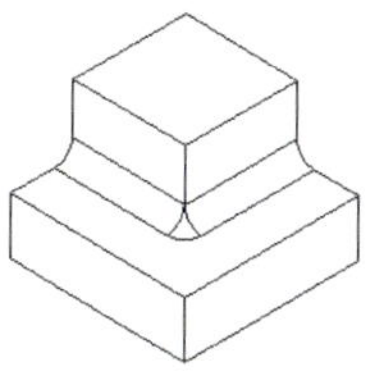	Creates a smooth transition by blending ONLY 2 edges. (Use edge/face where edge is perp to face.)

How do I specify a radius curve to use in blending edges?

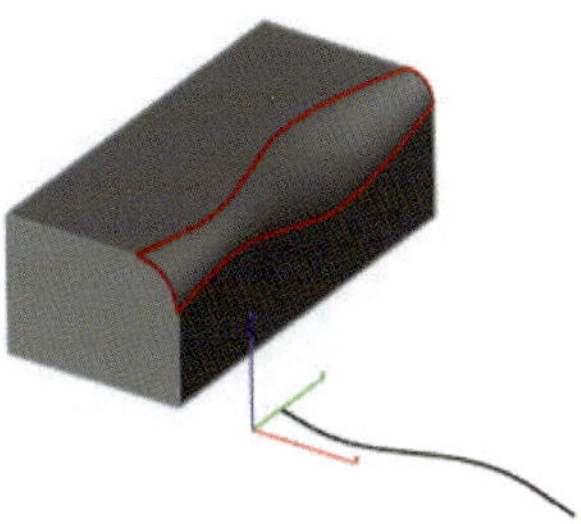

Figure 4.23- Specifying radial curves for blending edges

This unusual blend option uses a curve in the xy plane to specify the radius value along the edge of a solid. Use this option as an alternative to radial or linear blending when you need discrete control over the radial distribution along an edge.

When using a radial blend, the x direction represents a distance along the edge of the solid. The y direction represents the radius value at a particular x location.

How do I blend two bodies together?

It is possible to blend two separate solids using the *Blend* tool by following the steps below:

- After drawing your two objects, select the *Blend Edge* tool.

- From the options available, select *Constant Blend* tool.
- Depress the Shift key and following the tool prompt, click to the side of your objects to create a help point.
- Use the Data Entry Window to adjust the radius value. The radius value must be large enough to span the distance between the two bodies.

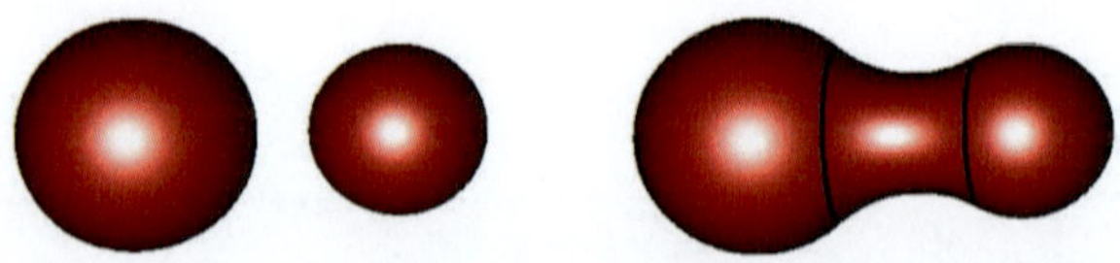

Figure 4.24- Blending two bodies

How do you create the rounded edges of a bolt head top?

- Select the *Prism* tool.
- Create a One Point Prism, setting the point at 0,0,0, diameter to 1, height to 0.25, and number of sides to 6.
- Next, create a three-point circle referencing the three middle edges of the prism.
- Extrude the circle down 1 inch with a 45°draft angle.
- Select the *Solid Intersect* tool; use this tool to pick the prism and extrusion parts.
- The resultant shape is your rounded top bolt head.

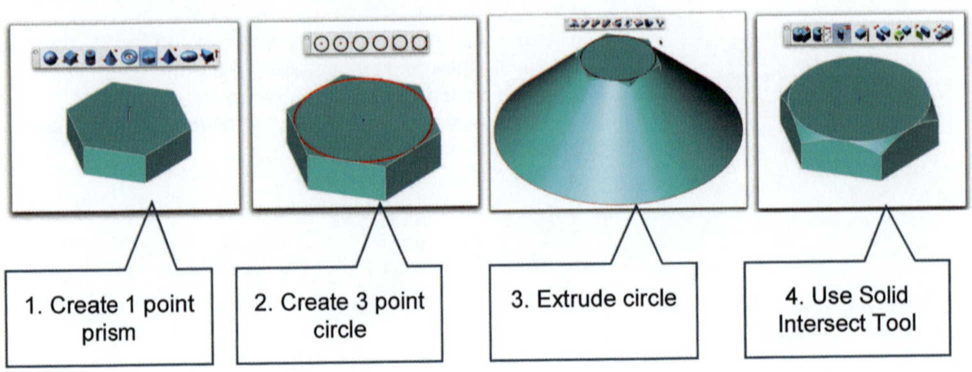

Figure 4.25 – Steps to create the rounded edges of a bolt head

What is edge based chamfering?

A chamfer feature adds or removes a flat section of material from a solid along a collection of one or more selected edges. The flat section creates a beveled surface between the surfaces common to the selected edges.

ViaCAD supports nine user interface options for creating chamfers. These nine options are classified into constant cross section and variable cross sections chamfers. Constant chamfers maintain the cross section properties from start to end whereas variable cross sections change lengths by a variety of options.

Table 4.4 – Chamfering Options

Constant Cross Section	Variable Cross Section
Length	Lengths
Two Lengths	Four Lengths
Length/Angle	Lengths/Angles
Vertex Corner	By Position
	Fixed Width

Each of the chamfer options has attributes for chaining neighboring tangent edges as well as allowing feature interaction.

- The **Neighboring Tangents** option will automatically add all tangent continuous edges to the selected edge.
- **Feature interaction** will search and account for additional intersections such as protrusions and cutouts within the chamfer region. The feature interaction option results in longer chamfering time.

Chamfering edges also support a user-defined setback. The setback is the distance measured back from a vertex common to the chamfered edges. Typically the setback only has meaning when three or more edges are involved with the chamfer operation.

The table on the following page lists several chamfer tools and includes illustrations of the different blending options.

Table 4.5 – Chamfer Examples

Chamfer Creation Tool	Sample Chamfer	Comments
Constant/ Length	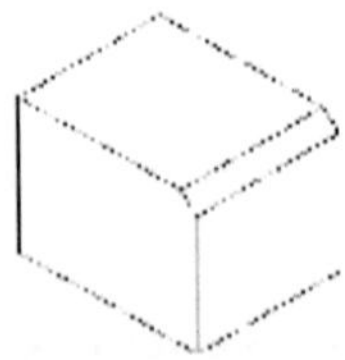	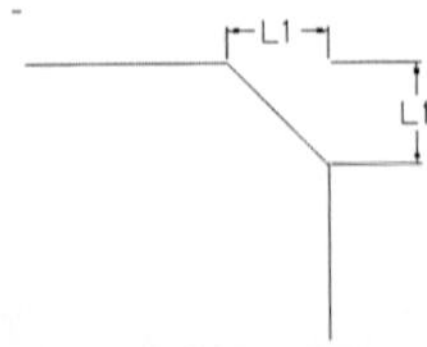
Constant/Two Lengths	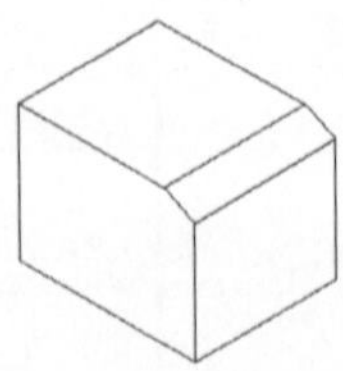	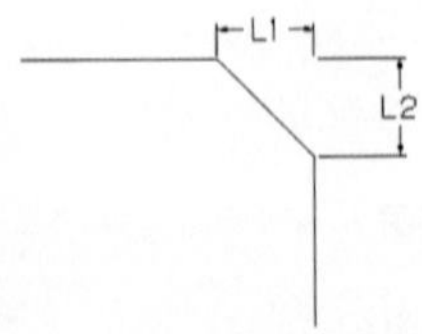
Constant/Length, Angle	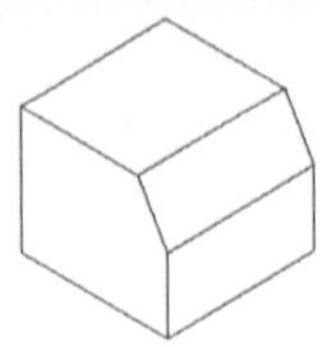	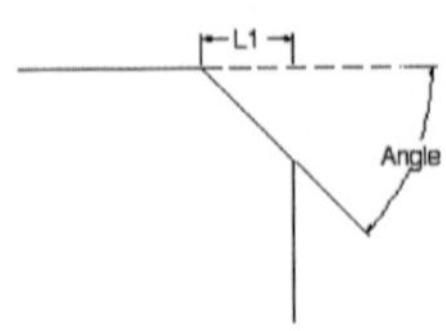
Constant/Vertex Corner	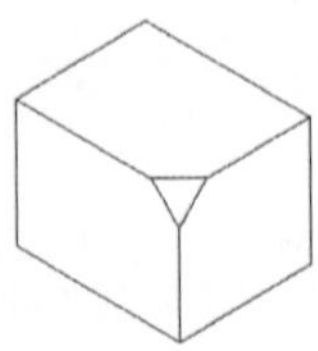	Planar Surfaces Only Same Convexity
Variable/Lengths	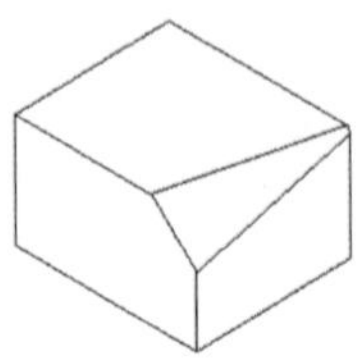	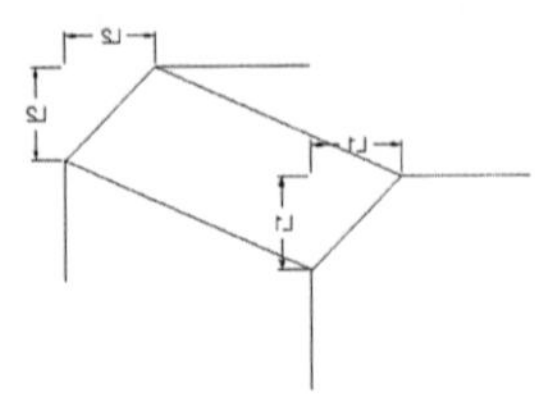

Variable/ Four Lengths	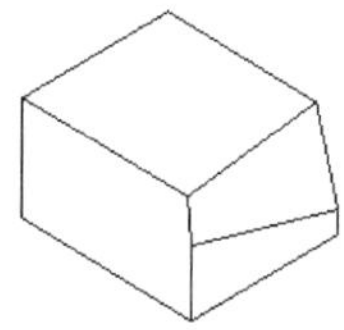	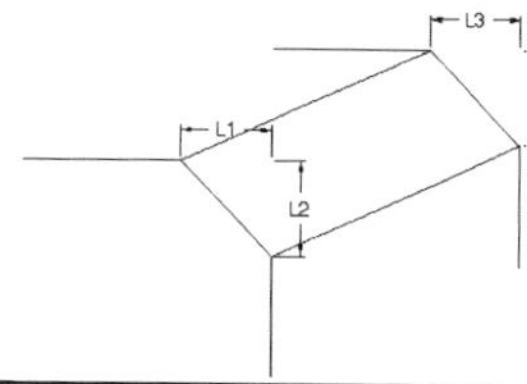
Variable/ Lengths Angles	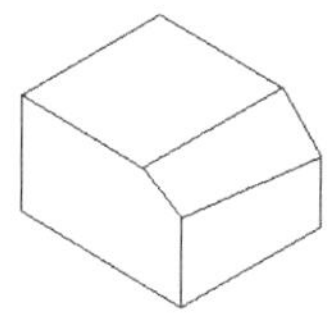	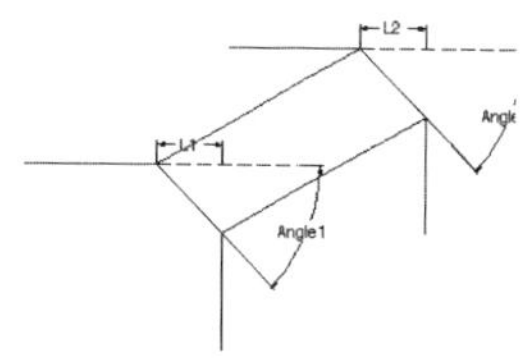
Variable/ By Position	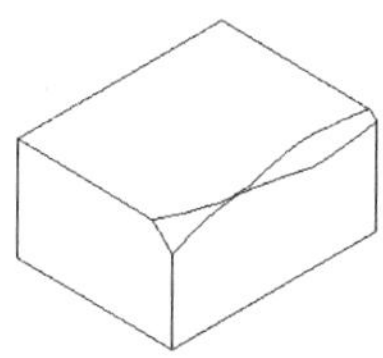	Specify Position/Length
Variable/Fixed Width	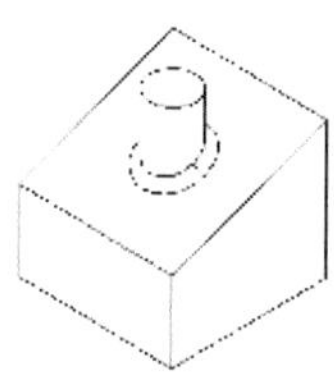	Distances vary to maintain constant width. 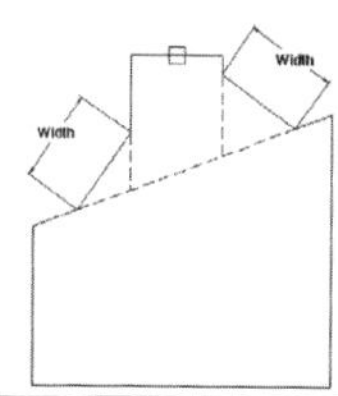
Multi-Edge Chamfer with constant lengths and no setback	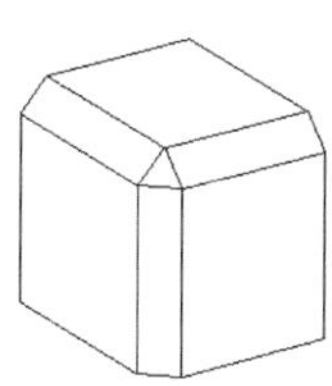	Creates a vertex setback at common point to that will create a triangular joining surface. Chamfering each edge one at a time will create a miter join.

Multi-Edge Chamfer with constant lengths and user defined setback	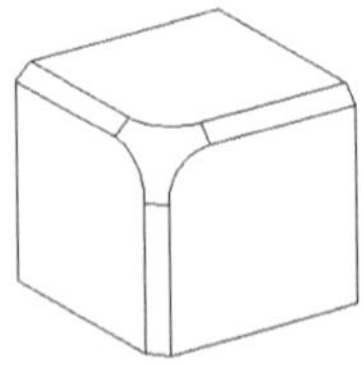	Setback is distance from shared vertex
Multi-Edge Chamfer with multiple edge lengths and user defined setback	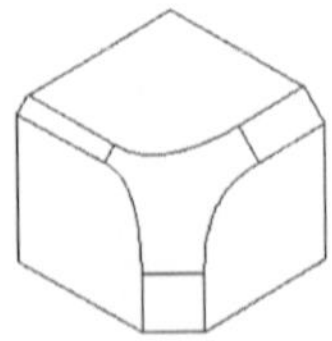	Use the Inspector Data Entry tab to change chamfer lengths per edge
Selected Edges, variable chamfer by position with degenerative start and ends	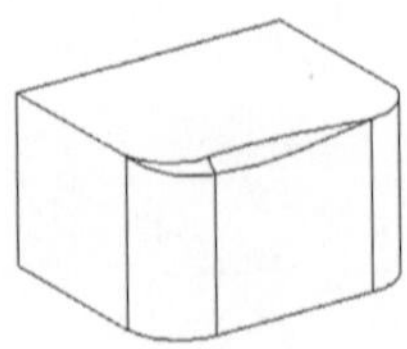	Chamfer distance/angle applied along the edge by position
Complex Chamfer with three cylinders and vertex setback	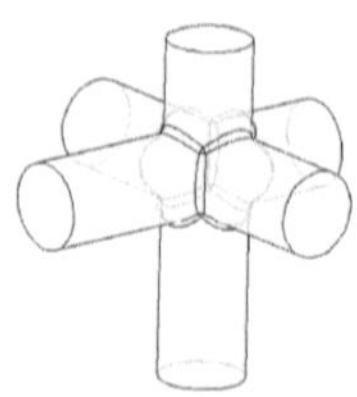	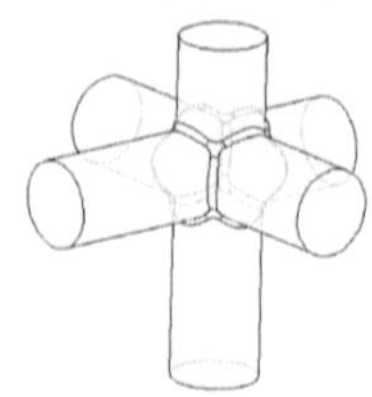
Select Only Edges	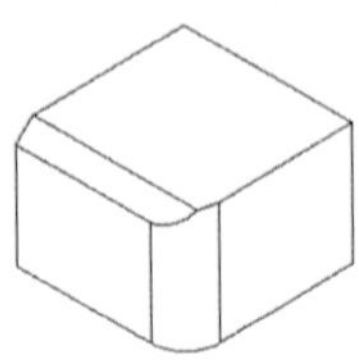	Turn off chained edges to prevent propagation along tangent edges
Chained Edges	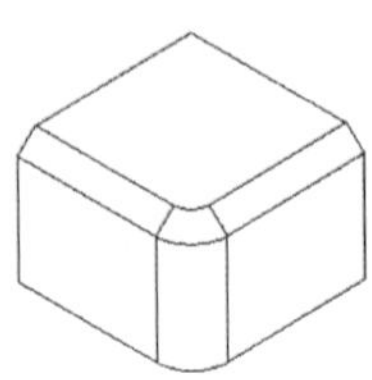	By default, edges that are tangent to the selected edge are used to compute the final chamfer

Feature Interaction (Protrusion)	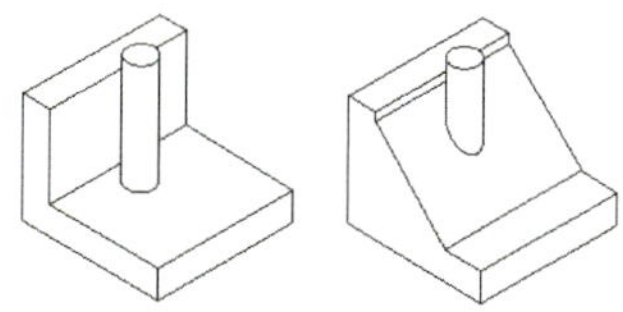	Be sure to check "Feature Interaction" in Blend options.
Feature Interaction (Cutout)	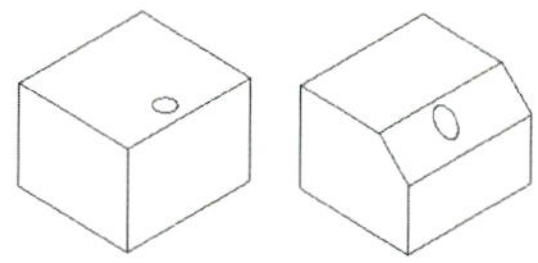	Be sure to check "Feature Interaction" in Blend options.

Can I flip the orientation for a length/angle chamfer?

The *Constant Chamfer Length/Angle* tool uses an edge, length, and angle parameters to create a chamfer. The orientation of the angle with respect to the edge is defined by underlying topology conditions. You can flip the default orientation at the time the chamfer is created using the option key.

Figure 4.26 - Chamfer Edge Flip

You cannot flip the chamfer using the Inspector after it has been created.

Can I chamfer over an existing feature?

The *Constant Chamfer* tool has the ability to create a chamfer that completely envelops another feature such as a hole. However, by default this behavior is turned off. To enable this feature:

- Press the Options button in the Data Entry Window.
- Enable the Feature Interaction option from the Advanced Chamfer Options dialog.

Figure 4.27 - Chamfer Feature Interaction

How is the angle defined for a countersink hole?

The *Hole* tool has the ability to create a countersink defined by an angle. The angle for a countersink is defined relative from the face the hole lies upon. If you are given the included angle of 86 degrees, the countersink angle would be:

180 = 2x+86,
x = (180 -86)/2 = 47 degrees

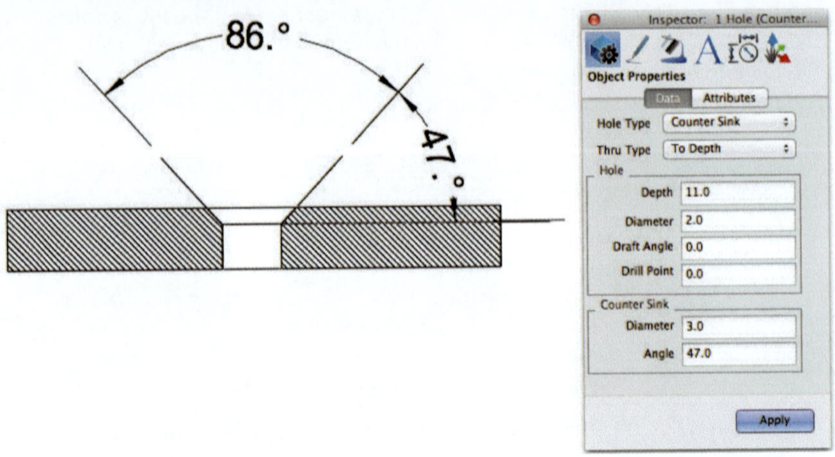

Direct Face Editing

What 2D shapes can be pushed or pulled into a solid?

The *Push/Pull* tool identifies closed regions defined by lines, splines, arcs, circles, conics, ellipses, smart polygons, and curves that lie across the boundary of a face. The curves must all lie in the same plane to create a push/pull region.

When pushing/pulling selected curves that line on a face, the face edges are automatically included as a region to push/pull.

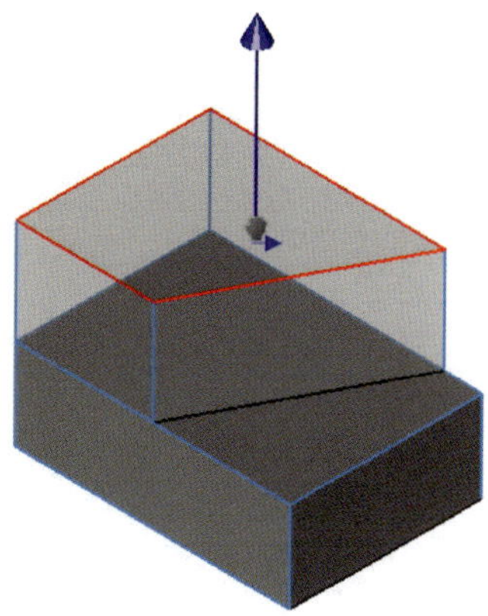

Figure 4.28 - Line on Face Pulled

Can I push or pull more than one face?

The *Push/Pull* tool modifies just one face at a time. However, you can use the Gripper to modify more one face. When you select the faces to modify, you must use the *Deep Select* tool.

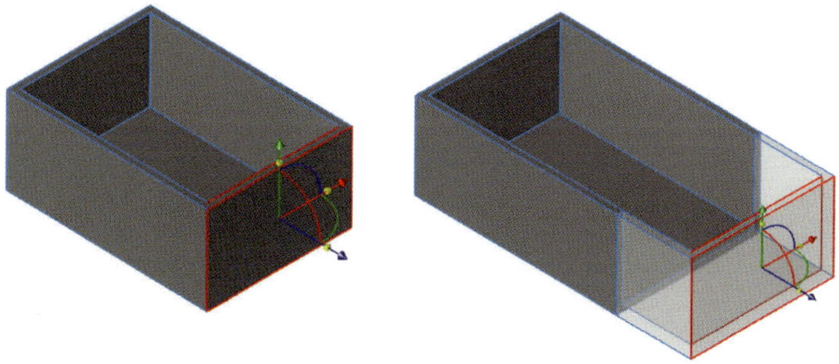

Figure 4.29

How can I defeature a model?

- Method 1: Use the *Remove Face* tool to delete faces from the part.

- Method 2: A faster way to delete faces is to select the faces to delete with the *Select Deep* tool and then hit the Delete key.

Figure 4.30 –Defeaturing a model

What is the reference face in the draft face tool?

The *Draft Face* tool tapers a collection of selected faces by a specified angle. One application of drafting faces is to make a molded part easier to remove from the mold. The reference face defines the pull direction through its surface normal. The draft angle is then relative to the surface normal as shown in the image below. The image below shows a negative draft angle.

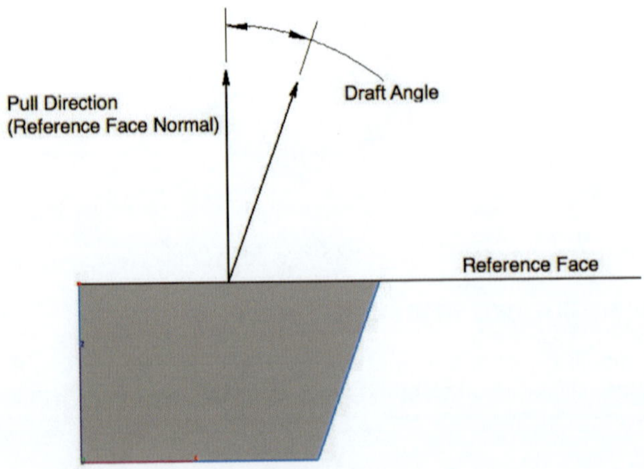

Figure 4.31 - Reference Face And Draft Angle

Can I thicken an entire body?

The *Offset Face tool* allows you to offset more then one face at a time. To thicken an entire body, simply box select the entire solid using the Offset face tool.

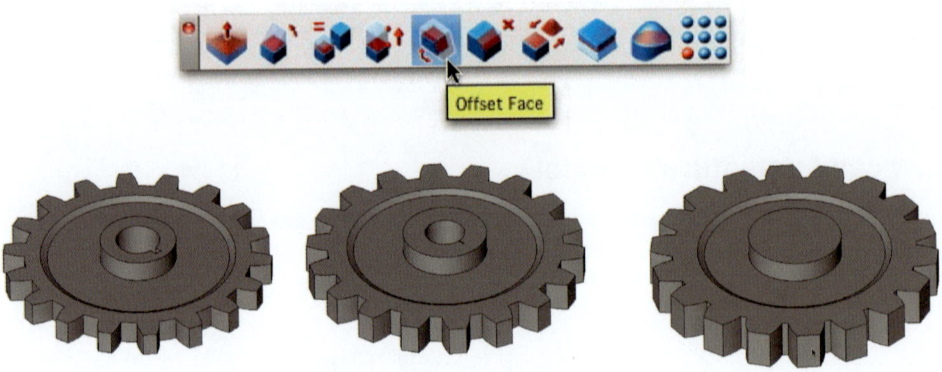

Figure 4.32 – Thicken All Faces

Solid Modeling Utilities

How can I convert facets to a solid?

When importing from facet based CAD systems, you may want to convert these facets into solids so you can perform solid modeling operations in ViaCAD. This tool is limited in the number of facets you can convert.

To convert facets to solids, select the mesh facets and then use the *Stitch* tool found in the Solid Modeling Utilities palette. You can then perform solid modeling operations, such as blending and shelling, on your model.

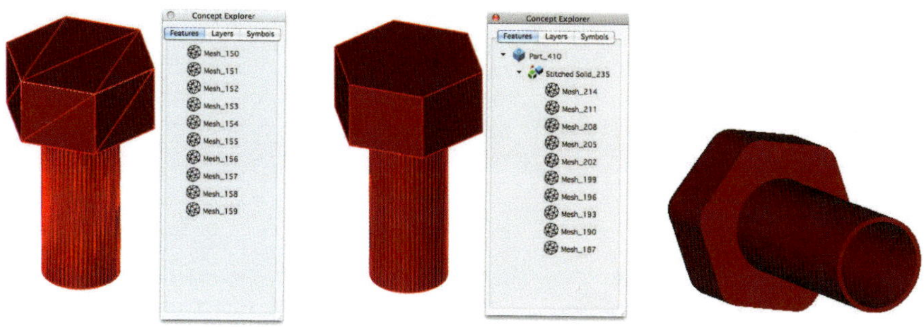

(a) Meshes (b) Solid (c) Shelled/Blended Solid

Figure 4.33 – Stitch meshed to solid

What does the "Change a Solid into Solids" option do?

The Change Object Type command (located under the Edit menu) has an option that lets you change a solid into solids. Many people have been confused about this option and to which conditions it applies.

The *Add Solid* tool can unite non-touching solids. To return these to separate solids, you can use the Change Object Type to Solids command.

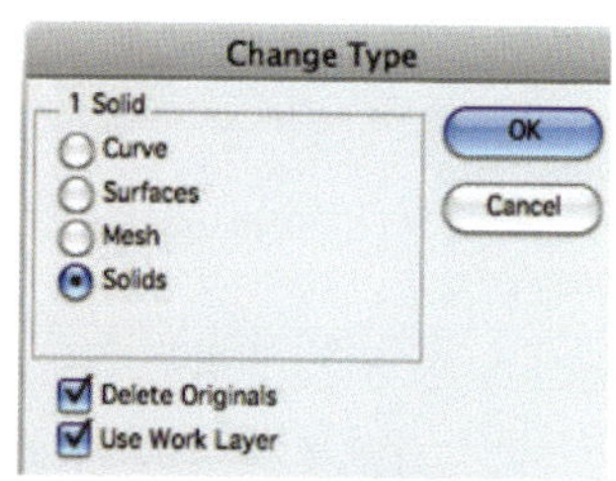

Figure 4.34 – Change type to Solids Command

What does the "Closed Volume Required" option do?

Turning off the "Closed Volume" check mark in the Stitching tool advanced options lets you have open edges in a part (the part is not water tight). This option allows you to perform solid modeling operations on surfaces. For example, you can use this to do a variable radius blend on two surfaces or to add a chamfer, hole, boss, cutout, or protrusion to a surface.

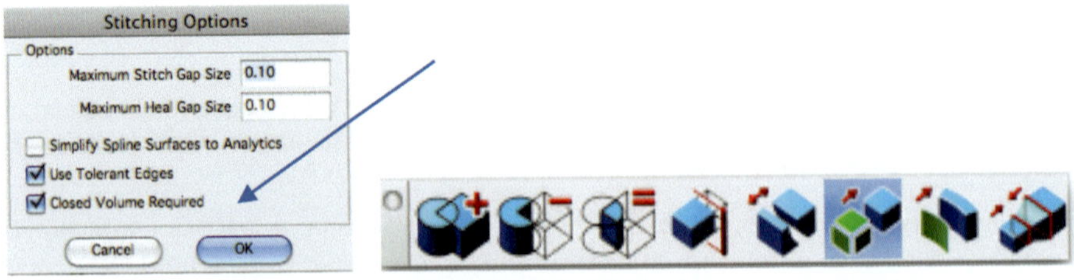

Figure 4.35- Disabling "Closed Volume Required" will permit open edges

Figure 4.36 below represents two open-ended surfaces stitched into a solid with a solid modeling feature operation (variable radius blend) applied. The Closed Volume Required has been disabled.

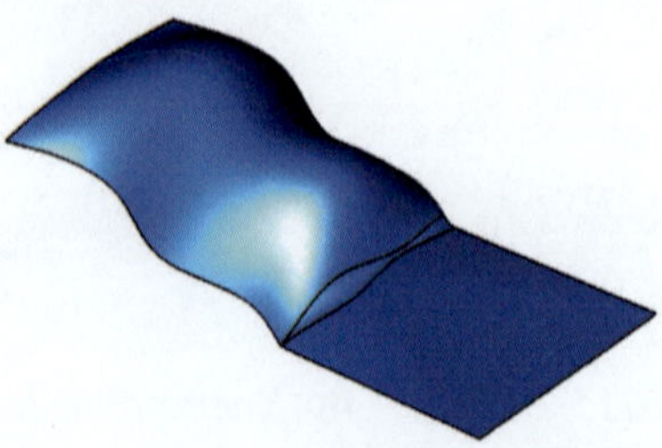

Figure 4.36 - Surfaces stitched with "closed volume required" disabled.

How can I change the twist continuity?

The *Twist* tool located in the advanced transform utility palette will twist a collection of curves, surfaces, or solids. The input options allow you to twist about an axis with a specified angle. If you twist a solid, additional options are available to control the twist continuity through the Inspector.

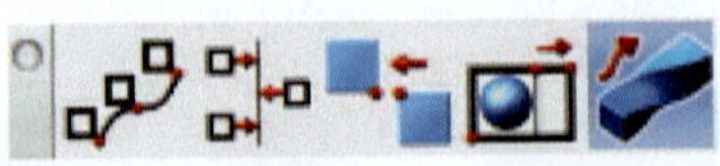

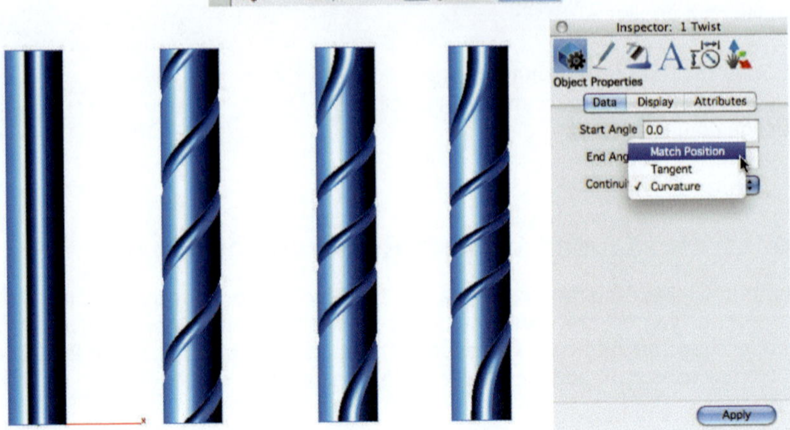

(a) Body to Twist (b) G0 (c) G1 (d) G2 (e) Inspector Continuity

Figure 4.37 - Twist Continuity

The continuity setting is applied where the twist starts and ends. Twisting can start and end anywhere along a body. Below is an image where twisting starts a distance away from the base.

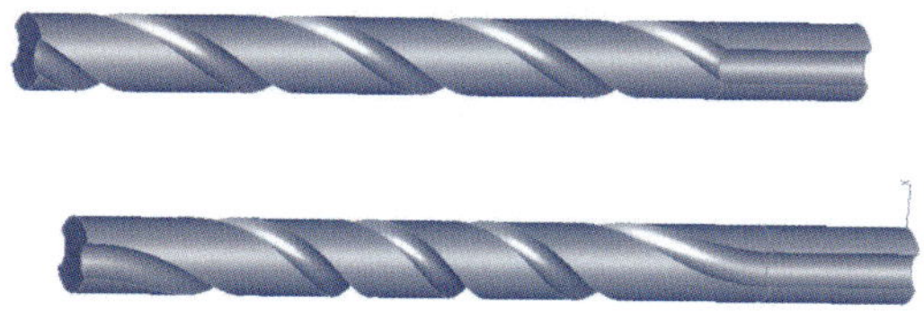

Figure 4.38 - Region Twist

What does the start angle do in the twist tool?

The *Twist* tool located in the advanced transform utility palette has a parameter that controls the start and end angle of the twist.

- The end angle minus the start angle defines the total amount of twisting.
- The start angle rotates the body about the twist axis.

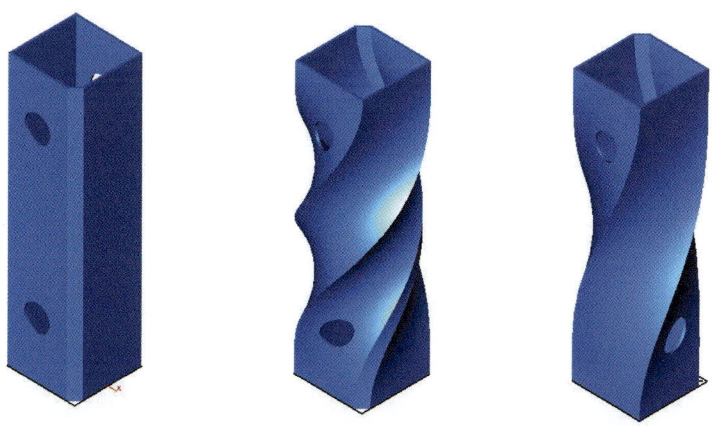

(a) Body To Twist (b) Start =0, End = 180 (c) Start =90, End = 180

Figure 4.39 - Start Angle Twist

How can I disable automatic part regen on surface updates?

- If you are a PC user, go to File. If you use a Mac, go to Application on your Menu Bar.
- From the pull down, select Preferences.
- Then, in the General category, uncheck the setting for Auto Resolve.
- Don't forget to re-enable Auto Resolve when done.

- You may now resolve manually whenever you desire by choosing Resolve Links from the Edit menu.

Is there a way to view and modify my history?

- Yes, as you are making a part with solid modeling operations, ViaCAD creates a history tree of your steps. With a history tree, you can go back and modify parameters to explore "what if" design options.

- The history tree is displayed and manipulated though Concepts Explorer.

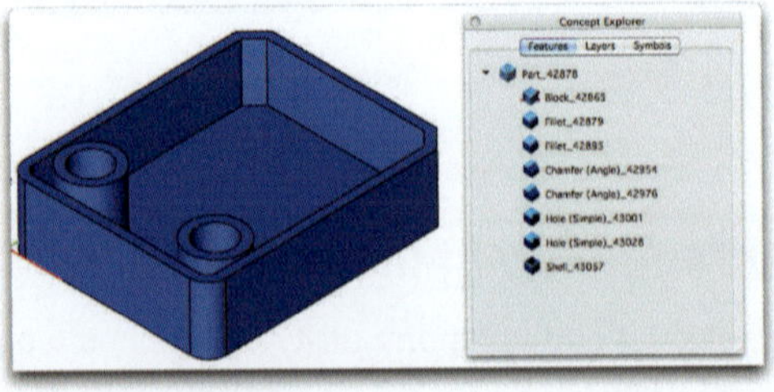

Figure 4.40 – History Tree

How do I add a material to the Mass Properties dialog box?

The Mass Properties dialog box calculates a variety of properties such as weight that are material dependent. Materials are specified in a drop down list in the dialog box. The material list is extracted from a file called Materials.ini. You can add custom materials to this file by modifying the file.

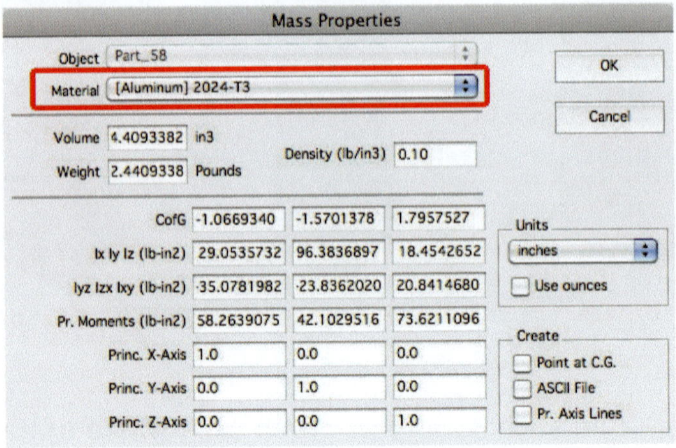

Figure 4.41 – Mass Properties

The example below shows how to add a new category and material to the Mass Properties dialog box:

- Locate the Materials.ini file in the Environ folder. The Environ folder is included in the application install folder or bundle. Make a copy of this file in case you need to revert to the original version.

- Open the Materials.ini file with a text editor.

- The first section defines the material categories such as Steel, Aluminum, or Copper. This entry is identified in the file as [_Categories].

- Add a new entry to the end of this list. As there are 14 default materials, give this new category (named MyNewMaterialCategory in this example) an index of 15.

```
[_Categories]
Misc=0
Steel=1
Aluminum=2
Brass=3
Copper=4
Magnesium=5
Nickel=6
Titanium=7
Zinc=8
Wood=9
Ceramic=10
Aggregate=11
Plastic=12
Composites=13
Liquids=14
MyNewMaterialCategory=15
```

- Next, scroll down in the file until you see the last entry called [Liquids]. Copy and paste the first two lines of this file. Change the name of the copied section to specify the name of your new material.

```
[MyNewMaterialCategory]
NewMaterial=1
```

- Now scroll down the in file until you see the material properties section. Copy and paste the first one you see. Change the name to your material category and name. Enter a density value for the material.

```
[MyNewMaterialCategory.NewMaterial]
Density=0.333
```

- Save the modified material file and launch the application. The Mass Properties dialog box will now include your new material.

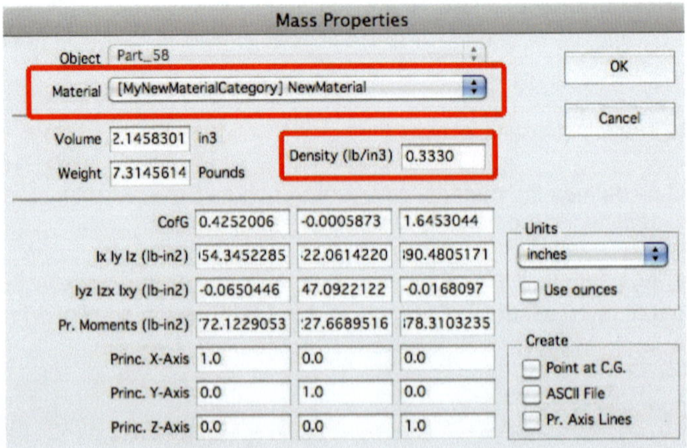

Figure 4.42 – Custom Mass Properties

If your material is not showing up, be sure to remove any white empty spaces after or before the equal sign.

Can I calculate the mass properties of an assembly?

Yes, you can calculate the properties of multiple parts as one unit. Select all the parts that you would like to calculate the properties prior to selecting the command from the Verify menu bar. Note that Object field will indicate ***ASSEMBLY***. However, if any of the parts do not share the same material, the Density and Weight fields will be empty.

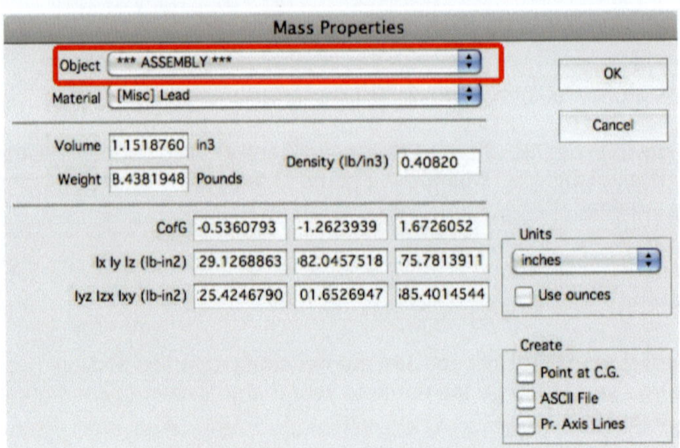

Figure 4.43 – Assembly Mass Properties

Chapter 5
Rendering and Display

Overview

The CAD shapes you create and manipulate using ViaCAD are displayed on the screen using a variety of methods. In some cases, how they are displayed is based on whether the shapes are curves or surfaces. Typically, curves are vectorized and displayed as polylines whereas surfaces and solids are triangulated and displayed as facets.

Object Display Resolution

Why does a circle appear to be a collection of straight-line segments?

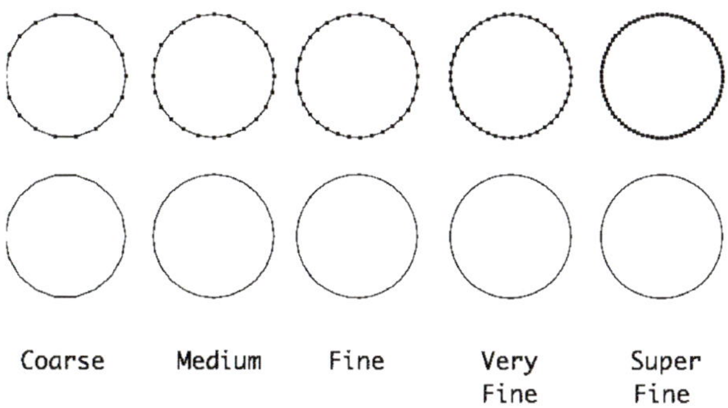

Figure 5.1 – Resolution Settings

It is because internally the circle is represented as a collection of line segments for the purpose of display. In the CAD application, all objects are displayed as vectors or facets through hardware accelerated OpenGL drivers. However, this is only for display purposes. Everywhere else the exact equation of a circle is used, such as in trimming, breaking, or LogiCursor references.

You can control the angular deviation between consecutive line segments (display smoothness) by adjusting the resolution. The object resolution can be set to one of the following: Coarse, Medium, Fine, Very Fine, or Super Fine. The fine setting, for example, will set the angular deviation to 11 degrees. Figure 5.1 above shows the various settings for a circle object. The row of circles on top have been exploded into line segments.

Why do prints appear to be a collection of straight-line segments?

Line segments are the result of vectorizing a curve into something that can be displayed on the screen. The amount of vectorization is controlled by the Object's display resolution located in the Edit menu. Since printing simply redirects the display from the monitor to a print driver, you must increase the resolution of the curve to reduce any straight line segments that might appear in your printed drawing.

How do I change an existing object's resolution?

- Method 1: After using the *Arrow* tool to select the objects you want to modify, go to **Edit** on your menu bar. Here you can find the Resolution command and the Coarse, Medium, Fine, Very Fine, and Super Fine options.

- Method 2: After using the *Arrow* tool to select the objects you want to modify, use the Context Sensitive popup menu opened by **right clicking** on an object. Figure 5.2 depicts the Context Sensitive Menu for a circle in which Very Fine Resolution has been selected.

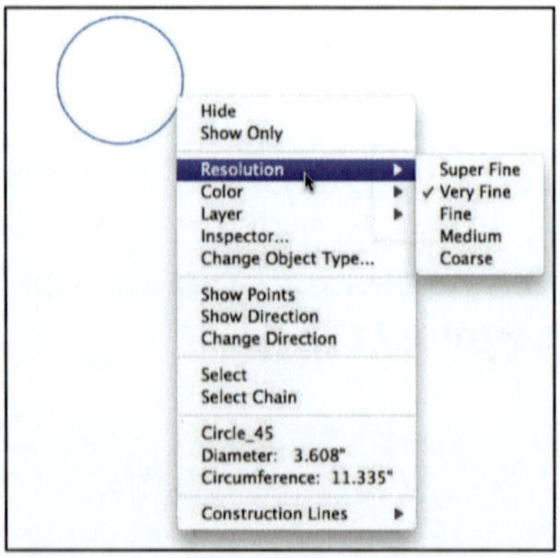

Figure 5.2 –Context Sensitive Menu for Circle

Can I change the default resolution?

Yes. You can change the default resolution by going to the Preferences dialog found under File for PC users and Application for Mac users. Here you can set the resolution for all future curves, surfaces, or solids.

Can I customize curve resolution angles?

Yes. ViaCAD version 7 products introduced a new feature that allows a user to change the definitions of each of the resolution settings. By default the curve resolutions are:

Coarse = 20 degrees	Fine= 11 degrees	Super Fine= 4.5 degrees
Medium= 15 degrees	Very Fine= 8 degrees	

These settings have been selected by the development team to provide the best all around performance for our users. However, if you have an unusual situation, you can change these defaults. Just remember that changing these recommended values will likely impact display performance.

To change the curve resolution angles:

- Go to Preferences found under File for PC users and Application for Mac users.

- Select Custom Resolutions from the menu to open up a dialog box.

- Here you can change the settings to automatically update all objects to the new setting.

It is easy to swap between two custom settings. For example, you can use a custom setting while creating drawings and another while printing!

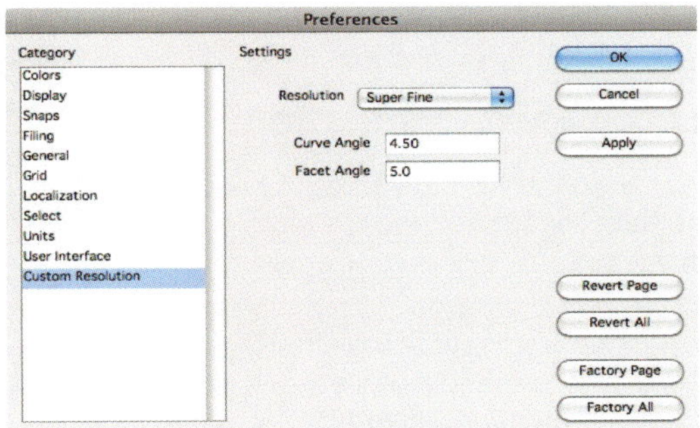

Figure 5.3 – Using Preferences to customize curve resolution angles

How can I display a faceted object beyond Super Fine resolution?

As stated above, the finest default resolution is Super Fine with a curve resolution of 4.5 degrees. However, you can temporarily increase the display resolution with a variety of custom settings using the trick below.

- Begin by selecting the object whose resolution you want to increase.
- Go to Edit on the Menu Bar and select the Change Object Type command.
- Select the change type to be Mesh.
- In the Mesh Parameters dialog box adjust the parameters.
- When finished, hit Cancel. **Do not hit OK.** Hitting Cancel will abort the conversion of object type, but it will leave the object display resolution at the mesh parameter settings.
- Your next regen of the object will set the object back to using the normal resolution modes.

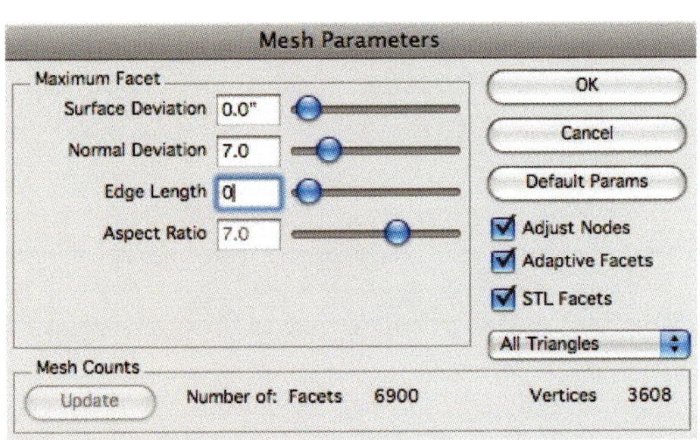

Figure 5.4 – Mesh Parameters dialog box

Use this tip to tweak the resolution of a part that is being exported for rendering formats such as OBJ.

Viewing Data

How can I change the View Orientation?

- Method 1: By going to the View Menu, you can change the view to Top, Left Side, Right Side, Front, Back, Isometric, or Trimetric views.

- Method 2: You can right click to display the Drawing Contextual Menu. This pop up menu has view options for Side, Front, Back, Isometric, and Trimetric.

- Method 3: To quickly change the view orientation, you can also use the keyboard shortcut keys found in Table 5.1 to the right.

Table 5.1 – Shortcut Keys

View Orientation Keys	
A	Right Side View
S	Front View
D	Top View
F	Isometric View
G	Trimetric View
View Zooming Keys	
W	Zoom to user specified area
E	Zoom to object extents

How can I rotate, pan, and zoom the view?

- Method 1: By going to the *View tool palette*, you can dynamically rotate, pan, and zoom the view.

- Method 2: You can also use the View Zooming shortcut key as shown in Table 5.1 to the right to quickly zoom.

- Method 3: By far the fastest way to rotate, zoom, and pan your drawing is to use the mouse. Pressing the middle button will rotate the view, scrolling the middle button will zoom the view at the cursor location, and pressing the space bar along with the left button will pan the view.

- Method 4: Pressing the arrow keys will pan the view. Pressing shift arrow key will rotate the view.

Figure 5.5 – View tool palette

How can I perform a zoom at anytime using the keyboard?

ViaCAD provides the user the opportunity to perform a zoom at any time without disrupting the current operation. For instance, imagine you are attempting to draw a line from point A to point B, but point B has more than one possible snap point in its hit radius. In this scenario, you could drag a line from point A to near point B, perform a Stroke Zoom to magnify the point in question, and complete the line.

- On a Mac: Hold the Command (Apple) key and drag a diagonal line as detailed below.

- On Windows: Hold the Shift and Control keys and drag a diagonal line as detailed below.

- *To Zoom In:* Stroke diagonally from upper-left to lower-right. As you're performing the stroke zoom, notice the box that ViaCAD generates. This box should encompass the area on which you wish to focus.
- *To Zoom Out:* Stroke diagonally from upper-right to lower-left.
- *To Zoom Previous* (zoom back to the original location after zooming in): Perform the opposite stroke. If you just zoomed in this would be from lower-right to upper-left. If you just zoomed out, this time the opposite stroke would be from lower-left to upper-right.

The Zoom Previous stroke can be of any length and at any location on the screen. A short stroke works just the same as a long one. It also doesn't matter where on the screen you perform the zoom previous; the only thing that matters is the **direction** of the stroke.

How can I save a view and zoom configuration?

Set your view orientation and zoom scale to the desired configuration. Then select the New View command from the View menu. Add in a name describing for your new view. To recall your user defined view, select the User View command from the View menu.

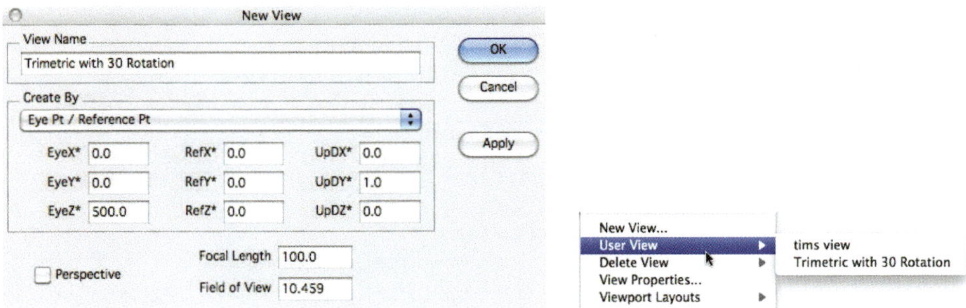

Figure 5.6

In addition to shaded, what other display modes exist to view objects?

You can change the display mode from the defaulted shaded to better suit your project needs by utilizing the six display features found in the lower left portion of the primary tool palette. Figure 5.7 shows these features labeled on the tool palette.

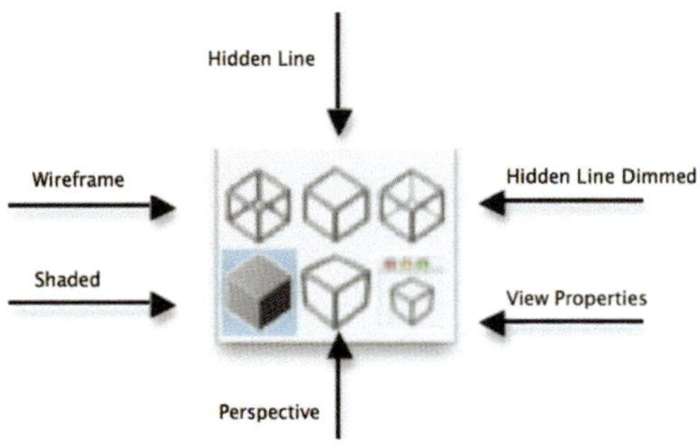

Figure 5.7 – Labeled Display Features on tool palette

- *Shaded* - Shaded mode draws meshes, surfaces, and solids as rendered images. Shaded images can take into account lighting. Objects behind other objects are hidden.
- *Wireframe* - In Wireframe mode,

meshes, surfaces, and solids are drawn only with their edges shown. Objects behind other objects are visible.

- *Hidden Line* - Hidden mode displays meshes, surfaces, and solids with only their visible edges shown. Objects behind other objects may be hidden.

- *Hidden Line Dimmed* – Hidden line dimmed mode displays meshes, surfaces, and solids with their visible edges shown in the object color. Objects behind other objects that are hidden are displayed with a less intense color.

- *Perspective* - Adds a perception of depth by foreshortening lengths of objects far away from the camera eye point. Perspective is a setting that works in conjunction with wireframe, shaded, hidden, and hidden line dimmed display modes.

- *View Properties* - The View Properties dialog box provides access to settings associated with the current view. You can modify the view orientation using parameters or adjust the focal length, which impacts the amount of perspective associated with the view.

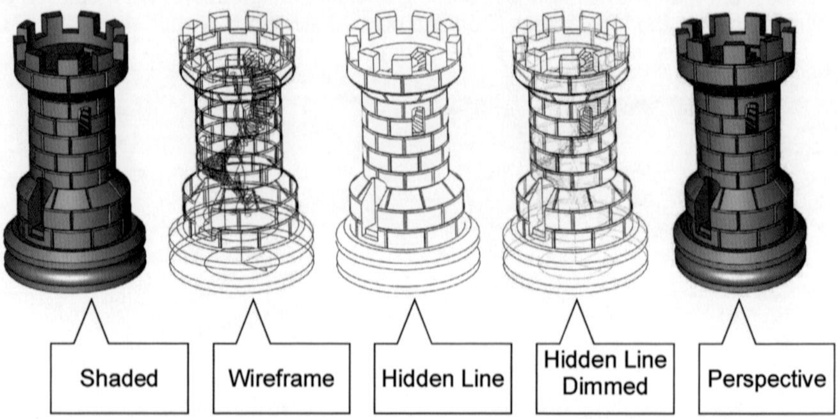

Figure 5.8 – Display modes displayed on chess piece

What is anti-aliasing?

Anti-Aliasing is a graphic technique of blending lines drawn to the screen to reduce stair-stepping or jagged appearance. In areas of pixel transitions, the edges are blended to give a smoother appearance.

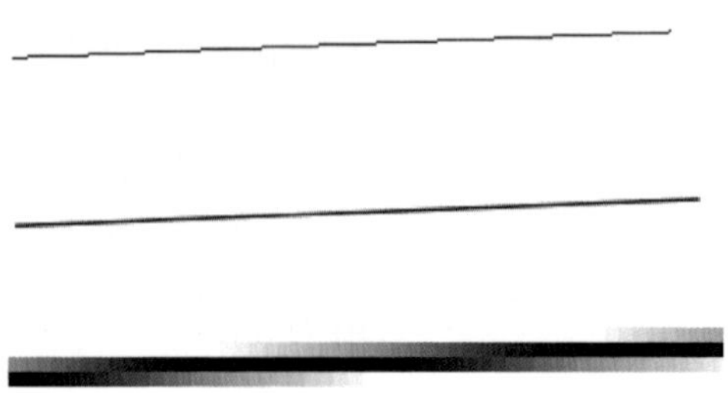

(a) line without anti-alias

(b) anti-aliased line

(c) enlarged anti-alias line

To turn on/off Anti-Alias, display the Shade Options dialog box and toggle the Anti-Alias option.

Does anti-alias impact performance?

While anti-alias is a great tool for reducing the jagged appearance of lines, this feature can impact your display sped performance. The amount will vary on your graphics board but could result in as high as a 15% performance penalty.

How can I change the direction of an OpenGL textured material?

ViaCAD 2D/3D includes several thousand textures that can be dragged and dropped onto your objects. This tip will help you control the orientation of the texture, especially on a solid with multiple faces.

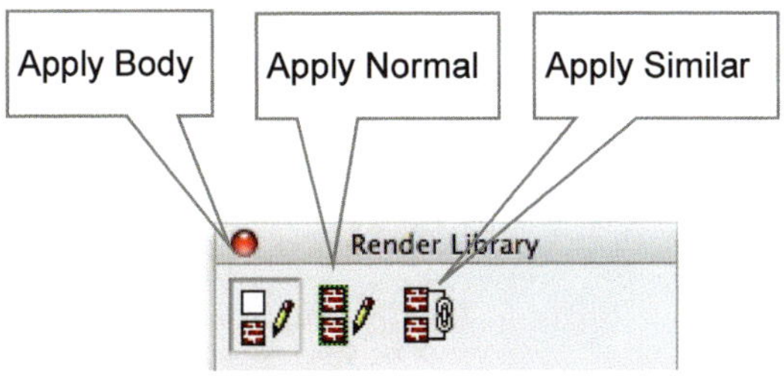

- Begin by dragging and dropping your texture onto the object. In Figure 5.9, we've used the "Apply Body" mode to drag and drop a roofing texture onto our object.

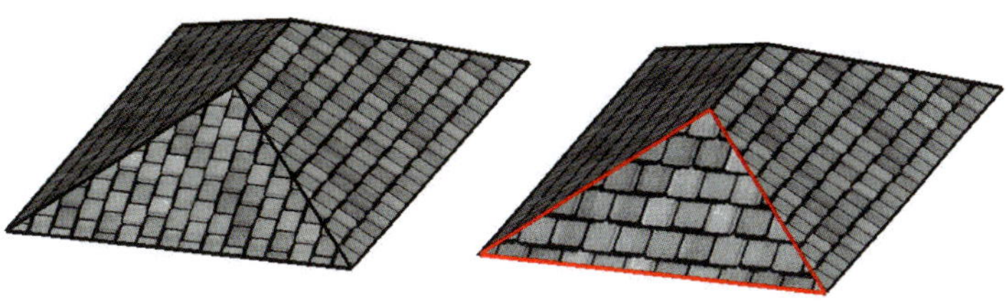

Figure 5.9 – Drag and drop texture onto object

- Next, select the "Apply Normal" mode, and drag and drop the texture onto the face whose orientation you want to modify.
- Pick the *Select Deep* tool and select the face whose texture orientation you wish to change.
- Display the Inspector and go to the Materials page.
- From here, you can change the angle to the appropriate degree. In this instance, we've changed it to 90°.

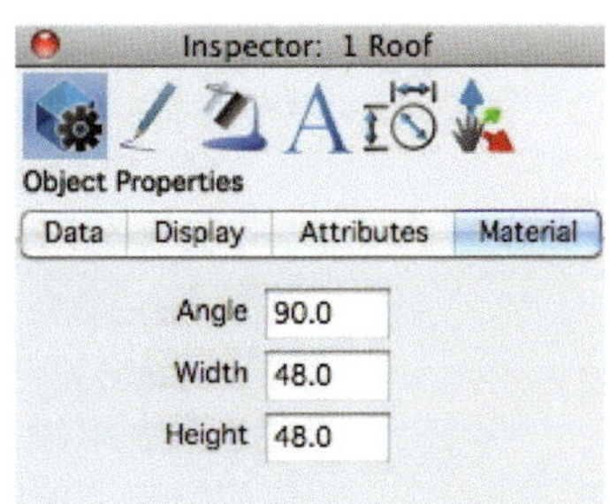

Figure 5.10 – Adjust angle using Inspector

How is the draft angle analysis tool used?

The Surface Analysis tools contain an option to display draft angles. The draft angle analysis option is used by designers of plastic parts and mold tool manufacturers to check for correct application of draft to their parts. Using draft analysis, you can visually verify draft angles within a part, as well as locate parting lines, injection, and ejection surfaces.

To use the draft angle analysis tool select your parts and then pick the Surface Analysis Draft Angle option located under the Verify menu bar. Using a default reference plane along the z axis, the part coloring is updated to reflect each facets angle relative to the reference plane.

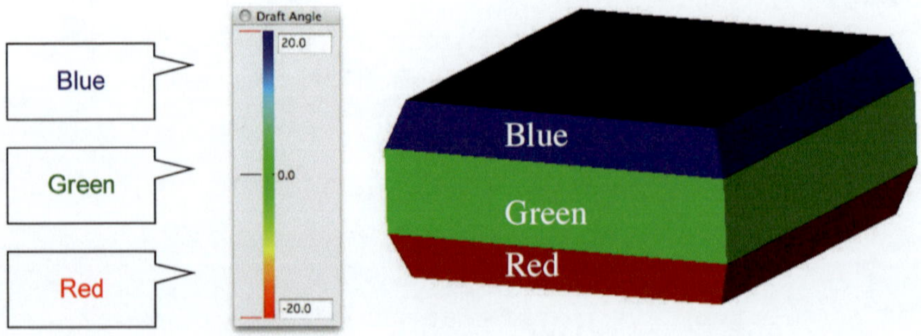

Figure 5.11

In Figure 5.11 above, the faces of the part are color coded by angle from blue to red. Using this information we can identify positive and negative draft regions as well as regions that may need correction.

Blue Displays faces with a positive draft. A positive draft means the angle of the face, with respect to the direction of pull, is more than the reference angle.

Red Displays faces with a negative draft. A negative draft means the angle of the face, with respect to the direction of the pull, is less than the negative reference angle.

Green Displays faces that may require correction. These are faces with an angle greater than the negative reference angle, and less than the positive reference angle.

CHAPTER 6
PHOTO REALISTIC RENDERING

Overview

Rendering is the process of generating an image from a scene that contains CAD shapes combined with texture, lighting, and shading information. These renderings typically take longer to generate then those methods discussed in Chapter 5 as images are built pixel at a time. However the output from photo-rendering produce impressive visual realism as shown in the image below.

(a) OpenGL Rendered Scene *(b) Photo-Rendered Scene*

Figure 6.1 – Rendered Scenes

Applying Materials

How can I apply a material to many objects?

Although normally you would drag and drop a material onto a single object, this can often be tedious when you have many objects.

A faster way to apply a material is to:

- First, select your objects.
- Then, right click on the material.
- Pick the "Apply Material to Selected Object(s)" to assign the new material.

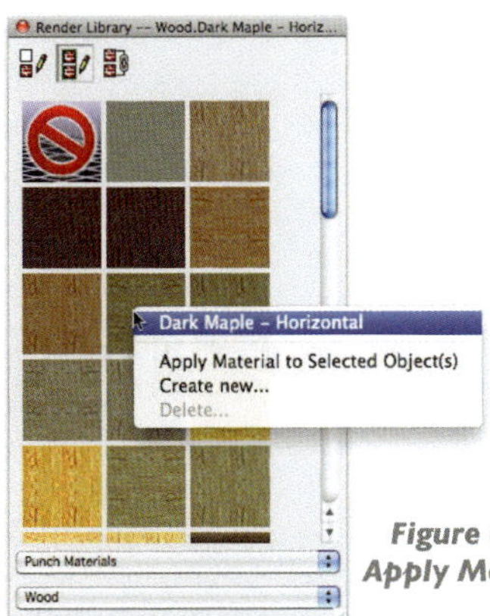

Figure 6.2 – Apply Material

How can I assign a material to an object within a group?

- Use the *Select Deep* tool to pick the object/objects you would like to assign a material to. To select multiple objects within a group, simply press the Shift key in conjunction with the *Select Deep* tool.
- Then, display the Render Library and locate the material you would like to add.
- Right click on the material to get a menu. Click on the "Apply to Selected" option.
- Render away.

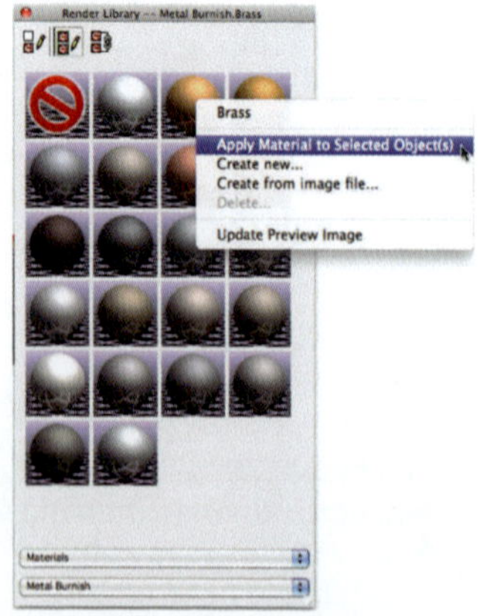

Figure 6.3 – Render Library Material Menu

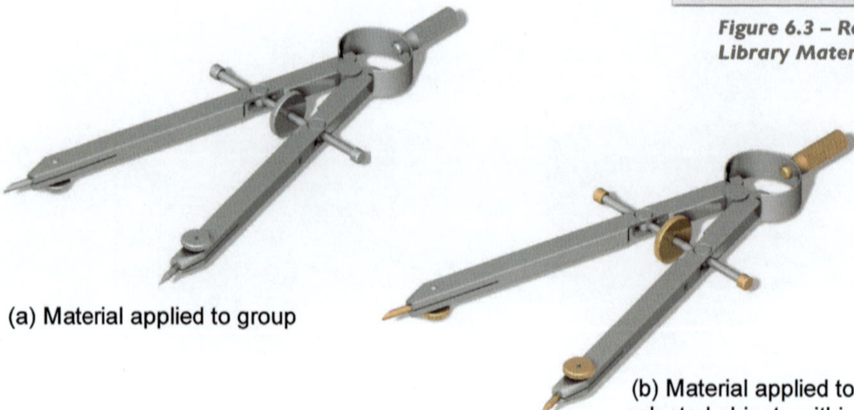

(a) Material applied to group

(b) Material applied to selected objects within group

Figure 6.4 – Assigning material to an object within a group before and after

How can I render an object to match a specific material?

Imagine you are trying to render a drawing of a floor to match a specific wood material's color and grain.

- First, you will need to capture the material you are trying to replicate. This can include scanning the image or downloading it as .jpg from an online source. You could even cut a sample piece of wood slightly smaller than your scanner and scan it directly!
- After getting your image, save it as a .jpg file and put it in your ViaCAD Pro product's textures folder.
- Open your drawing of the floor, grab any material in the Materials Window and drag it over and release on top of your floor image (surfaced image).
- Now, select the floor before clicking on Edit Objects.

- Go to Material and scroll down to your .jpg to select your own scanned/downloaded image.
- Next, click *Advanced* in the Materials editing window.
- Bring up the Render Materials Settings window.
- Set the parameters relative to your .jpg.
- Experiment with different texture spaces such as arbitrary plane and normal vector to achieve your desired results.
- Choose which axis you want for X and, in your drawing window, drag along the floor in that direction.
- Now your scanned grain is on the floor and you play with the other settings to get the desired effect.

Can I photo render curves, text, and dimensions?

By default, curves, text, and dimensions are not included as part of the rendered image. However, you can enable these objects from the Photo Realistic Render Settings dialog box located in the Photo Render tool palette.

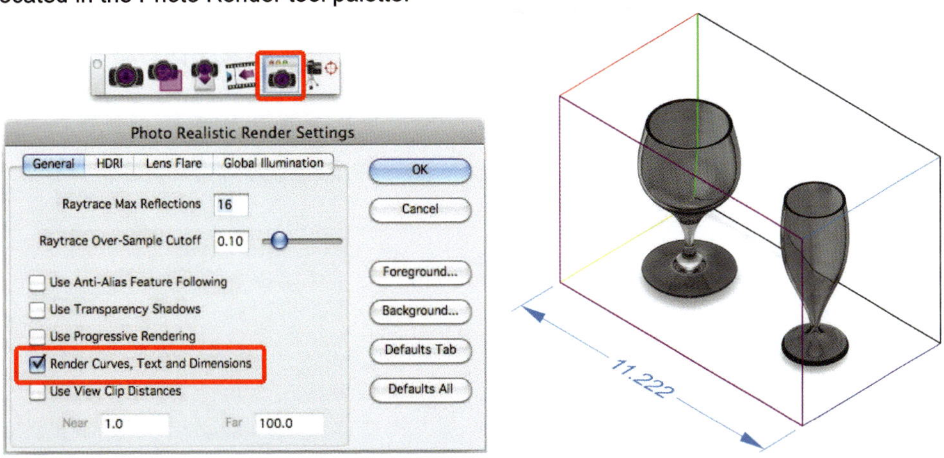

Figure 6.5 – Render curves, text, and dimensions

Adjusting Angles of Applied Materials

What's the difference between a procedural and texture mapped material?

- Procedural textures are mathematically generated, which enables you to alter some of the parameters by using numerical inputs. Procedural textures typically work in 3D space when the texture flows through shared edges, as shown in Figure 6.6. Example procedural shaders found in ViaCAD Pro and Shark include the color shaders for wood, marble, and granite. Additional benefits of using a procedural texture is that they typically tile perfectly, you don't always need UV mapping coordinates, and they also map through 3D depth, meaning that if you use a boolean operation to take a chunk out of the model, the texture will show correctly.

- Texture mapped bitmaps are any images that use pixels to define them. Things like hand painted maps or photos are examples of bitmap textures. Bitmaps generally need specific UV mapping coordinates, but once they are done, bitmaps offer more control over custom made textures. For example you can control the color on a procedural map, but with a texture bitmap, it is generally easier to put color exactly where you want it. ViaCAD 2D/3D uses texture bitmaps exclusively.

Figure 6.6 - Wood material applied to a block procedurally (left) and as a texture bitmap (right)

How can I adjust the angle of a wrapped image material?

- Select the solid and apply a material to it.

- Open up the Inspector dialog box and go to the Render tab. From here, click Advanced to bring up the Render Material Settings dialog box.

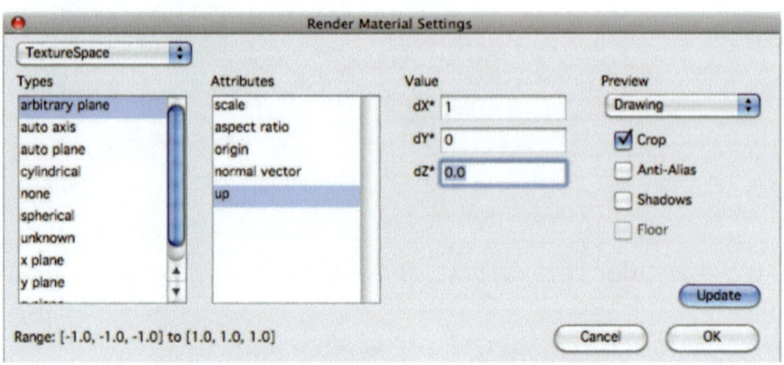

Figure 6.7– Render Material Settings dialog

The Render tab will only be available after a material has been applied so ensure you have already applied a material before going to the Inspector.

- In the dialog box, adjust the Scale Value appropriately.

- After the scale has been adjusted, select TextureSpace from the menu pull down.

- Select “arbitrary plane” under Type and then “up” under Attributes.
- Under Value, you can adjust the dX, dY, and dZ values to change the angle.
- Select Update to preview the changes. Hit OK and then Apply to save your changes.

(a) Original (b) dy value adjusted (c) Mouse defined vector

Figure 6.8 – Changing wood grain direction

In addition to inputting values to adjust the angle, you can use your mouse to define a vector directly on the drawing.

How can I change the direction of a procedural material?

The advantage of the procedural texture over a wrapped texture is that it will be unique on each piece and show the face side and end grains. Many of the properties can be edited and the end result is a much more realistic rendering, as it is a 3D texture. In the example below, an oak wood procedural material is being modified.

- Begin by applying the oak wood texture from the render library. Inserting the material from the library is advantageous, as appropriate displacement and reflectance settings will automatically be chosen for you. Additionally, the Render tab will only be available after a material has been applied.
- Then, in the Inspector, go to the Render tab and click on the Advanced button to bring up the Render Material Settings dialog.
- From the dialog, pick one of the procedural wood textures, and apply the correct setting for scale, trunk direction, and any other feature you wish to modify.
- In Figure 6.9 below, you can see the effect of adjusting the trunk direction and trunk center.

(a) Original (b) Changing trunk direction (c) Changing trunk center

Figure 6.9 – Adjusting trunk direction

- You can use the *Eye Dropper* tool (under the select tool) to copy the properties of this piece to the rest of the wood in your model.
- Later, you may want to explore applying different finishes using the displacement and reflectance tabs in the Advanced palette.

Achieving Realistic Renderings

What's a quick and easy way to improve the realism of an object?

If you were to examine the objects about you, you would probably notice the absence of sharp edges. This is because most objects have edge treatments to remove the sharp edges. In CAD, this is accomplished by applying small blends or chamfers to the part edges. When rendering, adding blends and chamfers will not only better model the actual part, but also it will also add subtle light reflections producing more realistic images.

Figure 6.10 – Using a chamfer to add realism

How can I reduce the facet appearance in my rendered images?

Photorendered images are created from facet approximations of the surfaces and solids based on the display resolution of the part. Change the display resolution to Super Fine to reduce the facet edges in the final rendered image.

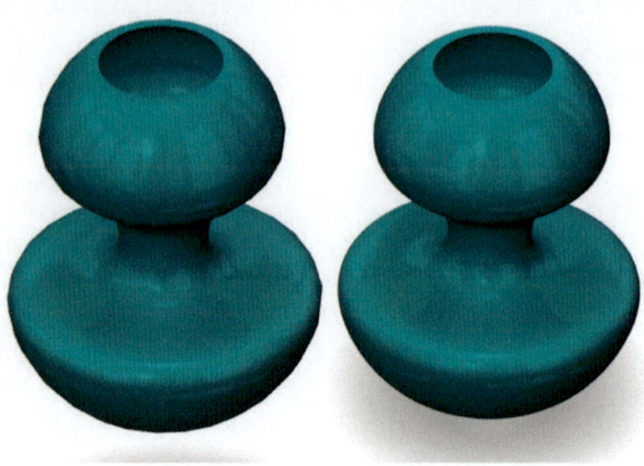

Figure 6.11 – Coarse and Super Fine Rendered Images

How can I make a light source glow?

- Insert your light sources. You can insert a distant light, spot light, or point light from the tool palette.

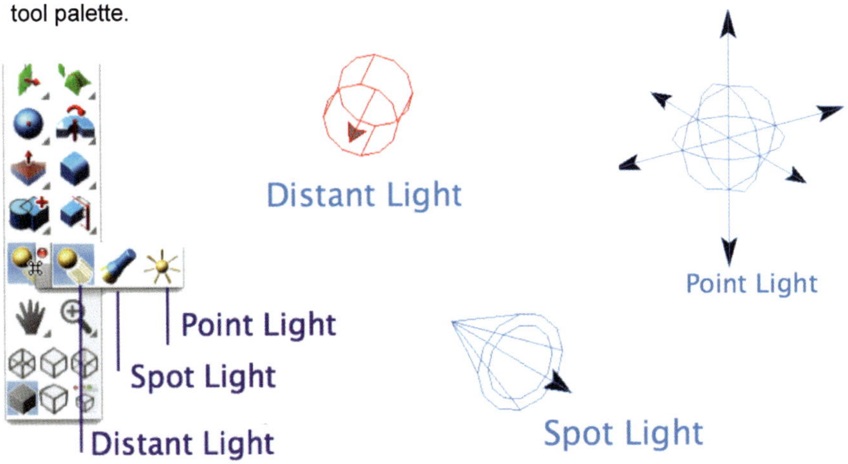

Figure 6.12 – Inserting light sources from tool palette

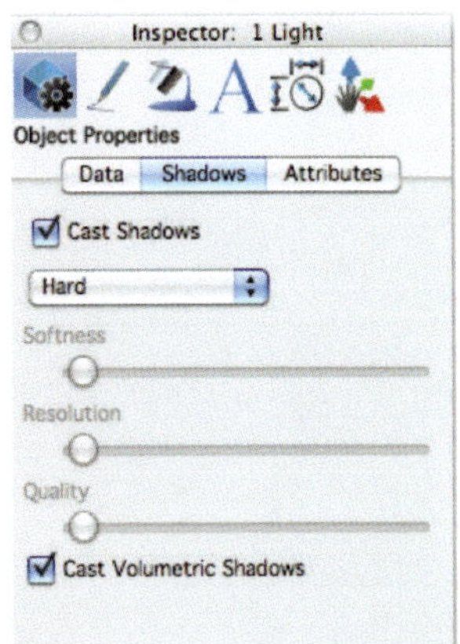

Figure 6.13– Use the Inspector dialog box to customize your light sources

- Next, go to the Object Properties tab found in the Inspector dialog box. To bring up the Inspector dialog box, simply right click on one of the light sources on your screen.
- Under the Object Properties tab, select the Shadow tab, check the box marked Cast Volumetric Shadow, and hit apply.
- To give your glow a more realistic falloff, you can adjust the light attenuation. This controls how quickly the intensity of the light will diminish. To change the attenuation, go to the Data tab found under Object Properties in the Inspector dialog box.
- To increase/decrease the brightness of the light, go to the Data tab found under Object Properties in the Inspector dialog box. Here, you can input values into the Intensity text field.
- Additionally, you can adjust the light color by assigning pen color attributes. To change the color of your light, go to the Pen Properties tab in the Inspector dialog box.
- Repeat these steps for each individual light source in your design.
- The light needs to display through an atmosphere to achieve the desired glowing effect. To insert such an atmosphere, right click anywhere on your screen to bring up the popup menu.
- From this menu, select Photo Render and then select Edit Foreground.

- From the Shader Setting Options, select fog light and your desired density value and click ok.
- Next, bring up the render library by going to the Window command on the Menu Bar.
- Insert a background so you will be able to see the glow from your light sources.
- Next, ensure your shadows are enabled. You can enable shadows at the top of your screen as shown in Figure 6.14.

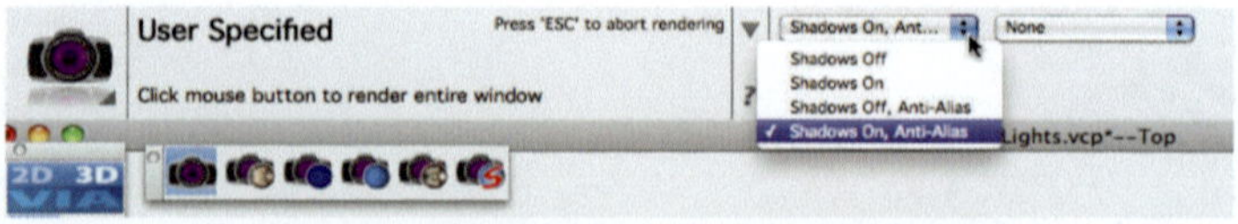

Figure 6.14- Don't forget to enable shadows

- Render away. The figure below displays a rendering of two spot lights and a point light.

Figure 6.15- Glowing Lights

How can I make light project through designed objects?

- Begin by setting up your lights. Refer to the tip above if you need assistance with making your light source(s) glow.
- Select your object and bring up the Inspector dialog box.
- Under the Object Properties tab, go to the Display tab.

Figure 6.16- Render Settings

- Check the box marked Transparency.
- Next, go to the Render tab.
- If you want the facets on the backside of the object to also cast shadows, you must enable Double Sided Facets.
- Next, click on the Advanced tab to bring up the Render Material Settings dialog. There are additional screen transparency parameters that are only available here.
- Next, go to Window on the Menu Bar and select Photo Render to bring up the Rendering tool palette.
- From this tool palette, click on the Photo Realistic Render Settings button to bring up the dialog box.
- Enable the "Use Transparency Shadows" option. Transparency shadows can slow down rendering significantly. Therefore, you should only use this option when really needed.
- Render away!

  Note: These additional settings are in the Shark FX rendering tool set.

Transparency shadows work for almost all transparency shaders. You can even get stained glass coloring effects.

How can I make a light cast a jpg image?

You can achieve some unique rendering effects by adding an image slide to your light. For example, you could set up light going through a stained glass window using the steps below.

- Create a Spot Light. The Spot Light type is the only light type that supports a slide.
- Enable the Slide check box and pick an image to cast.
- Adjust the Cone Angle to change the area of influence.

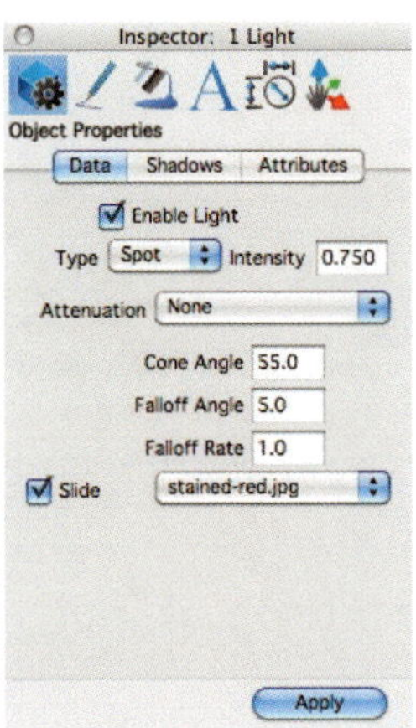

Figure 6.17

How can I make a clear glass material?

- Set your object to Super Fine. You may even want to go beyond Super Fine if your object has a lot of curvature.
- Go to the Inspector dialog box and check the box marked Double Sided Faces under the Render tab.
- Hit Apply.
- Set Object Color to white for clear glass
- Click the Advanced button tab in the Inspector dialog box under the Render tab.

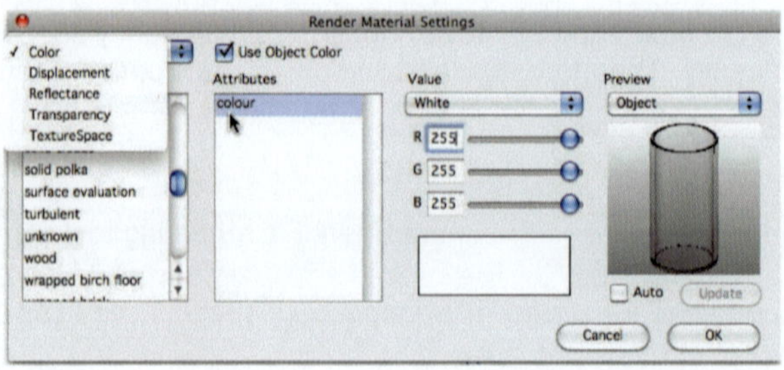

Figure 6.18

- Select the Color Shader and set the type to Plain, color white 255,255,255.
- Select the Displacement Shader and set the type to Rough.
- Select the Reflectance Shader and set the type to Dielectric.
- Adjust the settings to the following:

  - Ambient factor = 0
  - Diffuse factor = 0
  - Specular factor = 0
  - Transmission factor = 1.0
  - Mirror factor = 0.8
  - Roughness = 0.1
  - Refraction = 1.8

- Select the Transparency Shader and set the type to Plain.
- Make sure you hit Apply!

Figure 6.19

Within Edit Object>Material, what does “is backdrop object” mean?

Lightworks uses an internal ray-casting optimization method that sub-divides a model's extents into rectangular sub-volumes that are tagged as empty or not-empty.

Very large backdrop objects such as floors or walls can drastically increase the scene's extents volume and reduce the "precision" of the sub-volumes. This may result in longer rendering times. Keep in mind that "large" is relative to the other (important) objects in the scene.

On a related note, you should also turn off shadow casting on backdrop objects that will never cast shadows on other objects in a scene. This will result in better quality shadows and may significantly reduce rendering times.

Is there a way to tell which HDRI background I currently have applied?

- To view the current HDRI background, simply right click anywhere on the screen to bring up the pop up menu. HDRI's are available in the Shark products.
- From this menu, select Photo Render.
- Then, select Edit HDRI to bring up the HDRI Settings dialog. This will display the current HDRI background.

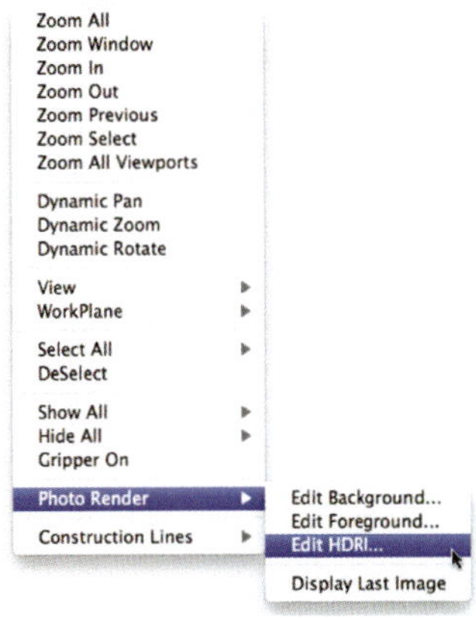

Figure 6.20

Shark FX has the ability to add high definition range images to a photo rendered scene, which is a quick way to define a lighting environment.

Can I change the Rapid Render settings?

The Rapid Render tools predefine settings for Metal, Glass, Plastic and Mirror materials.

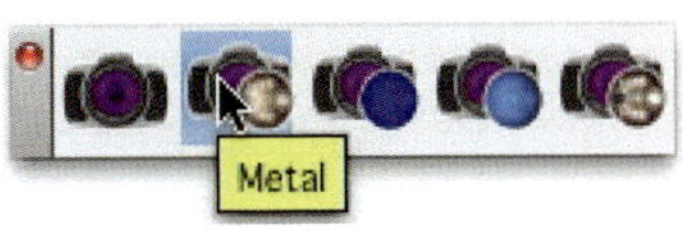

The definitions for these materials are specified in text files located in the Materials folder, which is located within the PhotoRender folder of the program install. You can edit these files with a text editor. The file contains categories of shader properties such as Reflectance, Color, Displacement, and Transparency. If you wanted to change the mirror setting for one of the presets, look for "mirror factor" in the [Reflectance] section and change the associated value.

Glass	OverrideGlass.csm
Metal	OverrideMetal.csm
Mirror	OverrideMirror.csm
Plastic	OverridePlastic.csm

7 CHAPTER 7
SHARING DATA

Overview

ViaCAD supports a variety of data formats that allow you to share your designs with other applications. Formats exist for importing and exporting to other programs, including CAD, CAM, rendering, publishing, and animation. The import and export commands for sharing data can be found under the File menu.

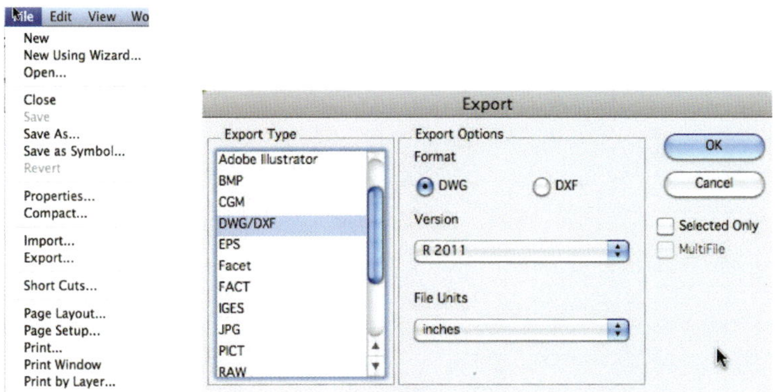

Figure 7.1

This chapter provides tips regarding the following aspects of sharing data with other applications:

- **Surface & Solid Formats –** These formats preserve the underlying geometry definitions in precise forms such as NURB and analytics. Example surface and solid formats include IGES, STEP, and SAT.

- **Facet Formats –** The facet formats triangulate the underlying definitions into less precise planar facets. This simpler format is easier to read into some 3rd party applications. Example facet formats include STL, OBJ, and RAW.

- **Other Formats** – Other formats include Adobe Illustrator, Excel, and SPLINE.

Surface & Solid Formats

What formats support NURB surfaces and solids?

NURB surfaces and solids provide a precise definition of the CAD objects, which makes it the preferred data-sharing format for manufacturing. The table below lists these various formats.

Table 7.1 – Surface & Solid Formats

Surface & Solid Formats	
.IGES	Initial Graphics Exchange Specification
.STEP	Standard for the Exchange of Product model data
.SAT	ACIS file format
.STEP	Standard for the Exchange of Product model data
.3DM	Rhino™ file format
.vcp, v3d, .sfx,	ViaCAD 2D/3D, ViaCAD™ Pro, Shark LT, Shark FX
.DXF/.DWG	Drawing Exchange Format DXF is a CAD data file format developed by Autodesk for enabling data interoperability between AutoCAD and other programs.
.CATPart .CATProduct	CATIA V5 (Shark FX PC)
.model .session	CATIA V4 (Shark FX PC & Mac)
.iam .ipt	Inventor Assembly (Shark FX PC) Inventor Part
prt	Pro/Engineer part (Shark FX)
.vda	Verband Der Automobilindustrie (VDA, Shark FX) VDA is a German standard and developed by the German Automobile Manufacturers Association

What is the best format to share 3D surfaces and solids?

Since ViaCAD's internal modeling engine is ACIS, the best file format to share precise data with is SAT. The SAT file format is considered the best, because the data is stored in its native definition and therefore not translated when read into another ACIS based system. AutoCAD and Inventor are based on a derived version of ACIS. As a result, ViaCAD has good compatibility with these products through the SAT format.

If you are sharing data with a non-ACIS based system, the best format is STEP. STEP does a very good job dealing with the various tolerances associated with curve, surface, and solids. Some applications such as Rhino support reading and writing SAT files which are not based on ACIS. In this case, you may want to consider STEP as the preferred system.

What does ACIS stand for?

ACIS contains the initials of the key team members who originally created the product:

Alan Grayer, **C**harles Lang, **I**an Braid, Dick **S**ower

What applications are based on ACIS?

> **Did You Know?**
>
> Grayer, Lang, and Braid are also known for having designed the ParaSolid kernel. Dick Sower was the founder of Spatial.

The 3D ACIS Modeler is a 3D modeling kernel owned by Spatial Corporation, a division of Dassault. ACIS is used by many software developers in industries such as computer-aided design (CAD), Computer-aided manufacturing (CAM), Computer-aided engineering (CAE), Architecture, engineering and construction (AEC), Coordinate-measuring machine (CMM), 3D animation, and shipbuilding. ACIS provides applications such as ViaCAD the underlying 3D modeling functionality.

The following CAD applications are based on ACIS:

ViaCAD & Shark, SpaceClaim, Alibre, KeyCreator, IMSI –TurboCAD Pro (Deluxe and Designer are facet based), and IronCAD.

What is the best format for SolidWorks?

Try using SAT R12 to share data with SolidWorks. ViaCAD uses the SAT file format, which is the standard file format for the ACIS kernel developed by Spatial. Since Spatial and Solidworks are divisions of Dassualt, technology components are shared between them that allow for precise reading and writing of SAT data.

Another excellent option for sharing files is STEP.

What is the best format for Inventor?

SAT is the preferred method to share surface and solid modeling data with Inventor.

Prior to 2001, AutoDesk licensed the ACIS kernel from Spatial to support solid modeling operations in their CAD applications. When Spatial was acquired by Dassault, AutoDesk exercised an option in their contract to buy a branch of the ACIS kernel, which they subsequently renamed as ShapeManger. Due to this common ACIS beginning, SAT is preferred method to share data with Inventor.

How can I confirm my exported STEP file is valid?

There are some instances when the receiving application has problems reading in a STEP file. If this occurs, you will need to determine if ViaCAD or the other application introduced the problem. The following steps will help determine if the STEP file you created in ViaCAD is valid:

- First, select the part and do a Check Object operation from the Verify menu. This will identify any geometry issues with the part.
- Next, export the part as a STEP file.
- Finally, import the file you just exported. Select the part and again do a Check Object from the Verify menu. This will confirm that the part was exported correctly through STEP.

If the above steps pass, potential translation issues are likely due the 3rd party application processing the file.

What happened to the 3D data in my DWG file?

DWG is the native file format for CAD applications such as AutoCAD and IntelliCAD. It's also a popular format to share data between other applications, as it provides robust definitions for curves, surfaces, solids, and annotation data. However, the 3D surface and solid modeling data stored in the file format is not always supported by applications. This is because that data is additionally encrypted and stored as SAT within the DWG/DXF format. SAT is a file format created by Spatial for the ACIS modeling kernel.

If your 3D data is not transferring into your 3rd party program, it's probably because it does not support the SAT format. One easy way around the issue is to export your file using the DWG R13 version. R13 did not support ACIS surfaces or solids so ViaCAD will automatically convert the data into facets that will likely be supported in the 3rd party system.

Figure 7.2 – Shade Options

Some tips regarding sharing data using R13 include:

- ViaCAD uses the default display resolution for facets. You can increase or decrease the number of facets using the Change Resolution command.
- To visually inspect the facets, turn on "Show Facet Edges" located in the Shade Options dialog box.
- To gain further control of the faceting, use the Change Object Type to Mesh command where you can specify the normal deviation and facet edge length.

Why do my DXF/DWG files appear scaled?

This may be a result of unit conversion. By default ViaCAD stores the unit in the DXF/DWG file. However, not all 3rd party applications properly process the file unit type. If you come across this situation, try using the File Units options in the Import/Export dialog box.

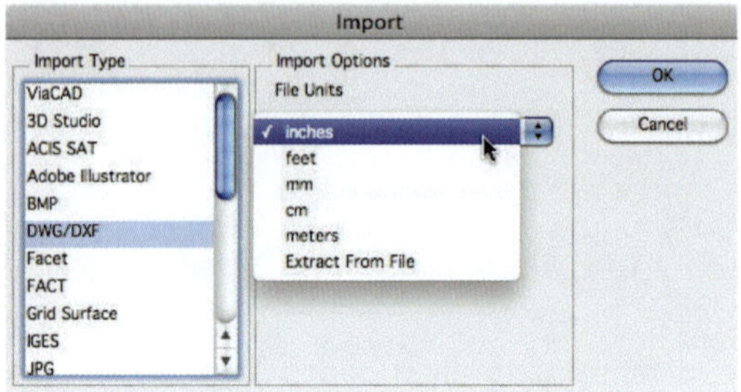

Figure 7.3 – Adjust Import File Units

Why is my text font wrong exported to DWG?

Text font types are not supported in some earlier version of DWG such as R12. If you export your file as R2011 or greater this will help ensure your font types are transferred.

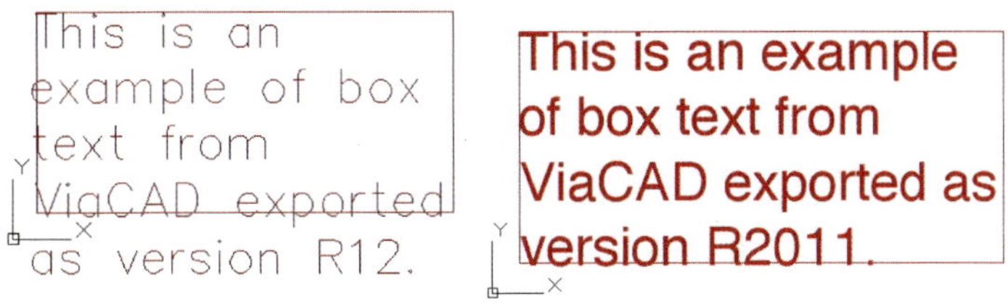

Figure 7.4 – Text imported into AutoCAD using two versions

Does IGES support text and dimensions?

The IGES definition does provide support for text and dimensions, however the licensed technology integrated into ViaCAD does not. If you need to read/write text and annotations, use the DXF/DWG file format.

When should I use the IGES format?

Use IGES as a last resort. IGES was replaced many years ago as the ISO standard because it did not support solids very well.

Why does my spline turn into a polyline in DXF/DWG?

The AutoCAD file format did not support splines until version R13. So if you export your drawing as an R12 file format, your splines are converted into polylines. Use a version greater than R12 to create nice smooth splines in your exported DXF/DWG files.

Facet Based Formats

What formats are based on facets?

Facet formats involve converting the more complex precision definitions into a format that is easily read and manipulated by applications that may not need the original accuracy. The table below lists these various formats.

Table 7.2 – Facet Formats

Facet Formats	
.3DS	3D Studio 3ds is one of the file formats used by the Autodesk 3ds Max 3D modeling, animation and rendering software.
.fact	Electric Image file format
.RAW	PovRay raw triangle format
.DXF/.DWG	AutoDesk standard file format Saving as a R12 version automatically exports all surfaces and solids as facets.
.Quad Mesh	File format used to share mesh data by Lockheed
.stl ,	.STL is the file abbreviation for **S**tandard **T**essellation **L**anguage used by the rapid prototyping industry for sharing data. This format approximates the surfaces of a solid model with triangles.
.vrml	The Virtual Reality Modeling Language (VRML) is often referred to as a 3D visual extension of the WWW. People can navigate through 3D space and click on objects representing URLs (including other VRML worlds). VRML is often pronounced like ``Vermal, not ``V-R-M-L.
.obj	Wavefront OBJ. Supports triangles and quadrilaterals. This format also supports normals and texture data.
.skp	SketchUp

How do I create a STL file?

STL is the file format standard used to create rapid prototypes. This format requires you have a closed, water tight body. The steps below show how to create a STL file:

- First, from the file menu select the Export option. In the dialog box that appears, select the STL option. At this point you have an option to create an ASCII or Binary STL file. The binary files create smaller file sizes. However, the ASCII file format compacts nicely if you post process it using a compression program such as Zip.

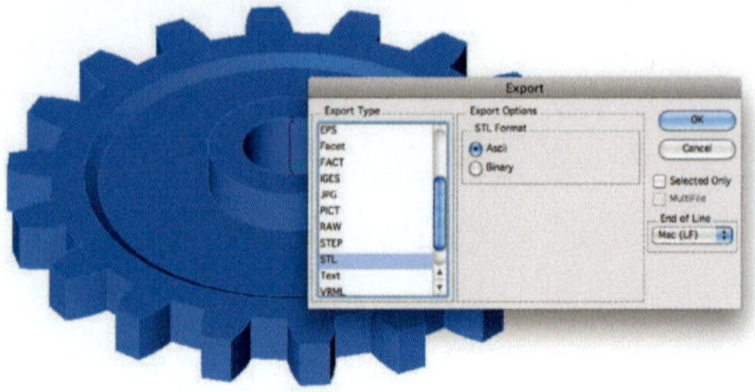

Figure 7.5

- Next, specify the file name and location to save the resulting file.

- The next dialog box that appears provides settings to adjust the facets that are exported to the STL file. By default, the dialog box displays the parameters associated with the objects display mesh.

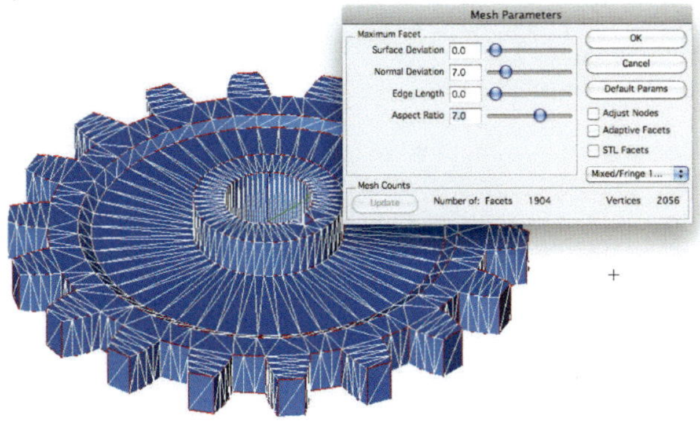

Figure 7.6

- Adjust these settings according to your needs. The facet outlines for the given settings is updated on the screen on your model. The best values to use will depend on the size, type, and complexity of the geometry, as well as requirements of by your rapid prototype supplier. If you are unsure, the default settings associated with Very Fine resolution will provide adequate results.

- STL file export complete, the file is saved.

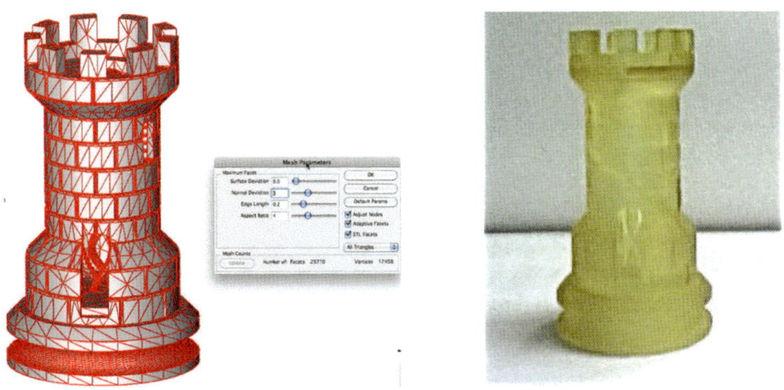

(a) Computer generated STL file (b) Manufactured STL File

Figure 7.7

What parameters are available for creating a STL files?

The STL file dialog box contains a variety of settings to fine tune the mesh exported to the STL file. Below you will find more information regarding these settings.

- *Surface Deviation* - The distance of a facet edge from the true surface. The default value of zero ignores this setting.
- *Normal Deviation* - The angular difference between two facets sharing the same edge. Use this as your primary driver to gain model resolution. Start with 3 degrees.
- *Edge Length* - Defines the maximum edge length of a facet. As a general rule, you should ignore this, as setting the Surface deviation small enough to get good resolution on the shallow surface yields a too highly faceted value on the highly contoured portion. It's a useful constraint when you have a model with both a highly contoured and shallow surfaced body (such as a wing/aircraft body), but otherwise, you should ignore this parameter.
- *Aspect Ratio* - Facets edge lengths are selected relative to your specified aspect ratio. This helps prevent long sliver facets. Aspects of 10/1 are fine, but when they get to be really thin slivers (20-30 to 1), the STL processing software will likely begin reporting either overlapping triangles or bad edges.
- *Adjust Nodes* - Facets are initially created on internal surface grid lines. By allowing the algorithm to adjust nodes, you can achieve better aspect ratios.
- *Adaptive Facets* - Facet density is increased more in high curvature areas without increasing density in lower curvature areas.
- *All Triangles* - Required for STL file format definition.

Check List

Creating ViaCAD parts for Rapid Prototyping:

✔ Stitch your surfaces into a solid to ensure the CAD model is "watertight". To confirm your part is watertight, do a Verify Volume.

✔ Check that your geometry is good. Use the Verify: Check Object, which will inspect for bad geometry that may create bad facets for the STL export.

✔ If you have a small feature, logo, or text on your model, a general guideline is to ensure these features are no less than 0.030 inches when working with plastics and 0.020 when working with metals.

✔ If your part has a void, be sure to model a hole to allow removal of support materials.

✔ There are no units in a STL file. ViaCAD saves the file in the current units. Be sure to coordinate with your STL partner regarding the units of the file.

✔ Export STL file as a binary file. This will save you time, as you will be sharing a smaller file.

✔Zip your file if sending over email

- *Mesh Counts* - Great feature for seeing the impact on your settings relative to the number of facets required to meet your conditions.

What are some of the manufactoring process that use STL?

The STL file format can be used in several rapid manufacturing processes, some of which are mentioned below:

- FDM (High tech hot melt glue gun):
    - Produces parts in what a final part might be (ABS, Polycarbonate, Ultem).
    - Generally this has the worst finish.

  - Difficult to build small features, and when small features are created, they are very delicate.
  - .005 min layers, with a normal of .010

- SLS (Sintered powdered plastic):
  - Usually Nylon 11 or Nylon 12
  - Material can be as rigid as a normal plastic. Some materials are glass, aluminum, or carbon filled. They can be flexible and porous, allowing their durometer to be changed by infiltrating with various polyurethane's (Adidas, Nike, etc prototype their shoes with this).
  - Gaps of .025" fuse together from residual heat in the part.
  - Protuberances of less than .025 don't tend to build.
  - Surface finishes like 120 grit sandpaper.
  - Layers from .003 to .006

- SLA:
  - Tends to have the nicest surface finish. Although they are resins, can have properties similar to engineering plastics.
  - Layer thickness from .0006 to .004

- DMLS (Direct metal):
  - There are a couple of companies making these machines (EOS seems to have the best surface finish and widest varieties of materials (Stainless (15-5 and 17-4), Tool Steel, Cobalt Chromium, Nickel Chromium, Aluminum ad Titanium).
  - Layers from .0008 to .006

Can I change the face edge color in the STL export command?

Yes, to change the face edge color:

- Go to Preferences.
- Select the Display category.
- From here, you can adjust color via the Edge Color option.

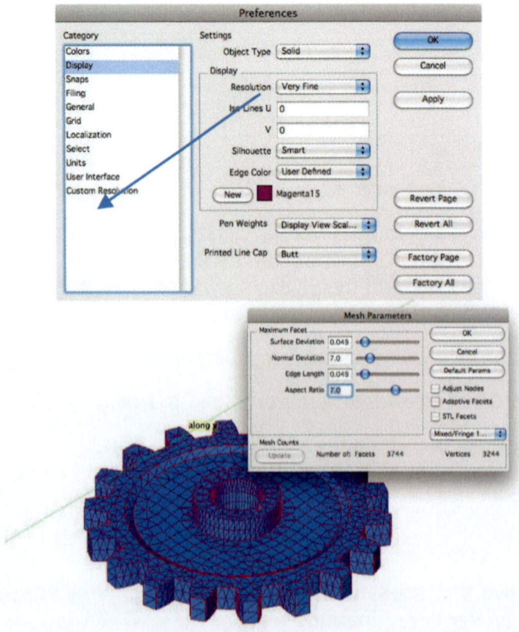

Figure 7.8

What facet format preserves surface normals?

Exporting facet data to file formats such as STL only write out the facet vertex information. However, the OBJ writes out the normal extracted from the underlying surface at each vertex, which is desirable for some rendering and animation applications.

How do I share data with the Electric Image Animation System?

The Electric Image Animation System (EIAS) is a collection of programs that render and animate a model. ViaCAD can share model data to and from EIAS using the FACT (.fac) file format. This format contains a facet based representation of mesh, surface, and solid objects from ViaCAD. Surfaces and solids are tessellated based on a dialog box presented to the user that controls such parameters as Surface Deviation, Normal Deviation, Edge Length, and Aspect Ratio.

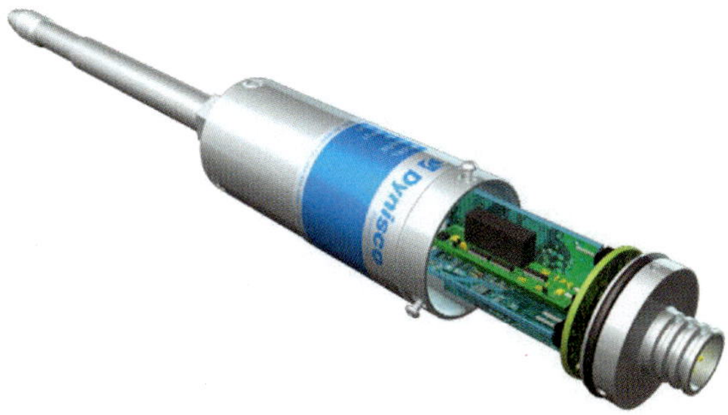

Figure 7.9 - Exported to FACT and with EIAS Rendering

What is the best format to export data to SketchUp?

SketchUp is a facet based modeler that does not support the precision formats mentioned earlier in this chapter. The preferred method is using DXF/DWG R13. It is important to use the R13 format or you will get an error reading the file into SketchUp as SketchUp does not read the precise SAT data embedded into the later versions. R13 will automatically convert the data into simple facet data that SketchUp understands.

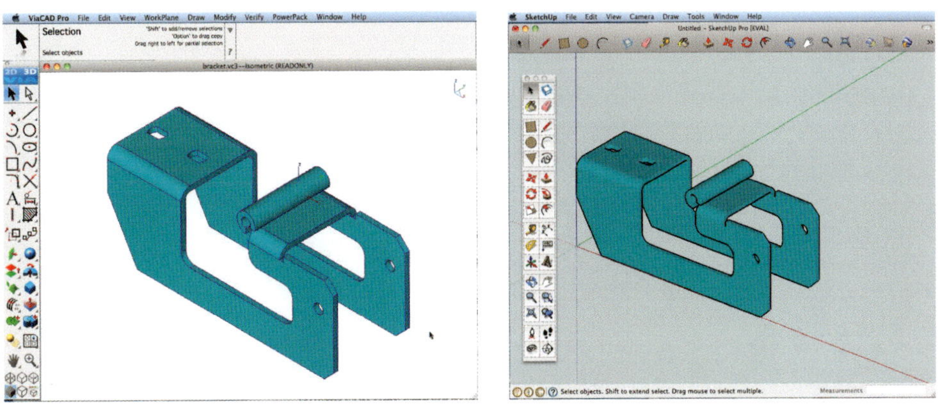

Figure 7.10 Export to SketchUp

What is the best format to import data from SketchUp?

ViaCAD supports a SketchUp importer that reads native .skp files. This is the preferred format as it reads in color, layers, and other attributes from SketchUp. Note SketchUp Import is available on PC for Version 9 products.

Figure 7.11

Is it possible to shell a model made in SketchUp?

It is possible to shell simple SketchUp models with ViaCAD. The steps to perform this operation are listed below.

- First, import the model into ViaCAD.

- Next, select the Stitch option from the main tool palette.

- Select the part to stitch. This will convert the facet model into a solid part suitable for solid modeling operations such as blending, chamfering and shelling. Note that many files from SketchUp will not stitch into a solid due to overlapping facets or other issues preventing an unambiguous collection of facets.

- Pick the faces that will remain open for the given shell thickness.

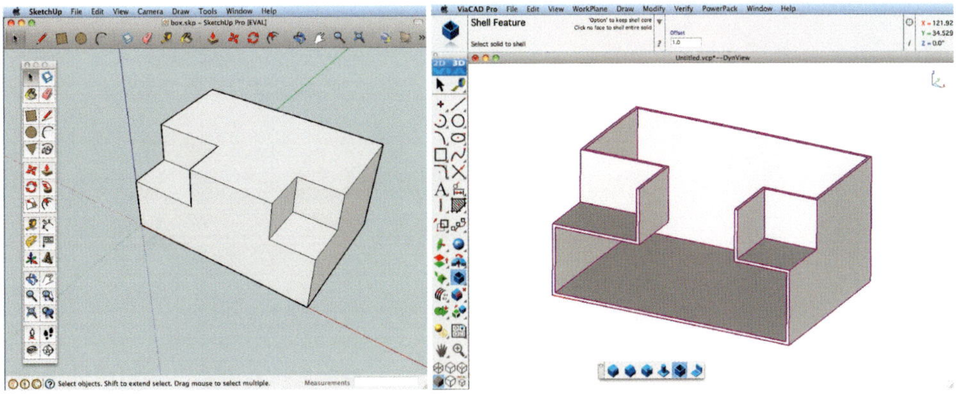

Figure 7.12

Can I export a quad mesh?

It is not possible to export a surface or solid as an all-quad mesh. However, you can export a model with mostly quads using the Change Object Type command. The key is to set the mesh type to Mixed/Fringe 1 Level and disable STL and Adaptive Facets. This will produce a mesh that consists of triangles along the edges and quads on the interior. To export the model, use the OBJ format, as it supports triangles and quads.

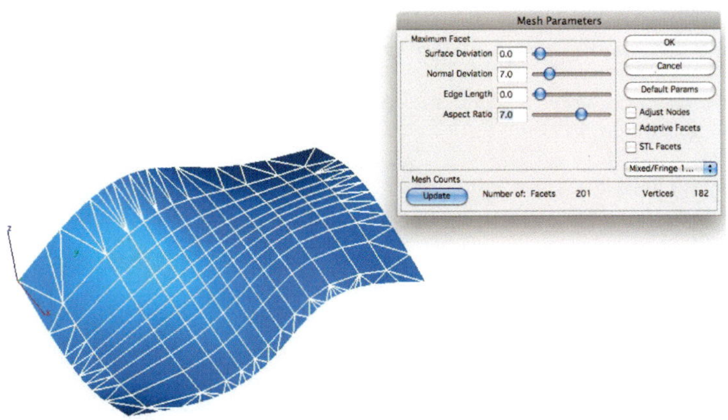

Figure 7.13

How can I reduce sliver facets when exporting?

The default facetter is set up to minimize the number of facets representing a surface or solid which may result in long sliver facets. Sometimes it is not desirable to have sliver facets when exporting to third party applications. You can reduce sliver facets by changing the object into a mesh and adjusting the Aspect Ratio mesh parameter. Note that you must set the Edge Length to a non zero value for the Aspect Ratio to activate.

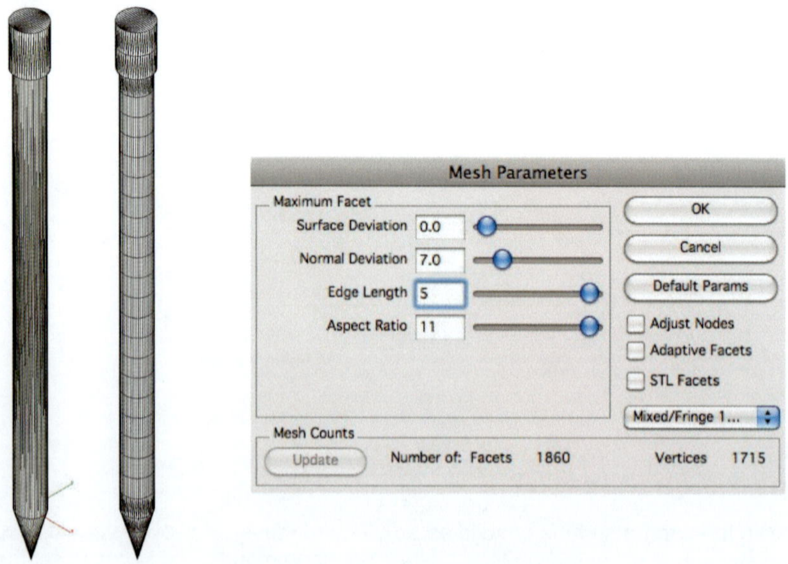

Figure 7.14– Setting the Aspect Ratio

Additional Formats

How can I import spline data from Excel?

Have you ever needed to import XY data from Excel to create objects? This tip shows you how you can share numeric data from Excel to create an object such as a spline.

- First, create your xy data in Excel, storing each component in a column. In our example, the points correspond to a parabola.
- In Excel, use the Save As command to select the *Tab Delimited Text (.txt) format.*
- Save the file.
- Launch ViaCAD and select the *File Import* option.
- Select the "Spline" Import type.

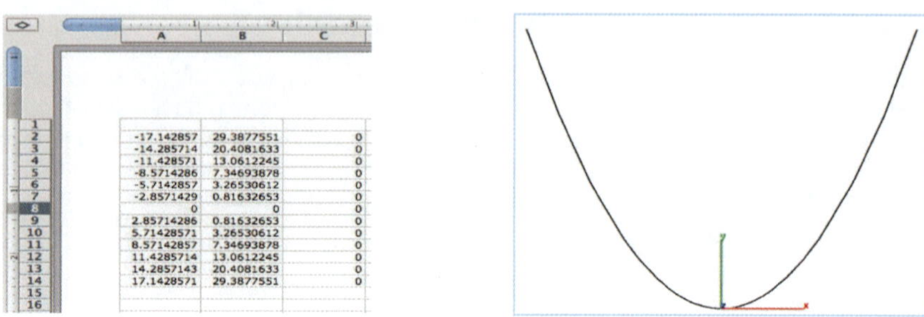

Figure 7.15 – Importing from Excel

How can I import point data from Excel?

Follow the steps from the previous tip on Importing Spline Data but this time edit the *.txt file* by adding “POINTS” to the top left of the file.

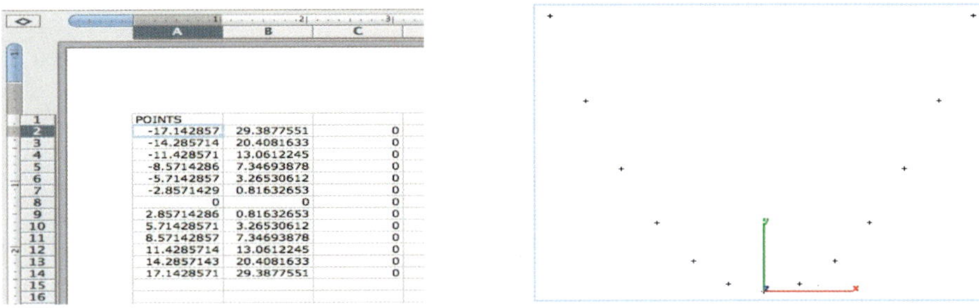

Figure 7.16 – Importing Points from Excel

Other keywords recognized by the Import Spline format include “LINE” and “POLYLINE”.

How do I set the scale of an export to Adobe Illustrator?

The Adobe Illustrator file format is 2D based on a fixed paper size whereas ViaCAD is 3D with infinite page size. To convert the data into 2D, ViaCAD will project the CAD objects currently displayed on the screen using the view plane. The flat objects are then scaled to the viewing plane scale which may be much larger then the Adobe Illustrate page size. The following steps provide a good estimation for choice of scale factor when exporting to Adobe Illustrator:

- Display the Page Layout dialog box from the File menu.
- Select the Single Page (this will match to an Adobe Illustrator single page).
- Select the Fit to Area option.
- Write down the scale factor displayed next to “Scale Ratio”.

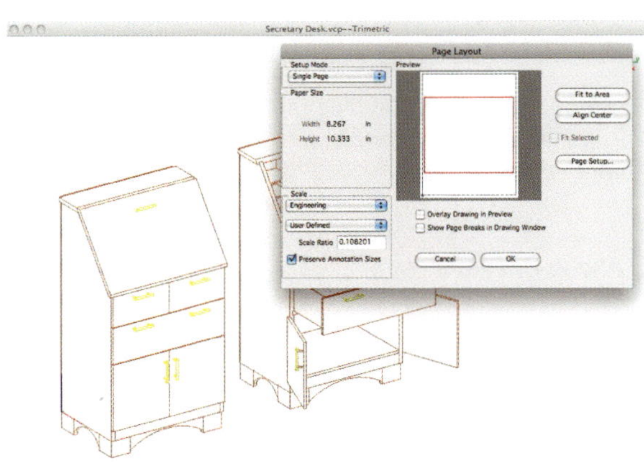

Figure 7.17

- Select Export from the File menu.
- Select Adobe Illustrator from the Export Type.
- Type in the Scale factor from Step 4.

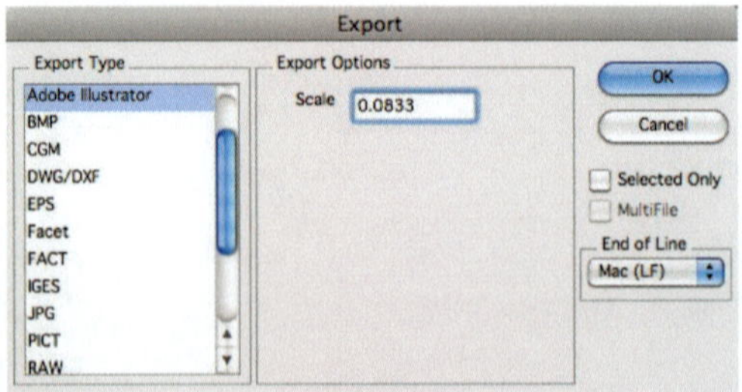

Figure 7.18

- Open the file into Adobe Illustrator.

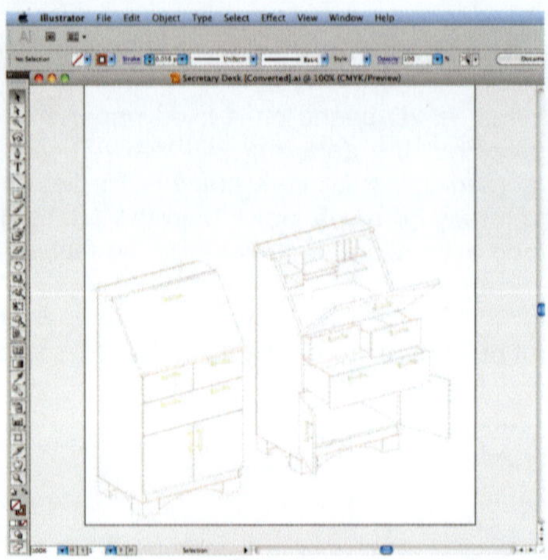

Figure 7.19

How can I import vectors from Adobe Illustrator?

ViaCAD provides an option to import Adobe Illustrator files (.ai). However, this import feature only imports vectors from version 8 or earlier. Fortunately, Adobe Illustrator provides an option to save files to older versions. The following steps demonstrate how to save a file and import into ViaCAD:

- Read the file into Adobe Illustrator.
- Select the Save As command, provide a file name and specify the Format as Adobe Illustrator.
- In the Illustrator Options dialog box, specify the Version to be Illustrator 8.
- Launch ViaCAD and select Import the file from the menu bar using the Adobe Illustrator

option.

- Turn of "Group curve segs," "Join Curve Segments," and "Polygon from fill option."

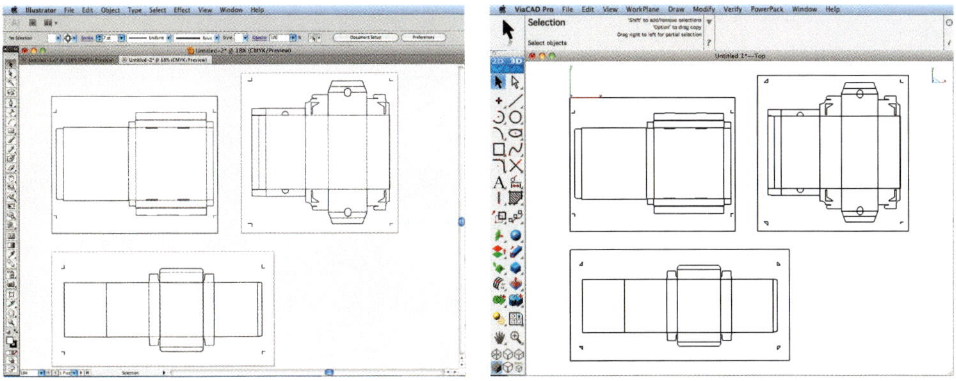

Figure 7.20

How can I import text from Adobe Illustrator?

Adobe Illustrator provides a comprehensive collection of tools to manipulate text including custom kerning and tracking, not found in ViaCAD. This tip shows how to import text created in Illustrator:

- Create your desired text in Adobe Illustrator.
- Right click on the text to export and select the Create Outlines option.
- Select the Save As file option and Adobe Illustrator format.
- Select the Illustrator 8 option for Version.

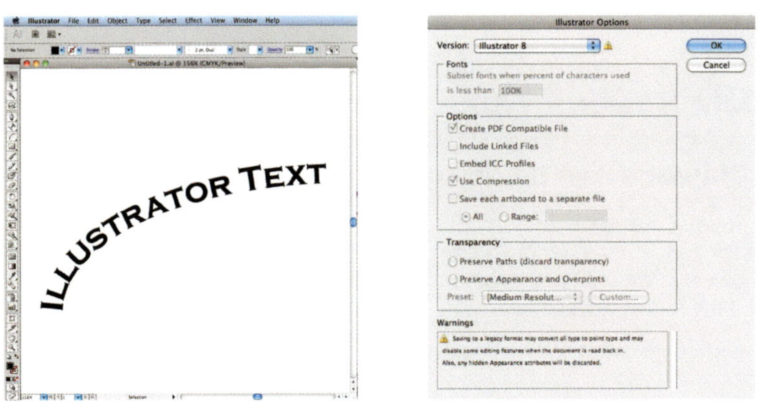

Figure 7.21

- Now launch ViaCAD and select Import from the File menu bar. This will display the import options available for Adobe Illustrator. Turn on “Group curve segs” and “Join Curve Segments”. Turn off the “Polygon from fill option”.

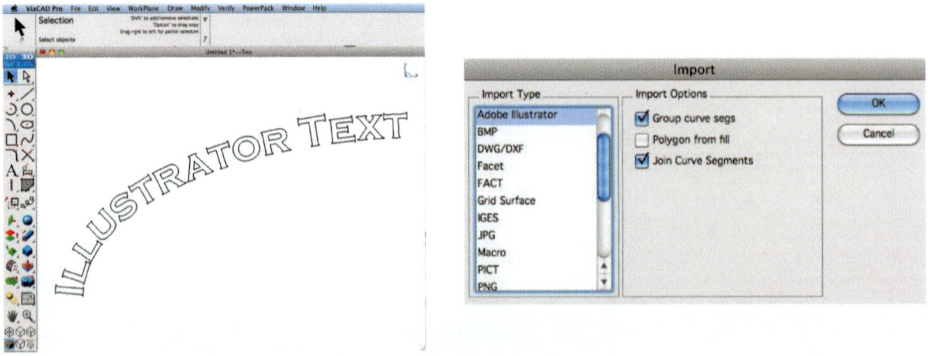

Figure 7.22

- Now that you’ve imported the text you can do some exciting 3D operations such as extruding the 2D shape into 3D and photo rendering!

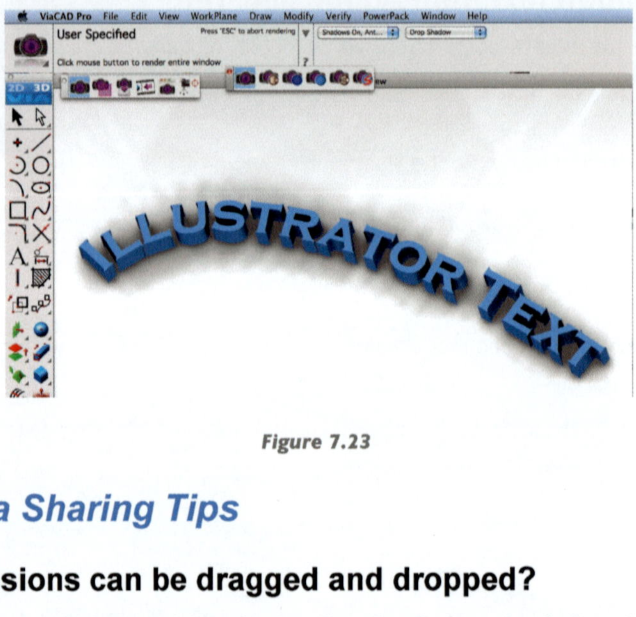

Figure 7.23

More Data Sharing Tips

What extensions can be dragged and dropped?

Did you know you could drag and drop foreign files directly from the desktop into ViaCAD? Normally users go to the Import dialog box under File to bring in files created from other systems. However, ViaCAD has an undocumented feature that allows you to drag and drop foreign files if they have a valid extension.

Table 7.3 – Drag and Drop

Extensions that can be Dragged & Dropped	
.igs, iges	IGES
.stp, .step	STEP
.dwg, .dxf	AutoCAD™
.STL	STL
.SAT	ACIS SAT™
.VCP	ViaCAD™ Pro
.v2D	ViaCAD 2D™
.v3D	ViaCAD 3D™
.sfx	Shark FX™
.shk	Shark™

You can drag more than one file at a time into ViaCAD. When dragging multiple files, these will be all dropped into the current drawing file.

How can I export a hidden line drawing to Illustrator?

To export a hidden line drawing to Adobe Illustrator:

- Set your display setting to Hidden. The Hidden option is located at the bottom of the Main Tool Palette.

- Select the File Export to Illustrator option.

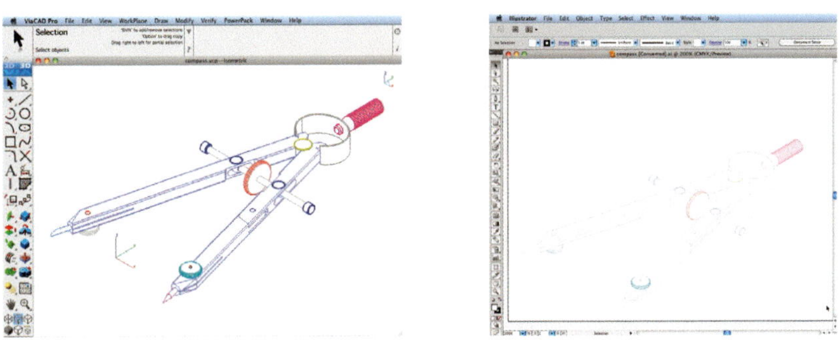

Figure 7.24

How can I export shaded drawings to Illustrator?

The Adobe Illustrator exports using the current display setting. To export a shaded drawing simply select the render mode from the bottom of the display palette. Shaded images are exported as sorted facets to Illustrator. One issue with this method is that each part's facets are only sorted relative to the part. This can result in parts being displayed on top of others

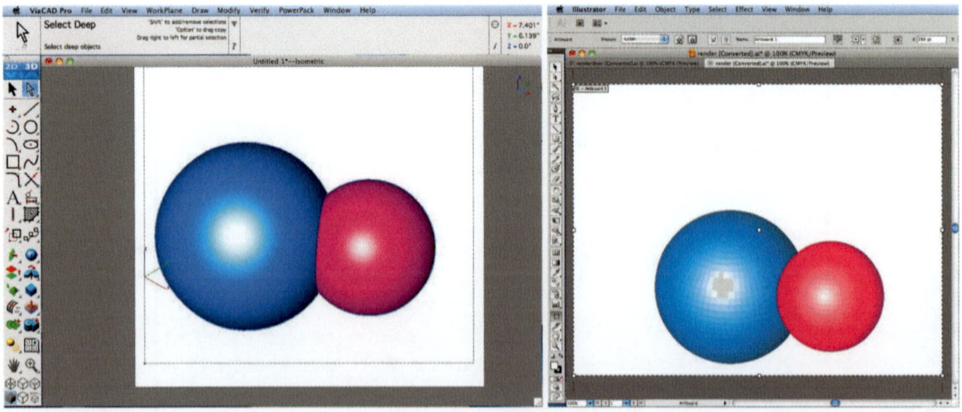

Figure 7.25

Can I read a ViaCAD V8 file into ViaCAD V7?

The file format of a ViaCAD file typically changes with a new release. However, if you have access to V8, you can use the Export option from the File menu to save the V8 file as a V7 file.

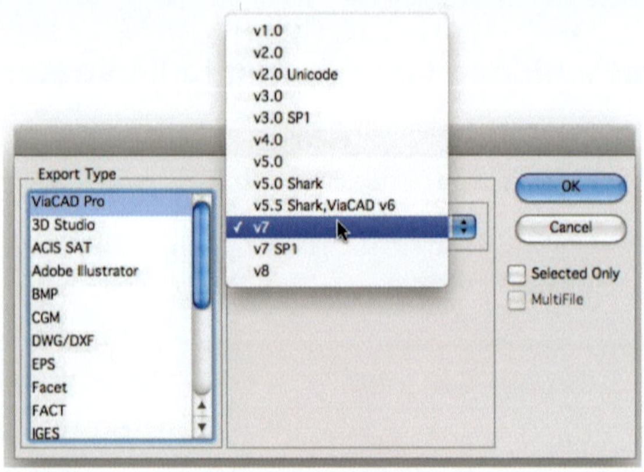

Figure 7.26

Can I read a ViaCAD Pro file into ViaCAD 2D/3D?

Yes, the file format within the same version is compatible. Objects created in Pro however that do not exist in 2D/3D will exist as entity types without parameters to modify.

What file formats contain unit settings?

Some file formats do not specify whether the values contained are expressed as metric (i.e. cm) or US standard (i.e. inch). This can result in your file being scaled by a factor of 25.4! The table below shows some of the common formats used in ViaCAD and whether the format supports unit specification as part of the format.

Table 7.4 – Surface & Solid Formats

File Unit Formats	
Units	No Units
.STEP	.STL
.SAT	.OBJ
.STEP	.3ds
.3DM	.ai
.dxf/dwg	.fact

What formats read/write text and dimensions?

The only format ViaCAD supports to read and write text and annotation data is .dxf/.dwg.

Is it possible to read airfoil data?

There are two ways to read in airfoil data. The first requires AeroPack, an addon from Darcorporation that supports a variety of tools specific for aircraft design. Aeropack includes the ability to generate an airfoil from equations as well as read data in from a variety of industry airfoil standards.

The second method requires a manipulating the original airfoil data into the spline file format. The steps needed are as follows:

- First, add a comment marker to any descriptions in the file. Comment markers in the spline format are "//" and tell the parser to ignore this line in the file.
- Add "THROUGHSPLINE" before the coordinate data.
- Remove any commas by replacing with a "space" character.
- Add a third value of "0.0" to all coordinate values.
- Read into PunchCAD using the File Import Spline option.
- The second method creates an interpolated spline with the provided points. It does nothing special regarding slopes at the leading or trailing edge.

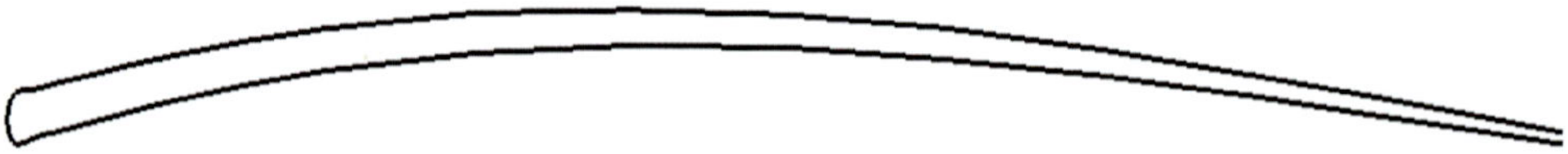

Figure 7.27 Imported Wright Flyer Airfoil

Table 7.5 - File Modifications for Spline Format

Eiffel 10 1903 Wright Flyer	//Eiffel 10 1903 Wright Flyer
1.000000, 0.006400	THROUGHSPLINE
0.950000, 0.014300	1.000000 0.006400 0.0
0.900000, 0.022000	0.950000 0.014300 0.0
0.800000, 0.037000	0.900000 0.022000 0.0
0.700000, 0.051000	0.800000 0.037000 0.0
0.600000, 0.062300	0.700000 0.051000 0.0
0.500000, 0.069300	0.600000 0.062300 0.0
0.400000, 0.071800	0.500000 0.069300 0.0
0.300000, 0.070100	0.400000 0.071800 0.0
0.200000, 0.061400	0.300000 0.070100 0.0
0.150000, 0.055000	0.200000 0.061400 0.0
0.100000, 0.046800	0.150000 0.055000 0.0
0.075000, 0.042300	0.100000 0.046800 0.0
0.050000, 0.037500	0.075000 0.042300 0.0
0.025000, 0.032300	0.050000 0.037500 0.0
0.012500, 0.029600	0.025000 0.032300 0.0
0.000000, 0.027300	0.012500 0.029600 0.0
0.000000, 0.000000	0.000000 0.027300 0.0
0.012500, 0.003200	0.000000 0.000000 0.0
0.025000, 0.006000	0.012500 0.003200 0.0
0.050000, 0.011700	0.025000 0.006000 0.0
0.075000, 0.017000	0.050000 0.011700 0.0
0.100000, 0.022300	0.075000 0.017000 0.0
0.150000, 0.031500	0.100000 0.022300 0.0
0.200000, 0.039000	0.150000 0.031500 0.0
0.300000, 0.048600	0.200000 0.039000 0.0
0.400000, 0.052700	0.300000 0.048600 0.0
0.500000, 0.051800	0.400000 0.052700 0.0
0.600000, 0.045600	0.500000 0.051800 0.0
0.700000, 0.037000	0.600000 0.045600 0.0
0.800000, 0.025500	0.700000 0.037000 0.0
0.900000, 0.012700	0.800000 0.025500 0.0
0.950000, 0.006500	0.900000 0.012700 0.0
1.000000, 0.000000	0.950000 0.006500 0.0

How do I import a surface grid?

This tip shows how you can import a structured grid of xyz points from a text file into a NURB surface using the Import:Grid Surface option. The steps needed are as follows:

- First, create an ASCII text file with a grid of xyz surface data. The first line in the file contains the number of u and v points ordered as a U x V grid. V is the number of points that are read U times. The first line of the file should appear as below for 4 x 3 grid of points:

```
4    3
```

- The next line of the file is the first point of the grid expressed as three floats. You will have u x v lines in this format. The line should look like:

  0.0 0.0 0.0

- If you data has commas, remove by replacing with a "space" character.
- Read into PunchCAD using the File Import Grid Surface option.

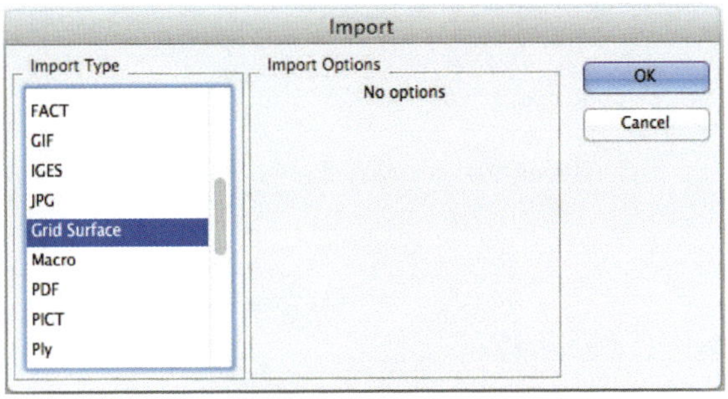

Figure 7.28 Import Grid Surface Dialog

The following table is an example 4 by 3 grid points

Table 7.6 – Import Surface Grid Example

4	3		// The number of points in a u x v array
0	0	0	// pt 1 u = 1, v=1
1	0	0	// pt 2 u = 1, v=2
2	0	0	// pt 3 u = 1, v=3
0	1	0	// pt 4 u = 2, v=1
1	1	0.5	// pt 5 u = 2, v=2
2	1	0	// pt 6 u = 2, v=3
0	2	0	// pt 7 u = 3, v=1
1	2	0	// pt 8 u = 3, v=2
2	2	0	// pt 9 u = 3, v=3
0	3	0	// pt 10 u = 4, v=1
1	3	0	// pt 11 u = 4, v=2
2	3	0	// pt 12 u = 4, v=3

The image below illustrates a 4 x3 grid of points.

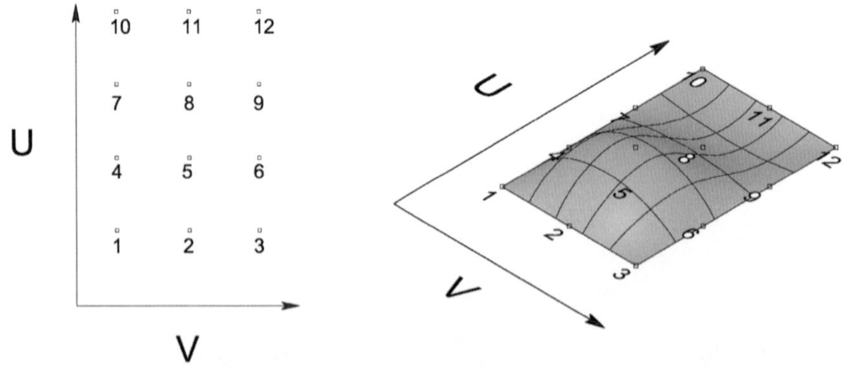

Figure 7.29 Import Grid Surface Expected Point Structure

Can I import a point cloud?

The Ply format supports point clouds as part of the file format definition. The data is marked inside the ply data as "range_grid". ViaCAD will read each range_grid definition as single point entity. In the example image below, a single point entity hold 47,000 vertices.

Figure 7.30 Import Ply as Point Cloud

Part II Create This! Tutorials

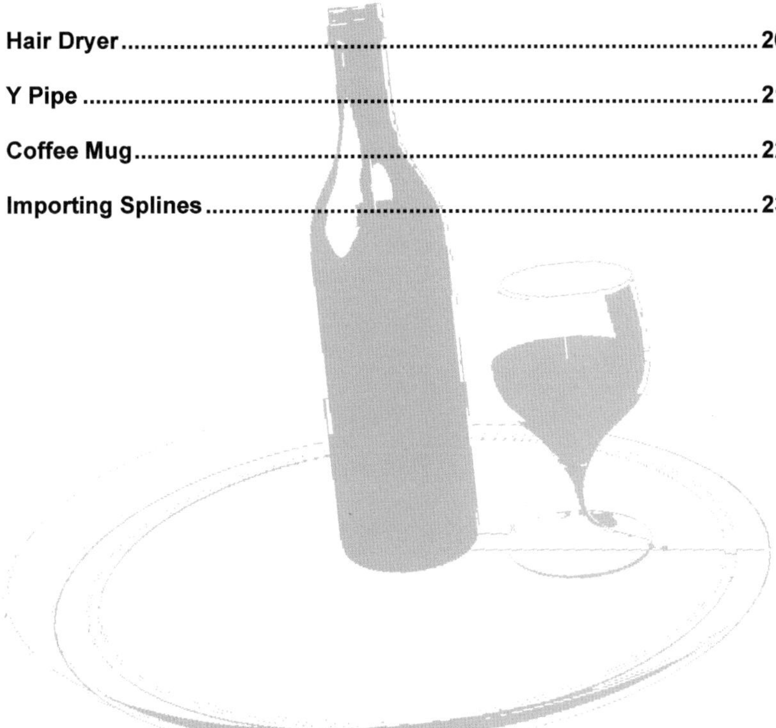

Paper Clip

Level: Beginner

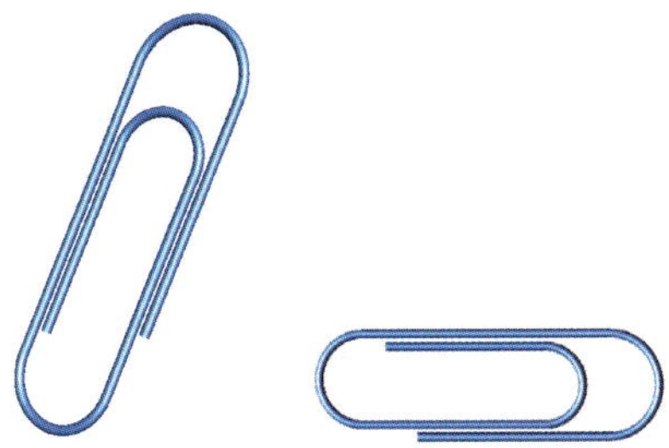

Description: In this tutorial, you will learn to make connected lines with the *Multi Line* tool, how to use the *Select Chain* tool, and how to apply the *Solid Pipe* tool. The end result is a model of a paper clip.

Key Tools: Multi Line, Fillet 3 Curves, and Pipe Solid

Overview:

Making the paper clip can be broken down into the following process:

1. Drawing the 2D curve Profiles from which to create the 3D model

2. Using the *Solid Pipe* tool to generate the paper clip from its profile

1. Drawing the Profile

- Begin by changing your view to Top view. This can be accomplished by going to View and selecting Top; alternately, you can right-click on the drawing window and use the context sensitive menu to select Top View.

- Now, select the *Multi Line* tool, which can be found in the line palette.

  - The *Multi Line* tool allows multiple segments of straight lines to be drawn consecutively. The endpoint of one segment will be the starting point of the next.

  - Once selected, the tool name in the top bar changes to read Multi Line. This is called the tool prompt. Refer to the tool prompt for step-by-step instructions for any tool you are using.

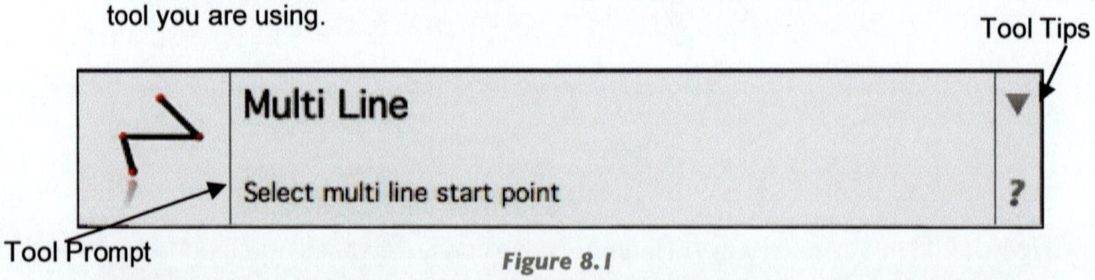

Figure 8.1

  - Additionally, the tool prompt will list any special operations that can be performed with the tool. For example, in the top right corner of the *Multi Line* tool prompt it states "Option to create arc." This is a special feature of the *Multi Line* tool that allows you to create an arc by pressing the Option key in conjunction with the *Multi Line* tool. Look to the tool prompt to find such shortcuts.

- Next, click on the origin to place the **1st point** of your multi line.

- Move your cursor to the right an arbitrary distance from the origin and click to place the **2nd point.**

To assist you in drawing a horizontal line, you will see a cursor helper line. Cursor helper lines will help you draw horizontal, vertical, perpendicular lines, etc. Use them!

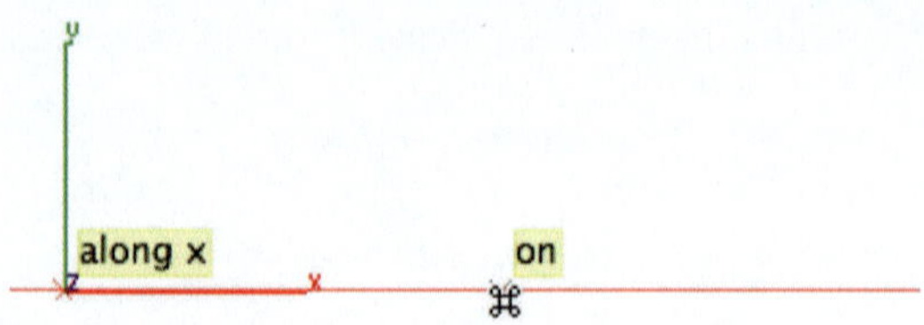

Figure 8.2 Cursor helper lines and tags

- From here, move your cursor up the screen about a third as far as the first part of the line, and click to place the **3rd point**. Again, watch for the cursor helper line to ensure that you are perpendicular to the first part of the line.

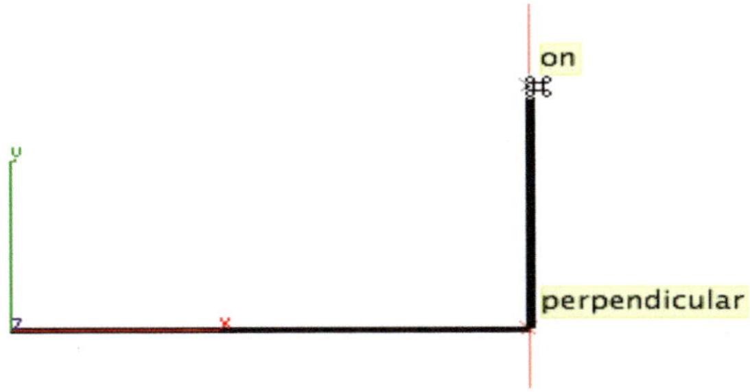

Figure 8.3 – Placing 3rd point. Note the red helper line and tags

- Next, move your cursor horizontally to the left by using the cursor helper lines. Pass the origin point by a short distance and place the **4th point.**

Figure 8.4 – Placing 4th point

- Continue this process until you have a Seven-Segment multi line that looks like Figure 8.5 below.

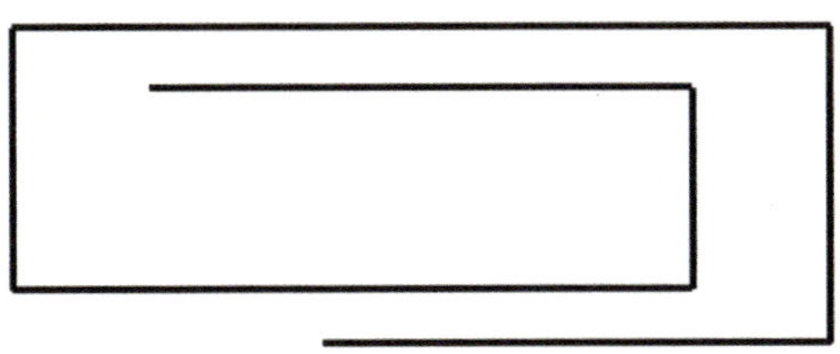

Figure 8.5 – Seven-segment multi line

- Once you have placed the **8th point** (seven segments) as shown in Figure 8.5 above, press the ESC key (or Right Button) on the keyboard to exit the tool.

2. Rounding the Paper Clip Ends

- Choose the *Fillet Three Lines* tool from the fillet palette. This tool constructs a fillet tangent to the three objects you choose.

- Click the 3 lines marked in Figure 8.6 to round the right end of the paper clip. You should see a dashed line similar to the one depicted in 8.6 as you click the lines. After clicking the 3rd line, the *Fillet Three Lines* tool will automatically round the paper clip end.

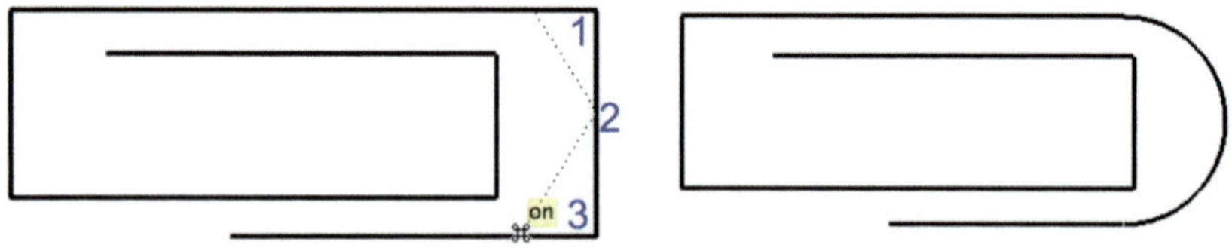

Fig 8.6 – Use Fillet 3 Lines tool to create round edges of paper clip

- Repeat this process on the left-hand end and inside curve of the clip. You should now have a drawing of a paper clip similar to the one shown below in Figure 8.7.

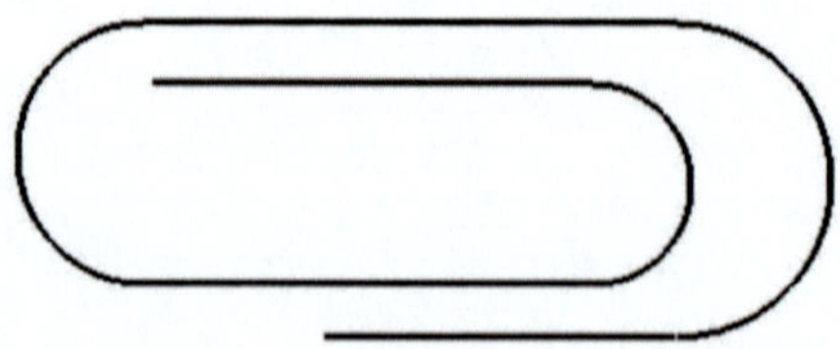

Figure 8.7 – Complete paper clip profile

3. Creating a Pipe Solid

- In order to give material thickness to the paper clip, you will now use the *Pipe* tool.
- Choose the *Pipe* tool from the Solids from Profile tool palette.
- Enter an appropriate value for the outside diameter of the solid pipe that the clip will be represented by. In this case, we will use 0.15 inch. Leave the inside diameter as zero.

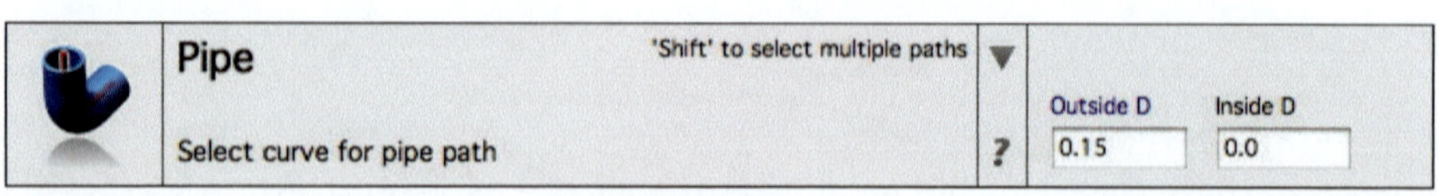

Figure 8.8

- Now draw a fence (a box) around the entirety of your paper clip.
- Provided the pipe diameter is not too large, the paper clip should now be seen with the stated material thickness, as shown Figure 8.9.

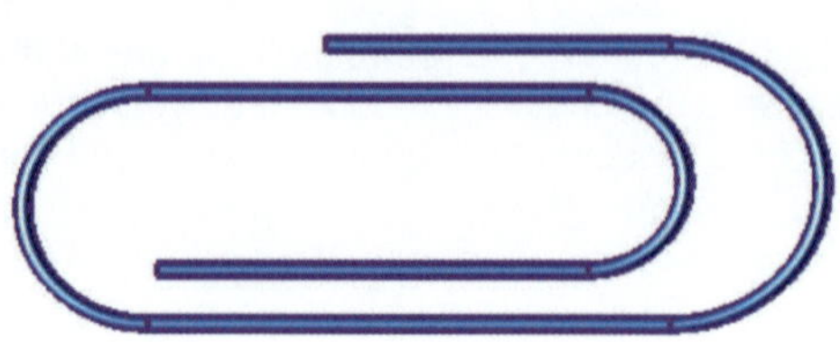

Figure 8.9 – Finished paper clip

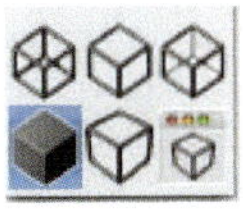

If you are not seeing the clip as it appears above, it may because you are viewing in **wireframe** mode as opposed to **shaded** mode. Try clicking the shade mode buttons at the bottom of the toolbar.

4. Extra Touches

- Try experimenting with the right-click context sensitive menu on your paper clip to change the color, resolution, and transparency of the object.

- Additionally, if you have ViaCAD Pro you can photo render the object to add further realism.

    - Simply go to Window on your menu bar. From the drop down menu, select Render Library. Use this dialog to apply your desired materials, backgrounds, and foregrounds.

    - To see the results of such applied materials, click on Photo Render under the same drop down Window menu. This will bring up the Photo Render tool palette, which contains several tools you can use to render your object.

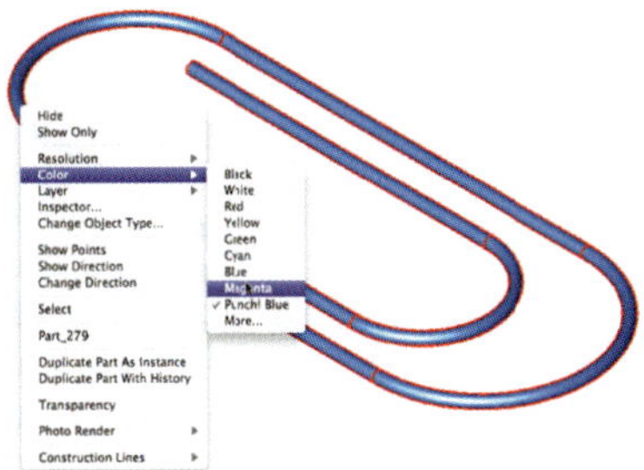

Figure 8.10 - Right click on any object to see a context sensitive menu of object related settings

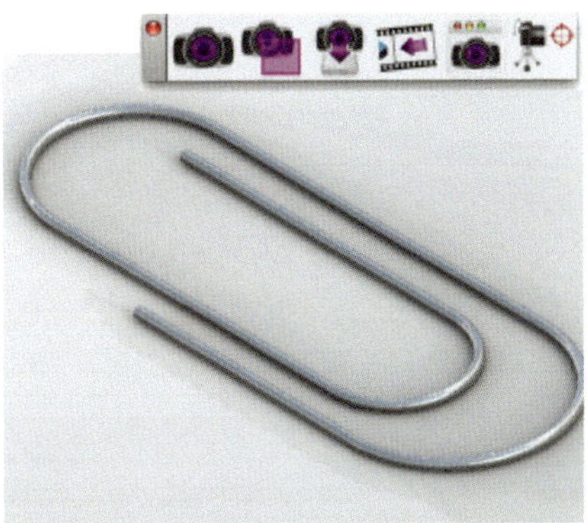

Figure 8.11 – Rendered paper clip shown with Photo Render tool palette

Get the Look

Material: Aluminum metal

Background: Graduated Gray to White

HDRI: Studio/lwhdr_studio5

_2k.hdr

HDRI Intensity: 2.0

* Shadows on, anti-alias

Breadboard

Level: Beginner

Description: This tutorial teaches you how to construct a solid by extruding a 2D profile and how to apply blends. The end result is a breadboard.

Key Tools: Single Line, Fillet Two Lines, Mirror, Extrude, and Blend tools.

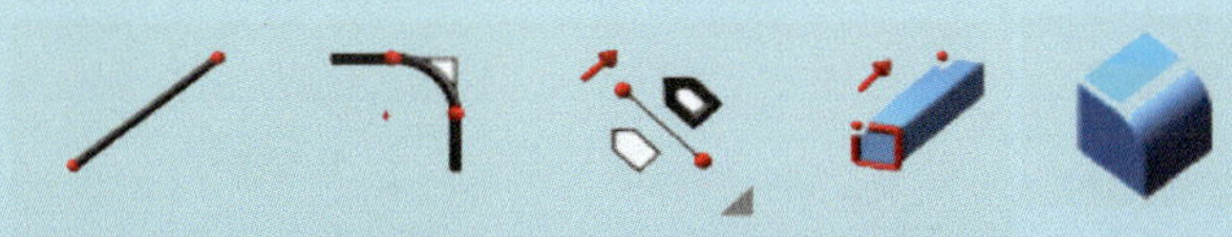

Overview: Designing a breadboard can be broken down into several steps:

1. Drawing the top profile using lines, arcs, and circles
2. Filleting the edges
3. Mirroring the profile
4. Extruding from 2D to 3D
5. Applying finishing blends

1. Drawing the Profile

- If not already in Top View, change your view to Top View by going to View and selecting top. Alternately, you can right-click on the drawing window and use the context sensitive menu to select Top View.
- Select the *Single Line* tool.
- Beginning at the origin, construct a 10-inch line along the x-axis. Type "10" into the length field of the Data Entry Window to quickly and accurately adjust the distance.

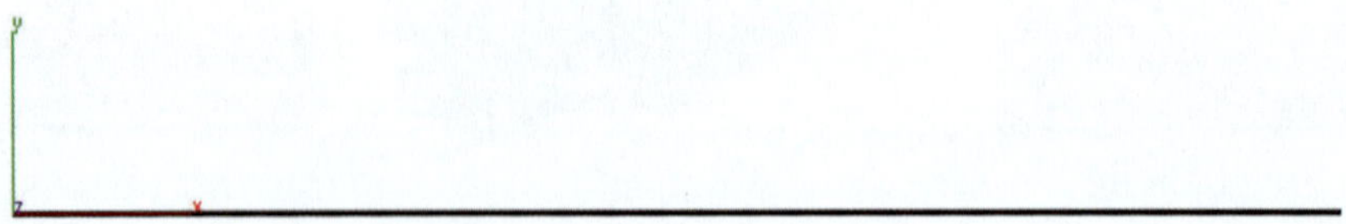

Figure 9.1

- Next, construct a 2-inch vertical line. Watch for the cursor helper lines and tags that will guide you in making the lines perpendicular.

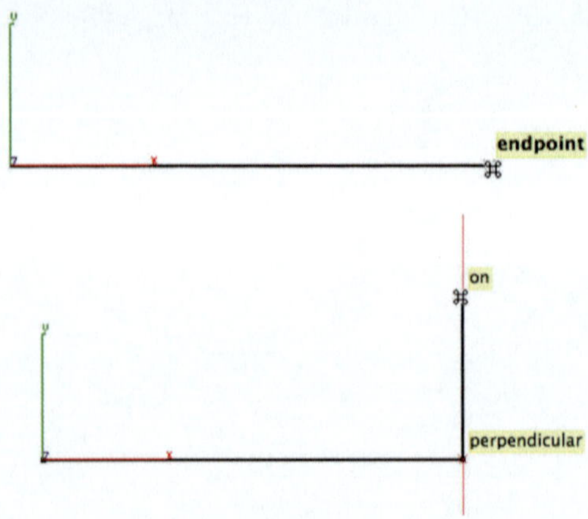

Figure 9.2

- Next, construct a 3-inch horizontal line followed by a 1.5-inch vertical line.

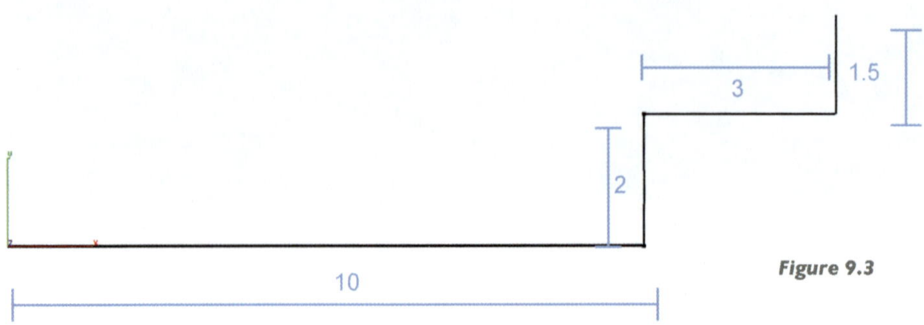

Figure 9.3

2. Filleting Edges of the Breadboard Profile

- We will now curve the edges of our breadboard profile.

- To do this, begin by selecting the Fillet Two Lines tool. This tool constructs an arc tangent to the two objects you select.

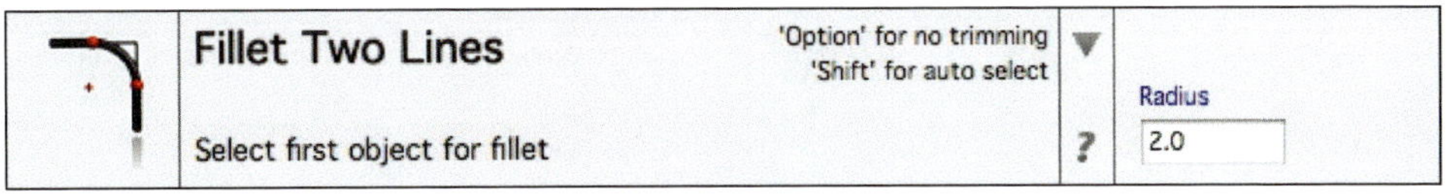

Figure 9.4 – Set radius of Fillet Two Lines tool to 2

- Next, adjust the radius to be 2.0 by going to the top of your screen and typing the value into the Data Entry Window.

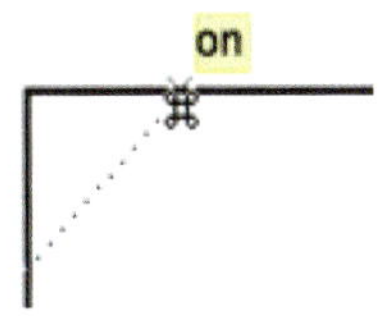

Figure 9.5

- Following the tool prompt, select the first object for fillet by clicking on the 2-inch vertical line. A little yellow flag saying "On" should pop up affirming you are indeed clicking a point on the line.

- Next, click a point on the 3 inch horizontal line. Again, a yellow flag should indicate when you have selected a point on the line.

- Upon release, the fillet will form similar to the one shown in Figure 9.6 below.

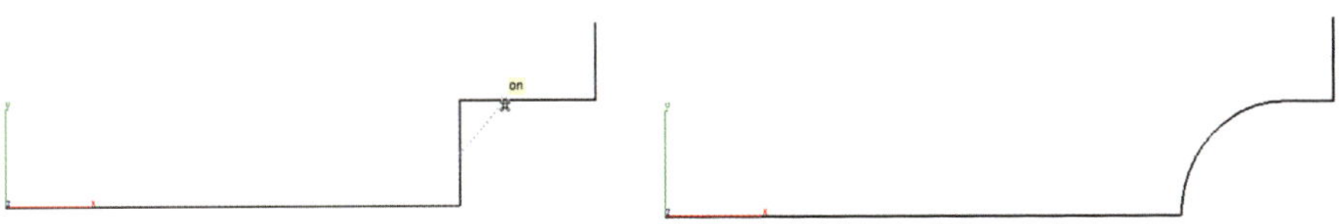

Figure 9.6 – Filleting edges

If you want to keep the original lines in addition to the newly created fillet, you simply need to press the Option key on a Mac or Control key on a PC. This will prevent the fillet from being automatically trimmed.

- As the Data Entry Window allows you to adjust the fillet radius value after creating the fillet, we must deselect the tool before creating our second fillet, because we will be using two different radii values. Therefore, switch to the arrow tool and then back to the fillet tool.

- Once back to the fillet tool, adjust the radius to 1 inch.

- Following the same steps as before, select the objects for fillet so you create a profile similar to the one illustrated in Figure 9.7.

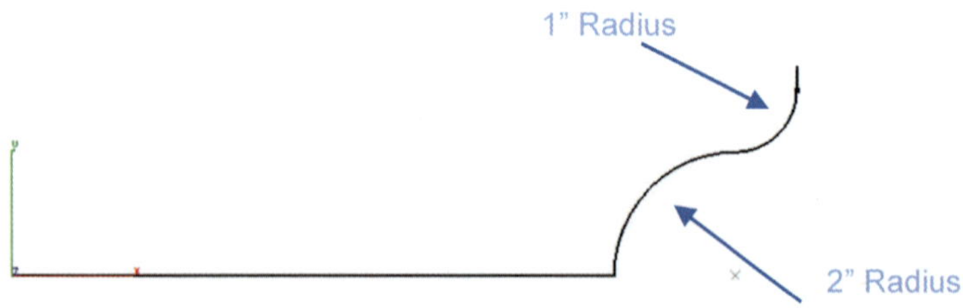

Figure 9.7

3. Mirroring Profile

- Begin by selecting the *Mirror* tool from the tool palette.
- Then, select all objects by pressing and holding the left button while moving from left to right. This will form a selection fence that will select all objects whose extents lie within the selection fence.
- Now, click on the endpoint at the top of breadboard profile.

Figure 9.8

- On a Mac: Press and hold the Option key.
- On Windows: Press and hold the Control key.
- Drag your cursor outward, perpendicular to the endpoint. A cursor helper line and flag should pop up to assist you. Click at an arbitrary distance.

Figure 9.9

- Upon release of mouse and Option/Control key, the profile should be mirror copied.

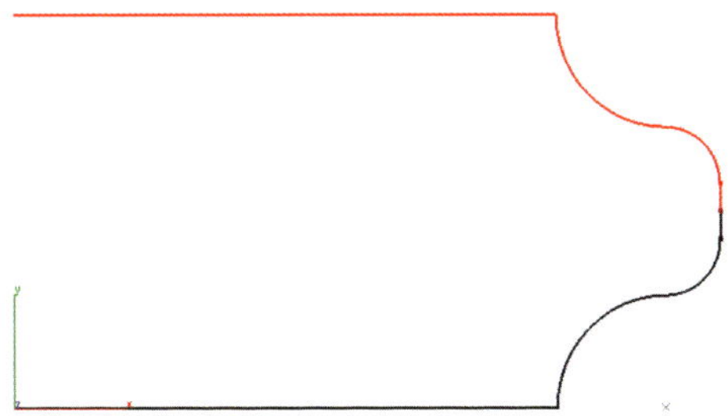

Figure 9.10

4. Finishing the Profile

- Now, use the *Single Line* tool to construct a vertical line to connect the newly mirrored profile to the original.

Figure 9.11

- To finish up the profile, we will now create a hole so that the breadboard can hang.
- Select the *Center Point Circle* tool.

Figure 9.12

- Go to the handle and move your cursor over the curve until the endpoint flag appears.

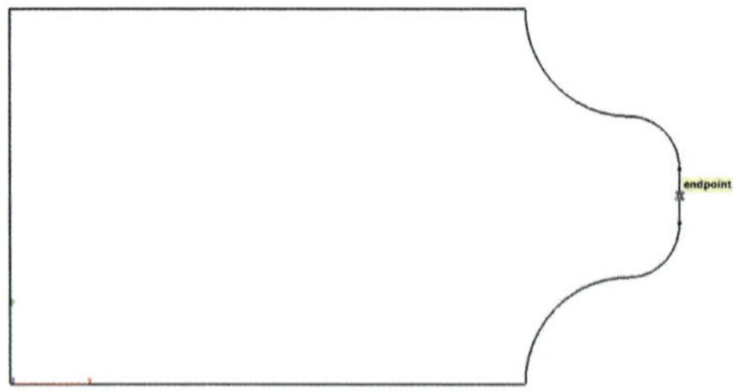

Figure 9.13

- Now, bring your cursor upwards to "awake" the y-axis line.

- Once the "along y" line appears, bring your cursor down to the approximate middle of the handle. The "along y" and "along x-axis" lines should appear to help guide you. Click to place the center starting point of your circle in the intersection between the y and x lines.

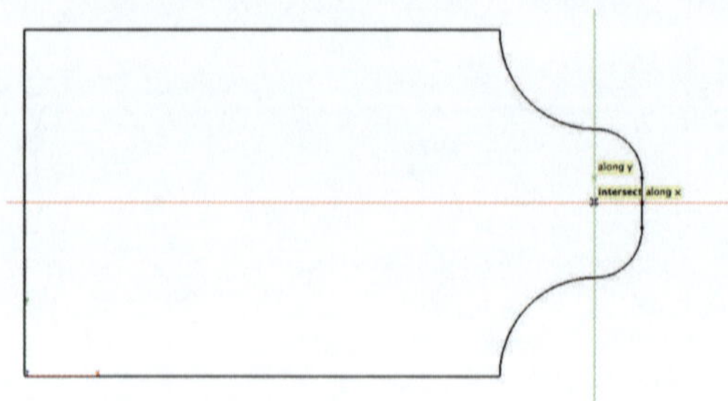

Figure 9.14

- Now drag your cursor outward an arbitrary distance to place the second point of the circle. Click to create a center point circle.

- Finally, enter 0.75 into the diameter text field.

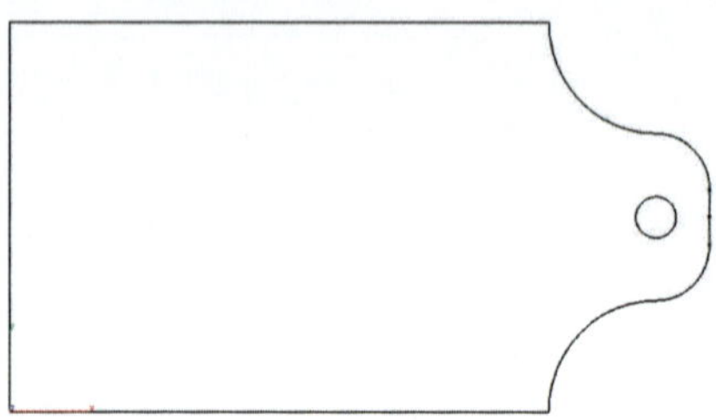

Figure 9.15

5. Extruding Profile into 3D Body

- We will now extrude our profile into a solid.

- Begin by switching the view to Isometric.
- Now, select the *Extrude Solid* tool from the tool palette.
- Select the Vector option from the Extrude Solid tool prompt bar.
- Select the entire profile by pressing and holding the left button while moving from left to right. This will form a selection fence that will select all objects whose extents lie within the selection fence.
- Following the tool prompt, we must now specify two points for extrusion height and length.
- As seen in the Figure 9.16 to the right, we have specified two points along the z axis by clicking the corner of our profile and dragging the cursor upwards along the helper line. At an arbitrary distance along the z helper line, click to place the second point.
- After the two points for extrusion height and length have been placed, the Extrude Solid tool will extrude the profile into 3D.

Figure 9.16 – Extruding Profile into 3D

- Next, adjust the thickness of the breadboard to your desired value by inputting the dimension into the distance text field. In our example, we have adjusted our thickness to be .75 inches.

6. Blending

- Next we will blend all the edges of our breadboard.
- Begin by selecting the *Constant Blend* tool from the tool palette.
- Adjust the Radius to be .2 by entering the value into the Radius text field.

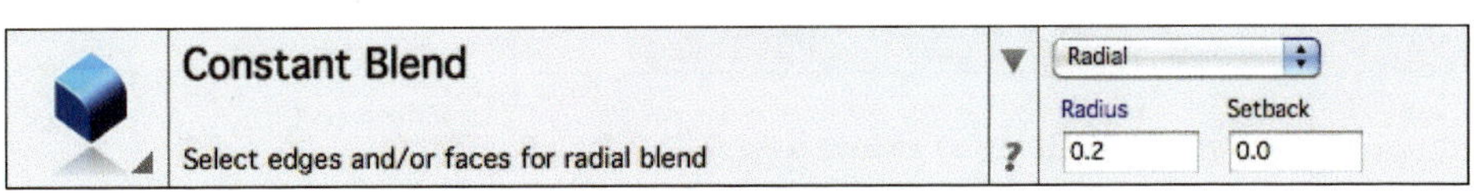

Figure 9.17 – Adjust Blend Radius to 0.2

- We will be blending all of our edges at one time so select the entire body by pressing and holding the left button while moving from left to right. This will form a selection fence that will select all objects whose extents lie within it.
- Click to blend all breadboard edges.

Figure 9.18 - Finished breadboard before rendering

10. Extra Touches

- You can add further realism to your design by photo rendering with a wood material. Figure 9.19 below shows an example rendering of the scene with ViaCAD Pro.

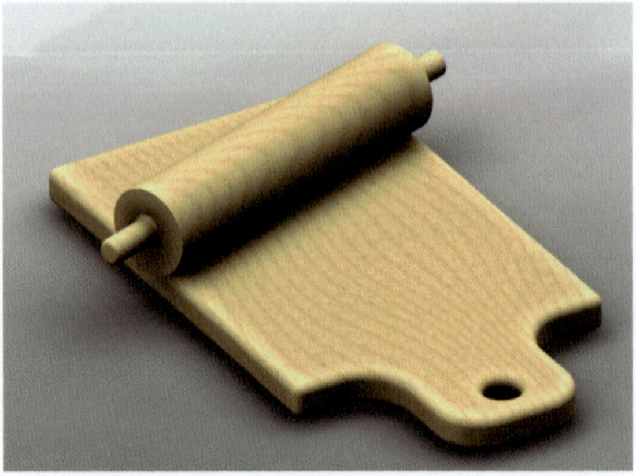

Figure 9.19 – Rendering of breadboard

- Additionally, try using Model to Sheet to generate 2D drawings of (and sections through) the breadboard. Figure 9.20 displays an image generated using Model to Sheet.

Get the Look

Breadboard shown with rolling pin

Material: Pine Wood (modified via the Advanced Material Render Settings: Scale Value .3, Wood Color R 234/G 201/B147, Grain Color R81/G38/B17, Ring Color R226/G187/B136, Ring Width .271)

Background: Graduated White to Gray

HDRI: Studio/lwhdr_studio2_2k.hdr

HDRI Intensity: 2.0

* Shadows on, anti-alias

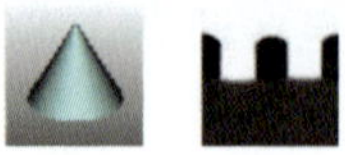

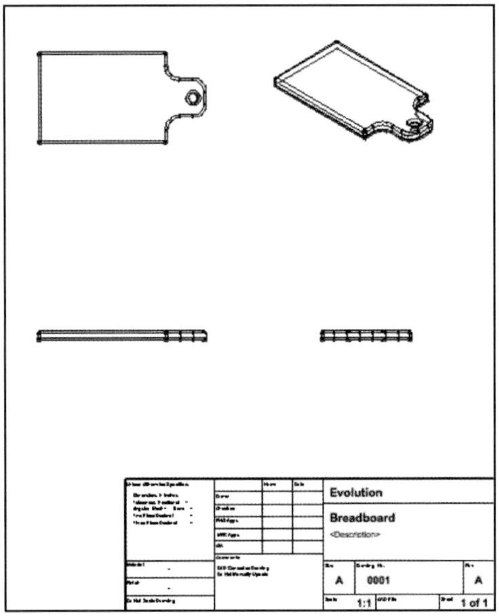

Figure 9.20 – Using Model to Sheet

WINE BOTTLE & GLASS

Level: Beginner

Description: In this tutorial, you will learn to draw profiles, to lathe, and to shell solids. The end result is a model of a wine bottle, glass, and tray.

Key Tools: Single Line, Spline, Revolve, and Shell

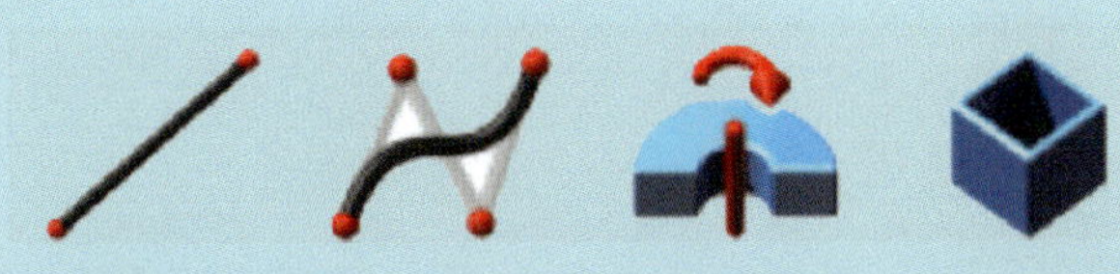

Overview:

Making the wine bottle & glass can be broken down into the following processes:

1. Drawing the 2D curve Profiles from which to create the 3D model

Important Note: Only half of the object need be drawn, as lathing the profile will generate the other half.

2. Using the *Solid Lathe* tool to generate the bottle, glass & tray from their profiles

3. Shelling out the body of the bottle & glass to an appropriate wall thickness

4. Using the *Split Solid* tool to create the wine in the glass and the bottle

5. Blending the edges of the objects to add realistic detail

1. Drawing the Profile

- Begin by changing the view to Front View by going to View and then selecting front. Alternately, you can right-click on the drawing window and use the context sensitive menu.

- Then, right-click on the origin and place a horizontal construction line. This will represent our base line (the surface on which the tray would sit). Figure 10.1 below shows the pop up menu with the option Construction Lines selected.

Figure 10.1 – Construction Lines

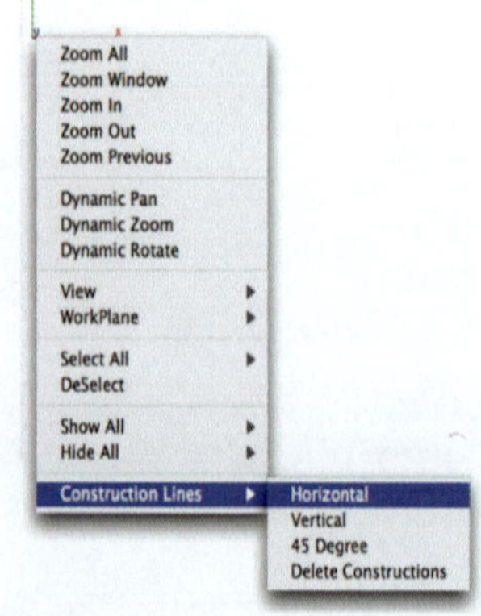

- Choose the *Single Line* tool from the tool palette.

- Use the *Single Line* tool to draw the centerline axis of the bottle and the glass. The tray beneath will share the same central axis as the bottle so that the bottle will sit right in the middle of the tray. To draw the centerline axis:

  - Click once at the origin.

  - Move the cursor vertically up the screen and click an arbitrary distance from the origin.

  - Type the height you wish the bottle to be from the base surface into the text field marked length. As can be seen in Figure 10.2 below, we have used a height of 12 inches. The line will adjust to the height you type.

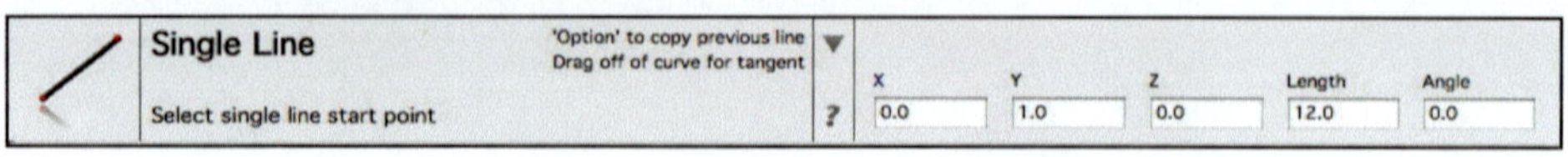

Figure 10.2 – Creating Centerline Axis for Bottle and Glass

  - Following the same process as above, draw the centerline axis of the glass. Move to the right of the bottle axis and draw another vertical line to represent the centerline axis of the wine glass. Ensure you leave a fair amount of space between the two lines, as you will be lathing the profiles later. The height of the glass should be about half the height of the wine bottle (we have used a value of 5.5 inches).

Figure 10.3 – Bottle and glass centerline axes

- Use a combination of the *Line and Spline* tools to generate the full profile of the glass as seen in Figure 10.4.

- Ensure you snap all endpoints together. If there are gaps, the lathe will fail.

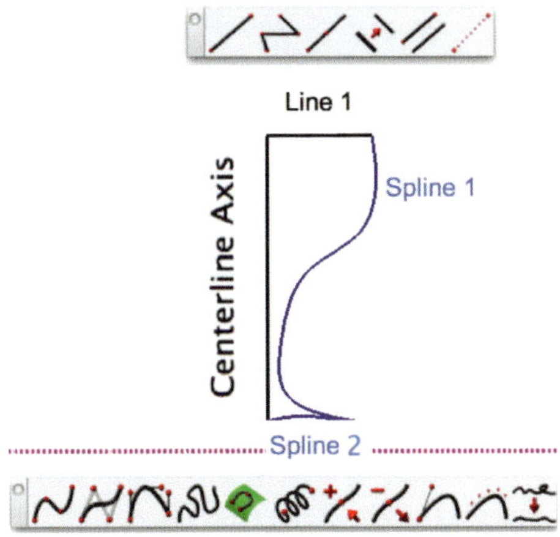

Figure 10.4 - Glass profile

You can easily to adjust the curvature of the glass profile by using the Gripper to modify the points on your spline.

- If the Gripper is not already enabled, simply display the Inspector dialog box and go to the Gripper tab. Check the box marked Enable Gripper.

- Next, to display the points of the spline, go to Edit on the menu bar and select the Show Points command.

- Use the same tools to then generate the profiles of the bottle and the tray to create a design similar to that seen in Figure 10.5 below. You may find it helpful to have a wine bottle and a glass at hand to study their shapes.

Figure 10.5 – Complete profiles for bottle, glass, and tray

- Ensure that there are no gaps in your profiles and that they are planar. These are the two factors that can cause a profile to fail when used with a tool such as solid lathe.

3. Lathing Profiles into Solids

- Choose the *Lathe Solid* tool from the tool palette.

Figure 10.6 – Lathe Toolbar

- Follow the prompts beneath the tool name.
- First, a profile must be selected. Begin with the glass.
- Instead of clicking one line at a time when selecting a profile, a profile can automatically be traced by right clicking on one of the curves that make up the profile of the glass or the bottle. A context sensitive menu will appear. From these menu options, choose **Select Chain.** Provided your profile is good (there are no gaps, duplicate lines, or branched lines), the entire profile will be selected.
- After selecting the profile, you need to select the line or axis around which to lathe it. This is its centerline. The lathed objects should appear immediately.
- After lathing the glass, lathe the bottle and then the tray following the same procedure.

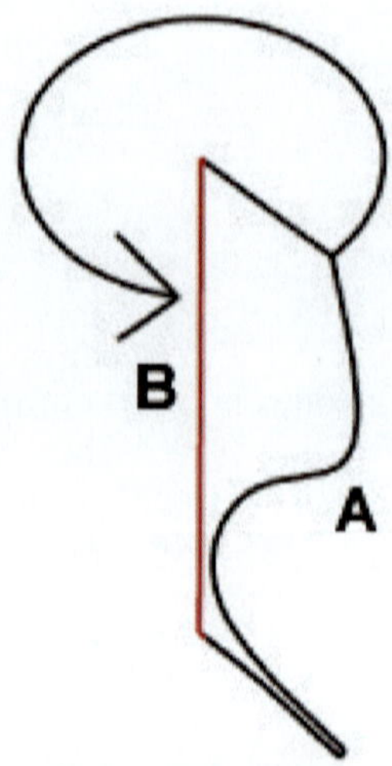

Figure 10.7 - Profile A shown is 'lathed' around axis B

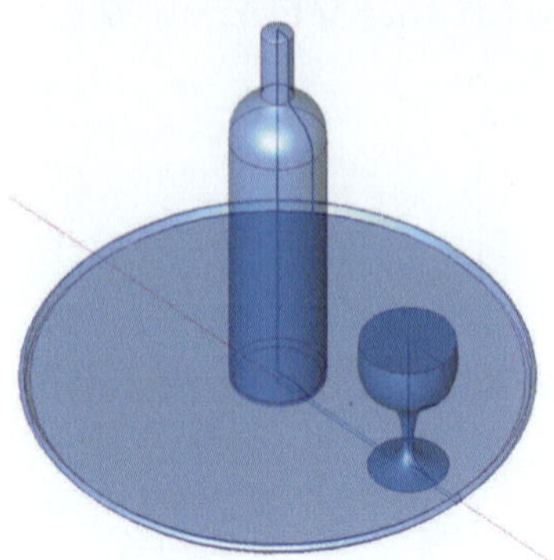

Figure 10.8 –The raw lathed solids before shelling

4. Shelling

- The new solid parts must now be shelled to an appropriate wall thickness.

- Because the constricted neck shape of a wine glass is difficult for the *Shell* tool to deal with, better results will be achieved if you split the glass at the neck using the *Infinite Plane* and *Split Solid* tools.
- Be sure to use a **Z-station** infinite plane at the neck of the glass when splitting.
- You can press Shift to select multiple open faces. Additionally, if you wish to have a hollow object but no open faces, you can click on the background. If you only want to keep the hollowed out section, press the Option key.

Figure 10.9 - Splitting the glass at the neck allows for a better result from the Shell tool

- After splitting the glass, choose the *Shell* tool from the tool palette.

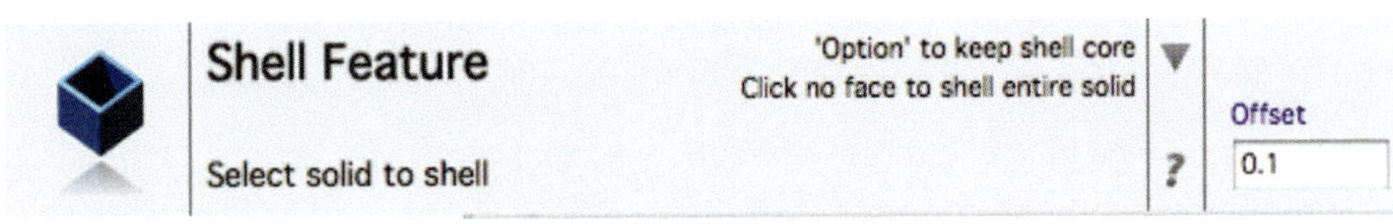

Figure 10.10 – Shell Toolbar

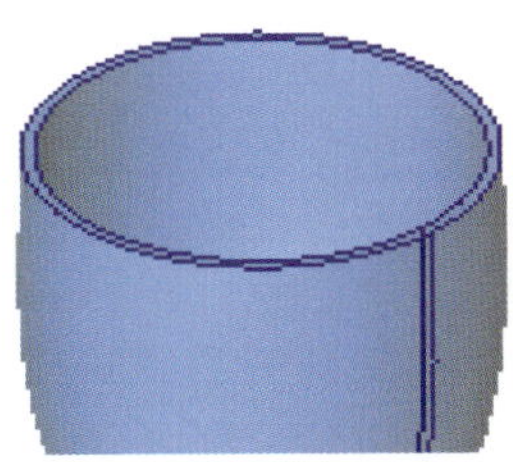

Figure 10.11 - Glass shelled to an appropriate wall thickness

5. Adding Realistic Details

- After shelling the objects, more details can be added for extra realism. For example, the hard edges of the objects can be softened, wine can be added to the glass, and decals can be added to the wine bottle.

- **Blending Edges**:
  - Choose the *Constant Blend* tool from the toolbar.
  - Enter an appropriate radius value into the input area of the top bar, as shown in Figure 10.12 below.

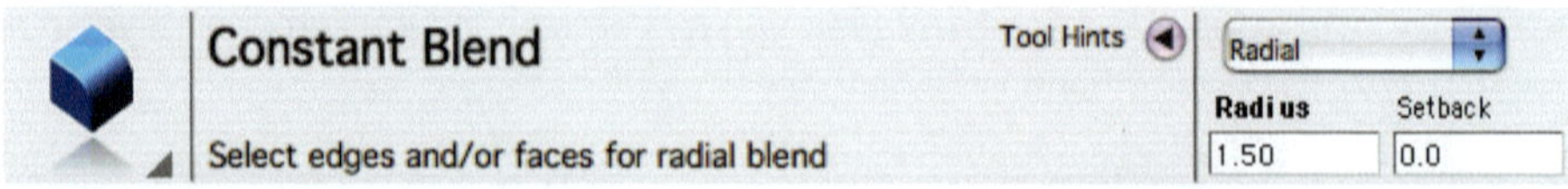

Figure 10.12 – Constant Blend

  - Following the prompts beneath the tool name, click on the hard edges of the glass top to apply constant blends.
  - A blend radius value typically needs to be less than the material thickness. On an object like a glass where the blends will be applied to both the inside and outside edges of the material, it is prudent to begin with a blend radius value of just less than half the material thickness.
  - Proceed following the same steps to blend the other hard edges of the glass, the edges of the bottle, and the edges of the tray.

Figure 10.13 - Application of a Constant Blend to the Top Edge of the Wine Glass

- **Adding Wine:**
  - You can add wine by splitting an overlapping block with the glass using the *Split Solid* tool. This will result in the block being split into three; however, only one of these is needed to represent the wine. Thus, the other two can be deleted.

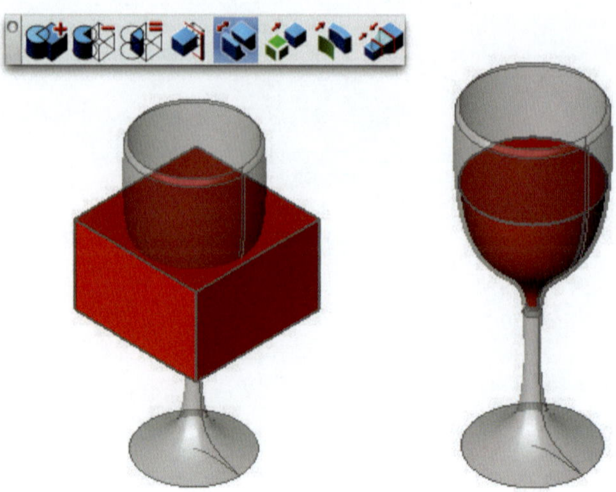

Figure 10.14 - Solid block split with wine glass to achieve a shape representing the wine

- **Adding Decals:**
    - Decals are a means to add a 2D image to a 3D rendered object. ViaCAD and Shark include a library of images that can be dragged and dropped onto your models, providing another level of photo realism to your finished image.

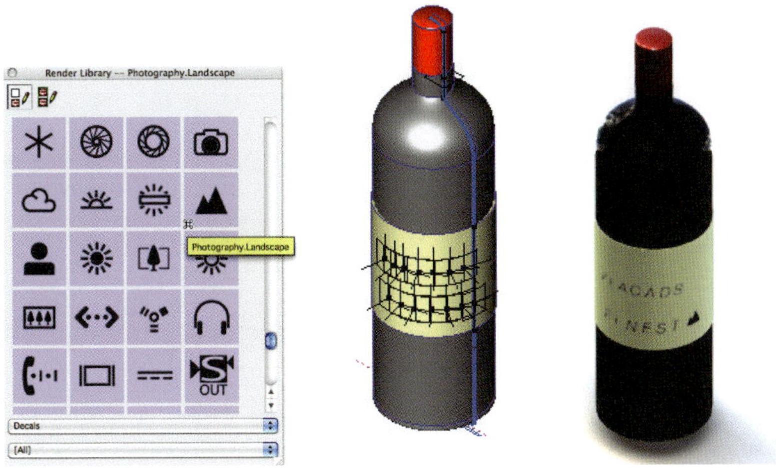

Figure 10.15 – Wine Bottle with decaled label

6. *Extra Touches*

- You can add further realism to your design by photo rendering with materials. Figure 10.16 below shows an example rendering of the scene with ViaCAD Pro.

Get the Look

Material: Metal Polish Silver, Glass Clear, Glass Reflect Black, Paint Metallic Red

Background: Environment. Restaurant Exterior

*Shadows on, anti-alias

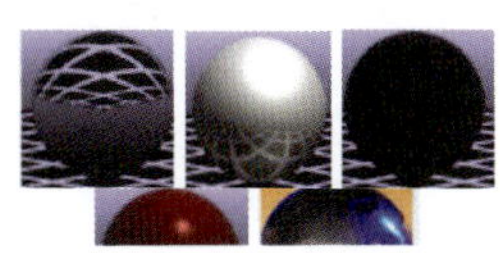

Figure 10.16 – Rendered Scene

- Additionally, try using Model to Sheet to generate 2D drawings of (and sections through) the scene. Figure 10.17 displays an image generated using Model to Sheet.

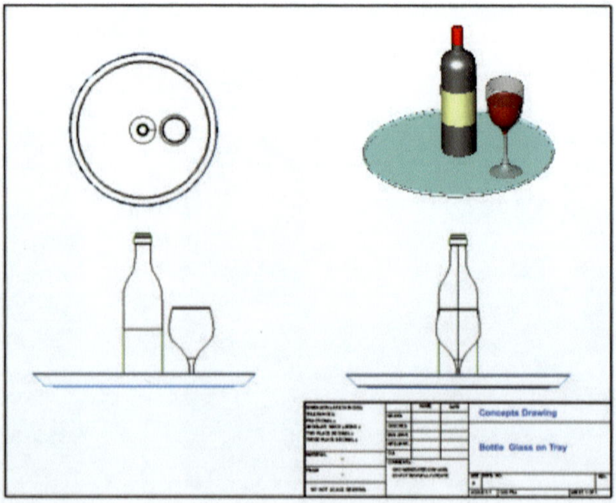

Figure 10.17 – Model to Sheet

HAIR DRYER

Level: Intermediate

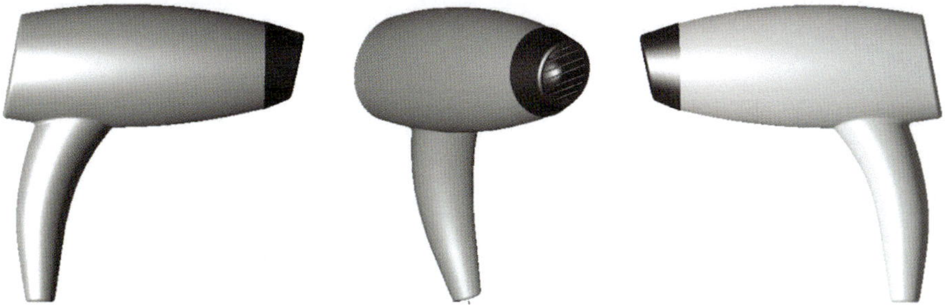

Description: In this tutorial, you will learn to skin a solid from profiles, to blend hard edges, and to shell solids.

Key Tools: Ellipse, Rotate, Scale, Plane, Skin Solid, Shell, and Blend

Overview:

Making the **Hair Dryer** can be broken down into the following processes:

1. Drawing the 2D section profiles using ellipses
2. Using the *Skin Solid* tool to generate both the body and the handle of the hair dryer
3. Joining the handle and body of the hair dryer using the *Add Solid* tool
4. Blending the intersection between the handle and the body of the hair dryer
5. Splitting the solids. As the object is symmetrical, we'll work on one half and mirror it later
6. Shelling the resulting solid to the appropriate wall thickness
7. Mirroring one half of the hair dryer to recreate both halves
8. Making the nozzle
9. Adding an air grill

1. Drawing Profiles

- Change the view to Right View by going to View and then selecting Right. Alternately, you can right-click on the drawing window and use the context sensitive menu.

- Use the *Single Line* tool and *Spline* tool to construct a guide for your hair dryer handle and nozzle.

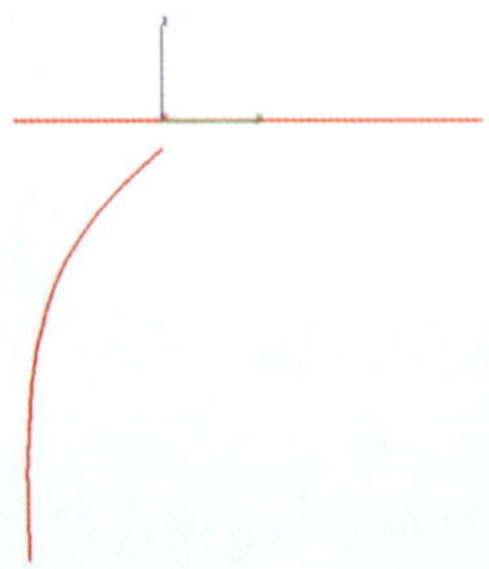

Figure 11.1 – in the right view, guide curves help in setting up the ellipse centers

- Choose the *Center Point Ellipse* tool.

- Now begin placing ellipses periodically along the body and down the handle of the hair dryer. The ellipse center points should be placed on the guide curves. Refer to Figure 11.2 below, which illustrates an example hair dryer profile viewed first in Right Side and then in Dynamic View. Using Dynamic View to rotate your view of the profile should help assist you in visualizing and constructing the profile.

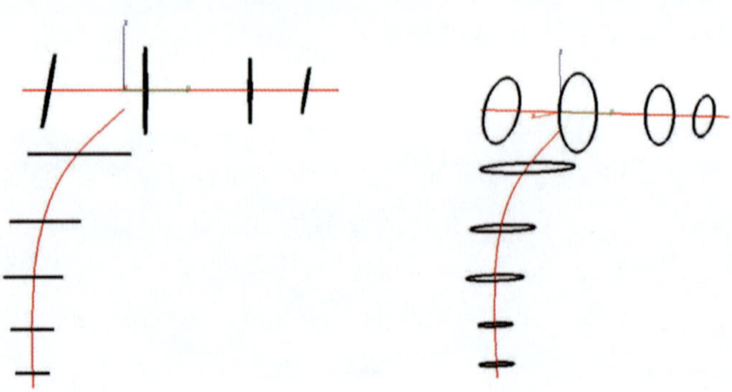

Figure 11.2

- Less profile sections will lead to a smoother form. Always use the minimum number of sections that can accurately describe the required shape.

- As seen in Figure 11.2 above, the first and last ellipses representing the front and end of the hair dyer have been placed at an angle. As there are many different styles of hair dryers, feel free to use this as an example, but don't be afraid to experiment with your own design. Take a look at some example hair dyers to get some ideas.

- The experience of creating a first skinned solid will lead you to understand how to better place and size the ellipses. Therefore, don't waste a lot of time trying to get the perfect placement and size. Once the profile is skinned into a solid, it will be easier to visualize, and you can adjust accordingly from there. As the software is fully associative, by adjusting the major and minor axes of each ellipse after the profile has been skinned, you will automatically change the solid as well.

2. Skinning

- Now we will use the *Skin Solid* tool to generate a solid from the main sections that make up the Hair Dryer body.

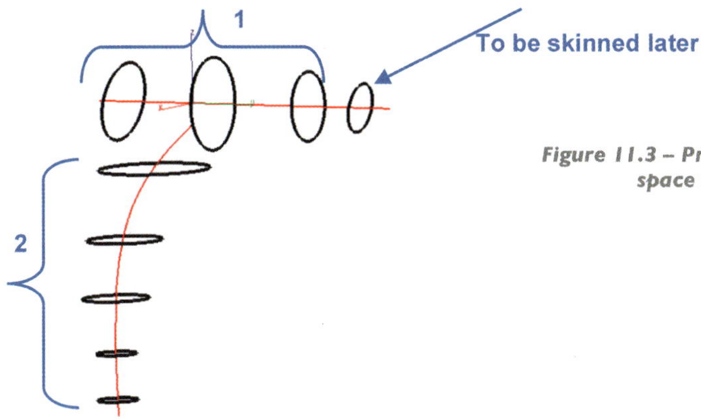

Figure 11.3 – Profile Sections created in 3D space to be solid skinned

- Begin by choosing the *Skin Solid* tool.
- Press the Shift key to prepare the *Skin Solid* tool to expect multiple profiles.
- Select three of the ellipses that compose the body. The fourth ellipse we will skin later as part of the nozzle of our hair dryer.
- The body solid will now be generated, as seen in Figure 11.4 below.

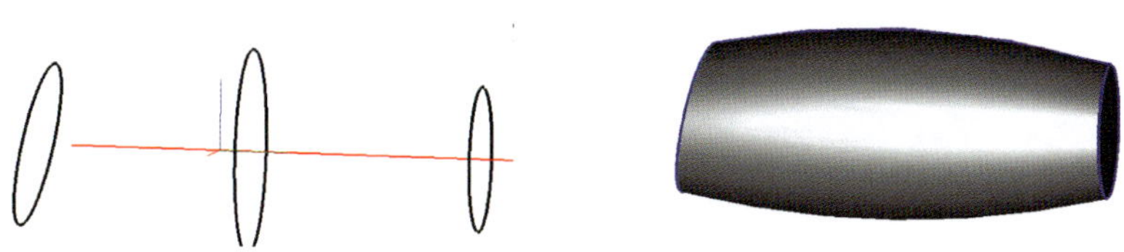

Figure 11.4 - Sections are selected for skinned solid

- Repeat these steps to skin the Hair Dryer handle, remembering to hold the Shift key while selecting.
- The handle solid will now be generated from the 5 main sections of the Hair Dryer handle profile.

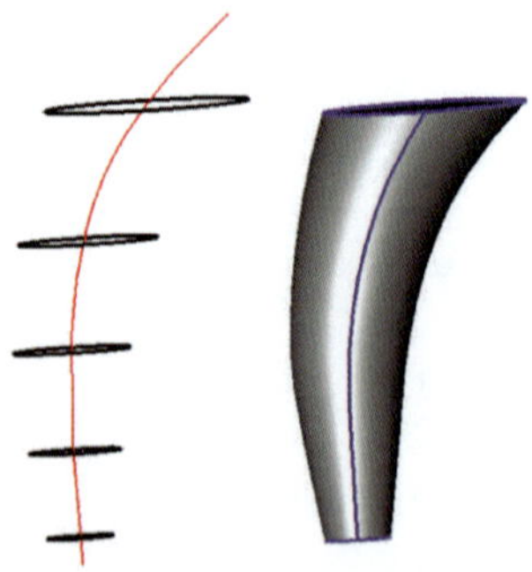

Figure 11.5 - Sections are selected for skinned solid

- Upon skinning your solid, you should now be able to better visualize the shape of the hair dryer. This is a good time to adjust the design. As seen in the figure below, the body of the hair dyer looks slightly out of proportion compared to the handle. We want the top base of our handle to be smaller than the hair dyer body so they can be seamlessly joined together. Therefore, we can enlarge the values of ellipses comprising the body to create a more realistic design.

- To adjust the values, select the ellipses and bring up the Inspector dialog box. Use the text fields to type in new values and hit apply to save changes.

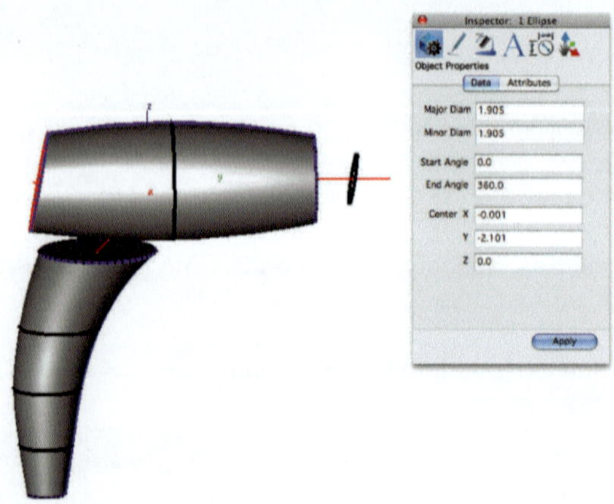

Figure 11.6

3. Uniting handle and body

- Now we will unite the handle to the body of the hair dryer.

- Begin by selecting the *Add Solid* tool.

Figure 11.7 – The Add Solid tool

- Simply click the body and then the handle of the hair dryer to join the two together to generate an image similar to the right dyer in Figure 11.8 below.

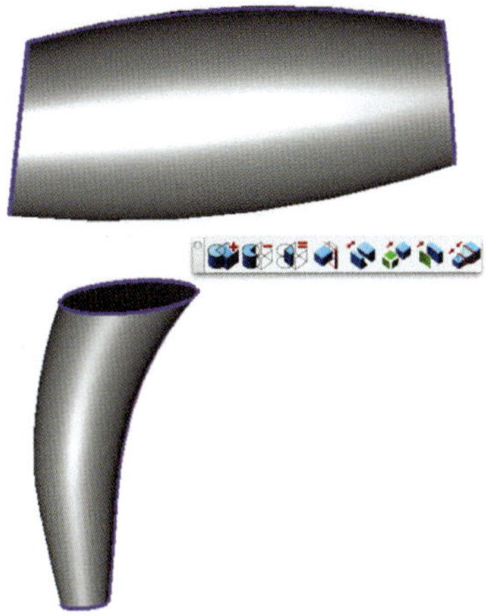

Figure 11.8 - Solid Union tool is used to join the handle to the body

4. Blending

- Choose the *Constant Blend* tool from the toolbar.
- Enter an appropriate value into the top bar input area.
- In this case, we have begun with a radius of .1 inches.

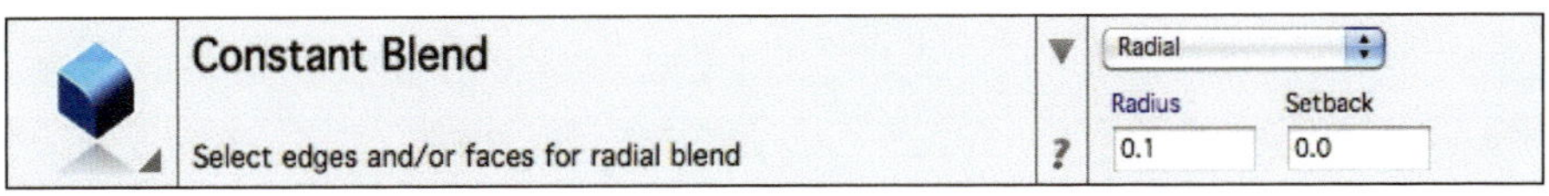

Figure 11.9 – Enter value into Constant Blend text field

- Click on the intersection between the body and the handle.
- Provided the input value is not too big, the fillet blend will run around the intersection.

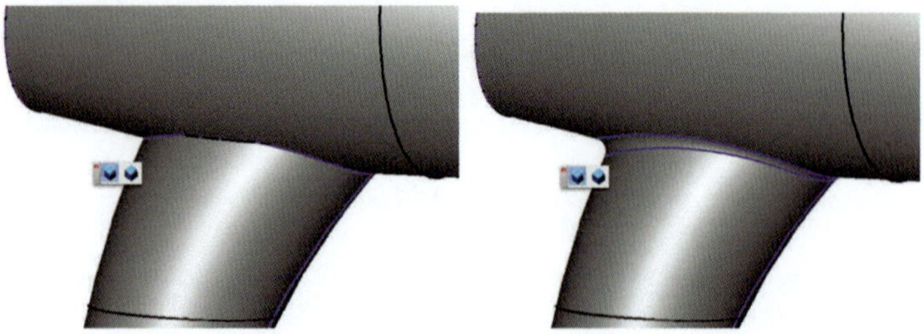

Figure 11.10 - Constant Blend tool applied to body/handle intersection before/after

- Next, blend the bottom of the handle and the back of the hair dyer as shown in Figure 11.11 below.

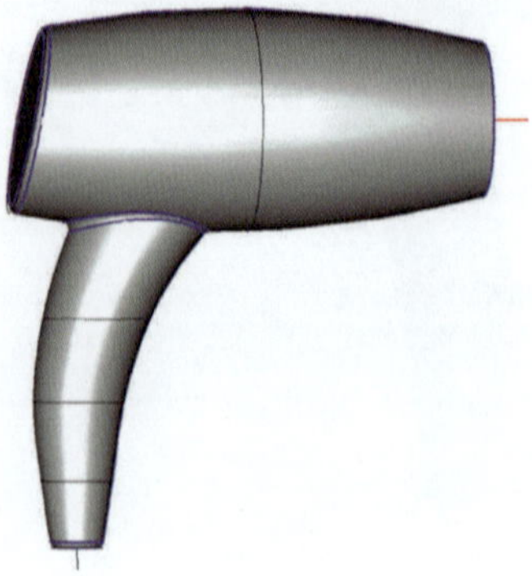

Figure 11.11

5. Splitting into Halves

- Because the Hair Dryer is symmetrical, we will continue by splitting the object, detailing one half only, and eventually mirroring back the missing half. Detailing only half will save time.

- Begin by choosing the *Infinite Plane* tool from the toolbar. The *Infinite Plane* tool will be used to cut the object down the centerline.

Figure 11.12 –Select Y- Station from the Infinite Plane top bar

- As our centerline is the X-axis, select **X-Station** from the tool input area (top bar). This setting infers that the plane will be created where the X value is constant. If you deviated from the example here and used a different construction axis, simply ensure you pick a plane that will split the hair dyer in half along the centerline.

- To help visualize the placement of the plane, we have changed the hair dyer to be transparent. As you can see from the image below, the infinite plane has been placed on the object centerline.

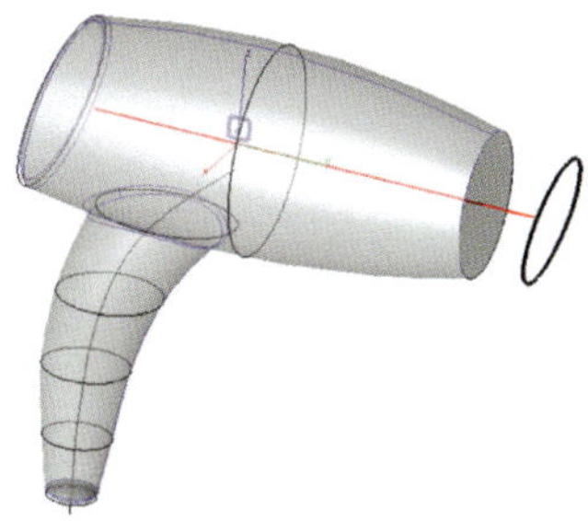

Figure 11.13

- Now choose the *Split Solid* tool from the toolbar.

Figure 11.14 – Split Solid tool

- Following the prompts, click the solid you wish to split.
- Select the surface to split the solid.
- The hair dryer is now split and selectable in two parts. Check that the split has occurred correctly and delete one half of the model.

Figure 11.15 – The Split Solid tool is used to split a solid with an infinite plane

6. Shelling

- Choose the *Shell Feature* tool.

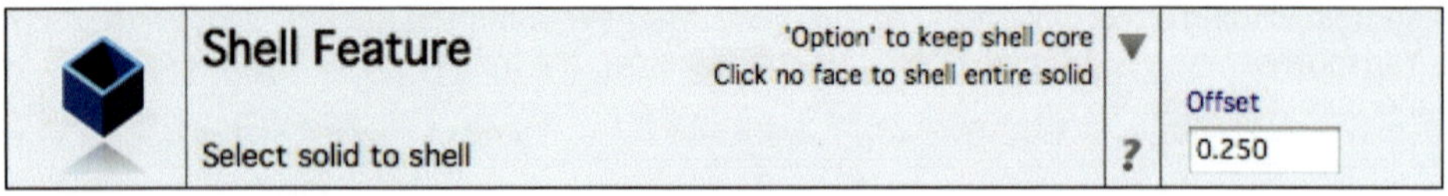

Figure 11.16- Set Offset Value on the Shell Feature Top bar

- Set the offset value to an appropriate wall thickness. We have used a thickness of .250 inches.
- Following the prompts beneath the tool name, select the object you wish to shell.
- You must now select the faces that you wish to leave **open**.
- Press the Shift key to tell the *Shell* tool to expect more than one entry.
- Click on the faces of the solid that **do not** represent outside surfaces of the Hair Dryer.
- On releasing the Shift key, the shelled solid is created.

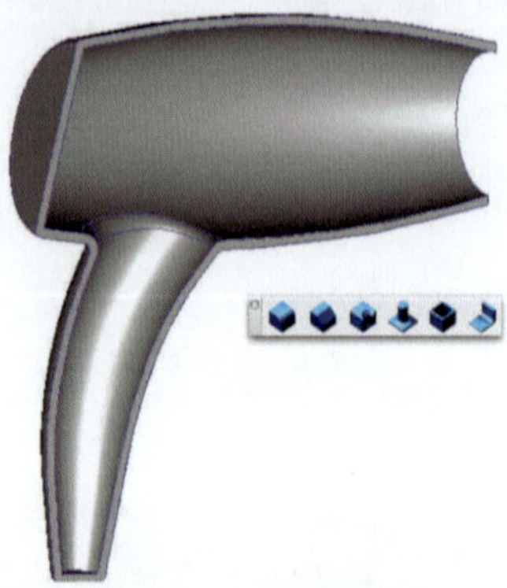

Figure 11.17 - The body of the hair dryer after the shelling operation

7. Mirroring

- Choose the *Mirror* tool from the tool palette to form the two molding halves.
- Select the shelled body half to mirror.
- Select ZX Plane from the *Mirror* tool pull-down.

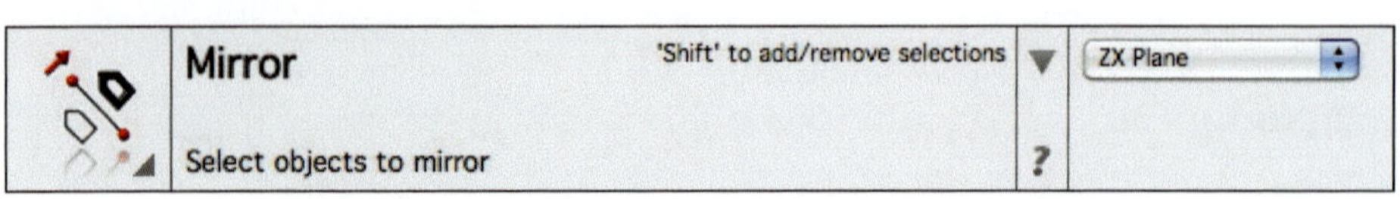

Figure 11.18 –Select ZX Plane from the Mirror top bar

- On a Mac: Press and hold the Option key.
- On Windows: Press and hold the Control key.
- Click on the axis of your hair dyer centerline (X-axis in our example) to choose a position for the mirror plane to be applied.
- The shelled body half will automatically be mirrored.

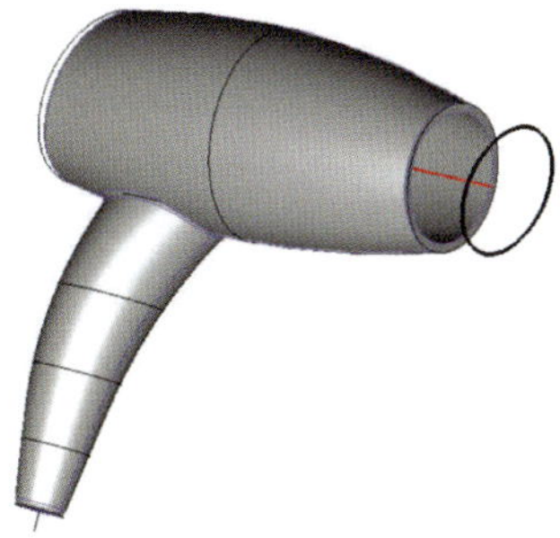

Figure 11.19 – The body of the hair dryer after the mirror operation

8. Making the Nozzle

- Use the same skin solid method described above in Section 2 to generate the optional flow nozzle for the hair dryer.

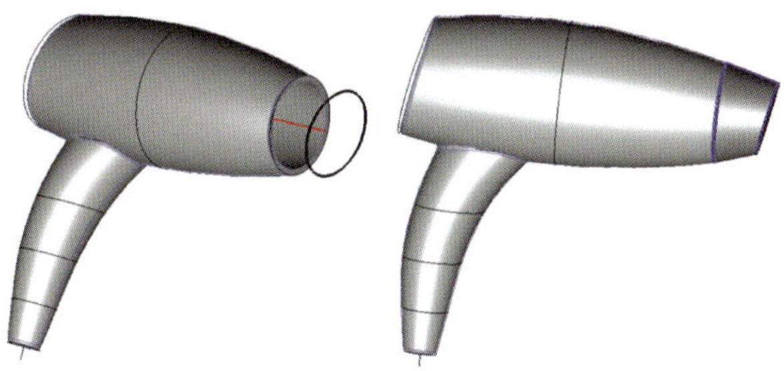

Figure 11.20 - Nozzle is skinned between 2 profiles before and after

- Now, shell the nozzle using the same process as with the body. Refer to Section 6 above if you have any questions.
- This time there will be two open faces so the air can flow through. Remember to hold the Shift key while selecting.
- We will now blend the edges of the nozzle.
- As before, use the *Constant Blend* tool and select an appropriately small radius setting. Refer back to Section 4 if you have any questions.

Figure 11.21 – The nozzle is shelled leaving 2 open faces

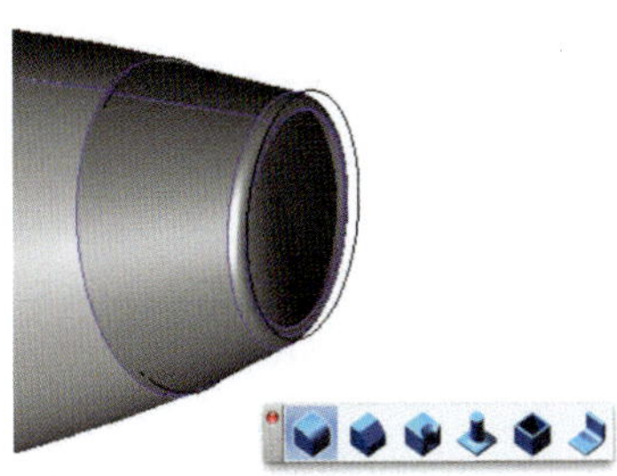

Figure 11.22 - Blended edges

- To complete the nozzle, you may want to change its color so it will noticeably appear as a different part.

9. Creating the Air Grill

- You may wish to add other details. For example, internal elements, an on/off switch, an air grill, and a cable will add additional realism to the hair dyer. Below, we describe how to construct an air grill.

- Before we begin constructing the air grill, it's beneficial to use the Show-Hide command found under Window on your menu bar to hide the rest of the hair dyer so we can better see the air grill as we design it.

- Selecting the Show-Hide command will bring up the Show-Hide tool palette. Select the ellipse we used to make the nozzle and click on Show-Hide from this palette.

Figure 11.23 – Show-Hide tool palette

- Now you can begin designing the air grill. Different hair dyers utilize varying air grills. You can examine one to get ideas. Below, we have used a traditional air grill with horizontal components.

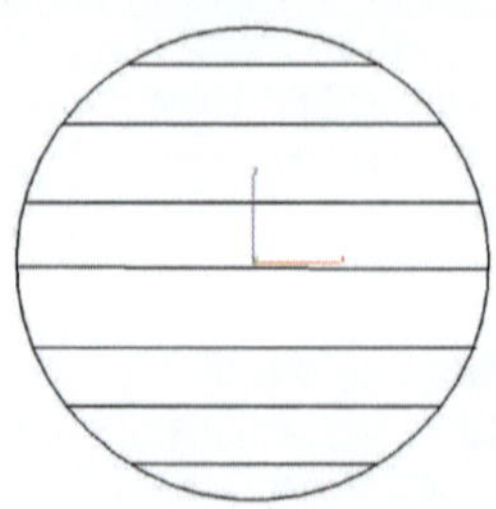

Figure 11.24

- Now select the *Pipe* tool from the main tool palette.

- We have set our outside Diameter to be .050 inches.

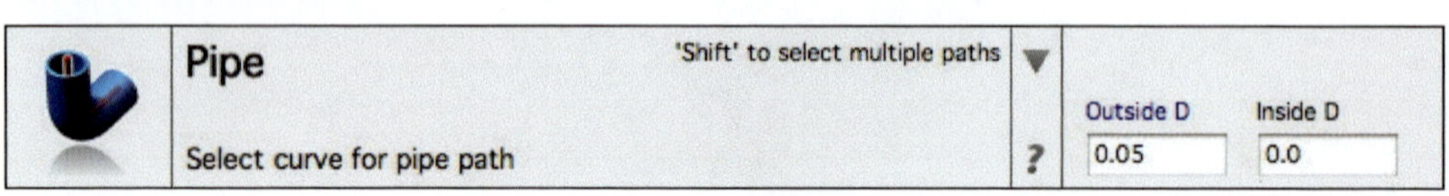

Figure 11.25

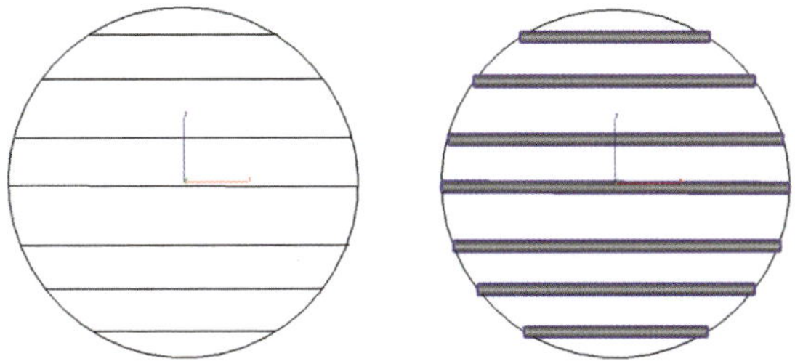

Figure 11.26 – Before and after pipe

- Next, use the *Add Solid* tool to join the air grill to the ellipse.
- Finally, use the Show All command from the Show-Hide tool palette to view the entire hair dyer.

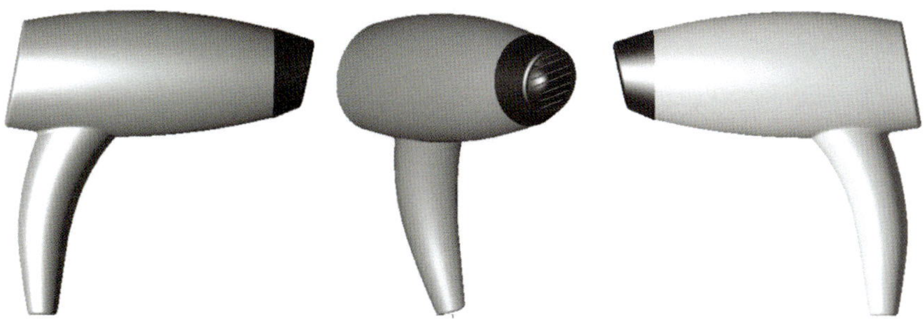

Figure 11.27 – Finished hair dryer before rendering

10. Extra Touches

- You can add further realism to your design by photo rendering with materials. Figure 11.28 below shows an example rendering of the scene with ViaCAD Pro.

Figure 11.28 - Rendering of the hair dryer

Get the Look

Material: Magenta Plastic Polish, White Plastic Polish

Decal: Keyboard letters and numbers

*Shadows on, anti-alias

- Additionally, try using Model to Sheet to generate 2D drawings of (and sections through) the hair dryer. Figure 11.29 displays an image generated using Model to Sheet.

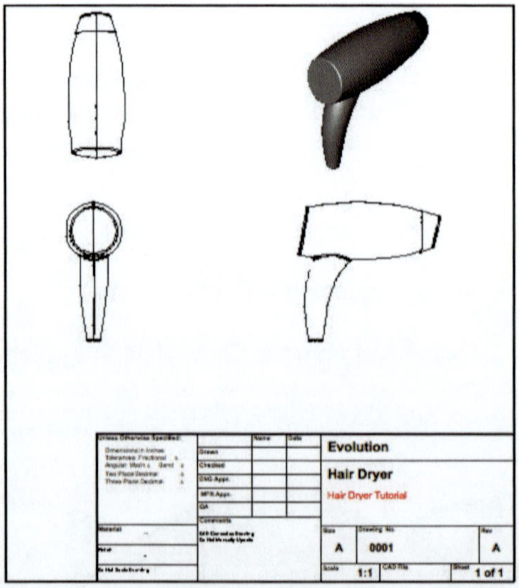

Figure 11.29 – Model to Sheet

Y PIPE

Level: Intermediate

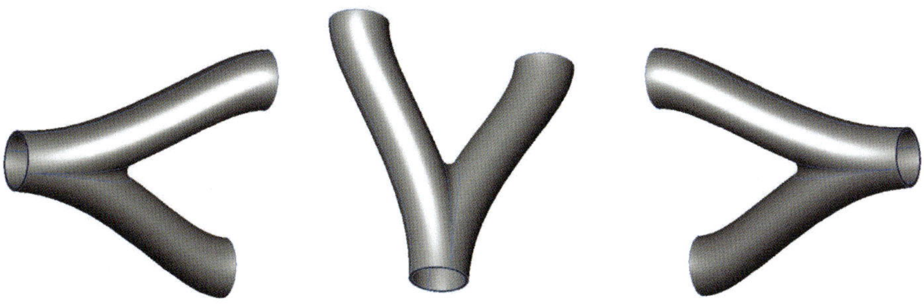

Description: In this tutorial, you will learn how to use the Skin Solid tool to generate a 3D body from a profile, how to use the mirror tool, and how to use the Shell tool to hollow out a body.

Key tools: Skin Solid, Mirror, Add Solid, Constant Blend, and Shell tools

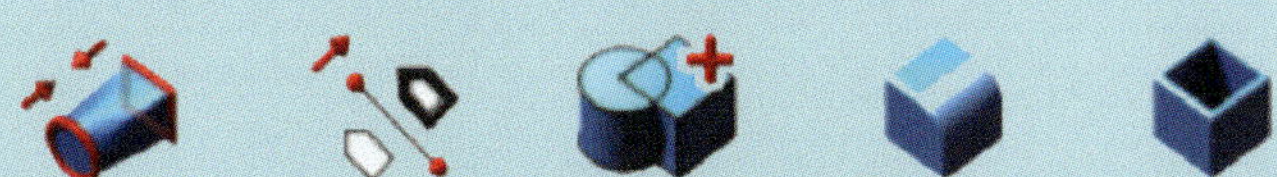

Overview: Creating a Y-Pipe part can be broken down into these steps:

1. Drawing the profile of the branch
2. Skinning this profile into a solid
3. Mirroring the solid
4. Uniting the branches by using the *Add Solid* tool and blending to smooth the intersection
5. Shelling

1. Drawing the Profile

- Change the view to Right Side View by going to View and selecting right side. Alternately, you can right-click on the drawing window and use the context sensitive menu to select Right Side View.

- Choose the Center Point Circle tool from the tool palette.

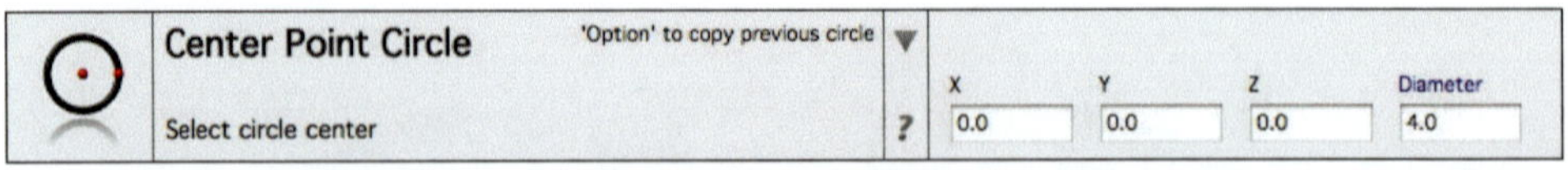

Figure 12.1

- Click on the origin.

- Drag out and release your mouse at an arbitrary distance.

- Type the diameter you wish the circle to be in the text field marked diameter. As seen in Figure 18.1 above, we have used a diameter of 4.

- Switch to the arrow tool and click on the circle to bring up the Gripper.

- Hold the Option key with the Gripper and drag to the right to copy the circle.

- You should now have created the profile of two identical circles as seen in Figure 12.2.

- Switch to Isometric view.

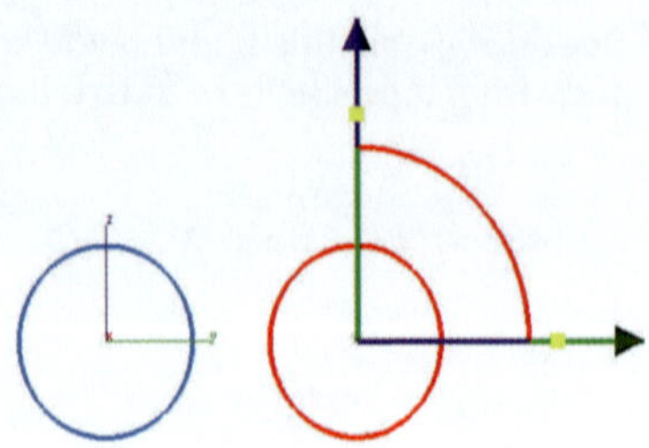

Figure 12.2 – Create 2 identical circles with diameters of 4

- Now, select your original circle.

- Use the Gripper's handles to drag the circle down. We have set the distance between our circles to be 17 units.

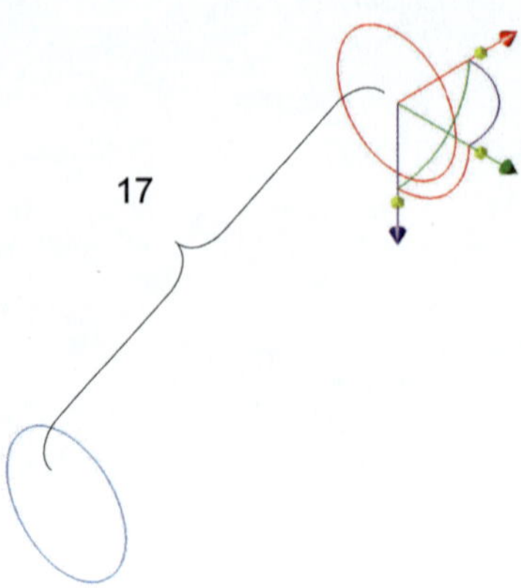

Figure 12.3

2. Skinned Solid

- Use the *Skin Solid* tool to generate a solid from the two circle profiles.
- Select the *Skin Solid* tool from the tool palette.
- Select the sections in turn.
- The body solid will now be generated, as seen in Figure 12.4 to the right.
- We will now adjust the tangencies of our solid.

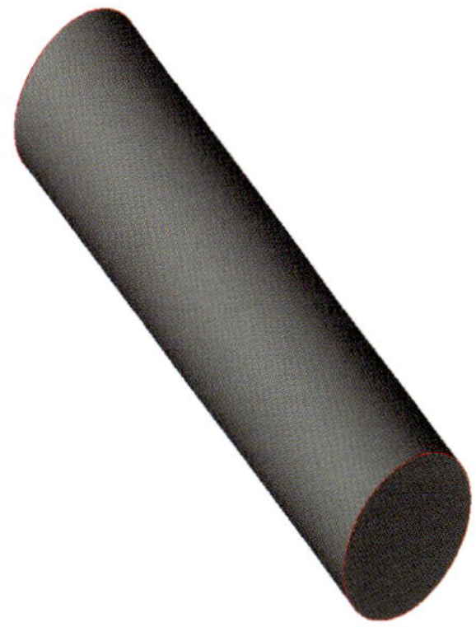

Figure 12.4 – Skinned Solid

- To do this, begin by selecting the solid.
- Go to the Inspector dialog box.
- Once in the Inspector, go to the Data tab under Object Properties.
- From here, check the Use Draft box.
- Now input your desired values into the data entry fields. We have set them to be:
    - Start Angle to 90°
    - Start Mag to 22
    - End Angle to 90°
    - End Mag 11

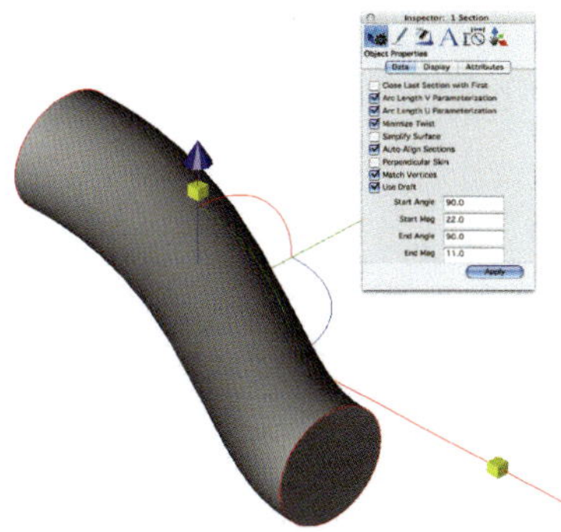

Figure 12.5 – Adjusting tangencies of solid using Inspector

3. Mirroring

- Select the body.
- Now choose the *Mirror* tool from the tool palette.

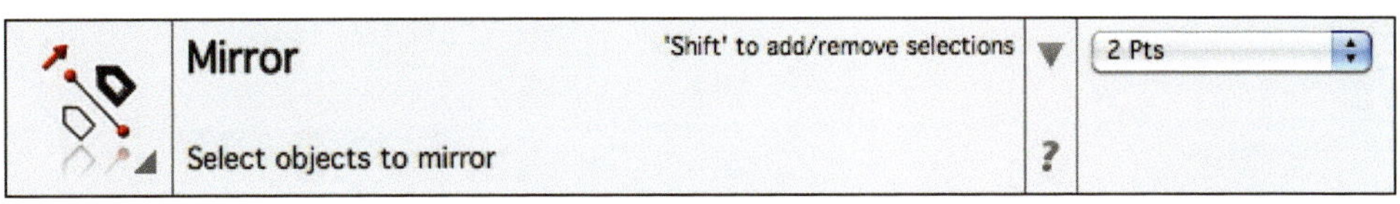

Figure 12.6

- Go to the bottom face and select the center so that the center tag appears.

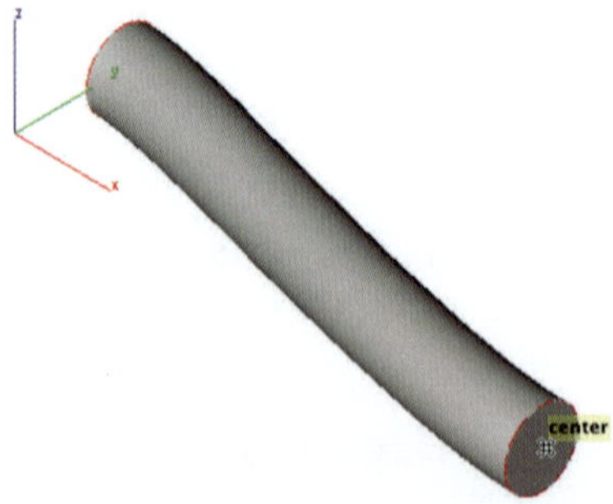

Figure 12.7

- On a Mac: Press and hold the Option key.
- On Windows: Press and hold the Control key.
- Drag out along the x-axis as shown in Figure 12.8 below. Click at an arbitrary distance.

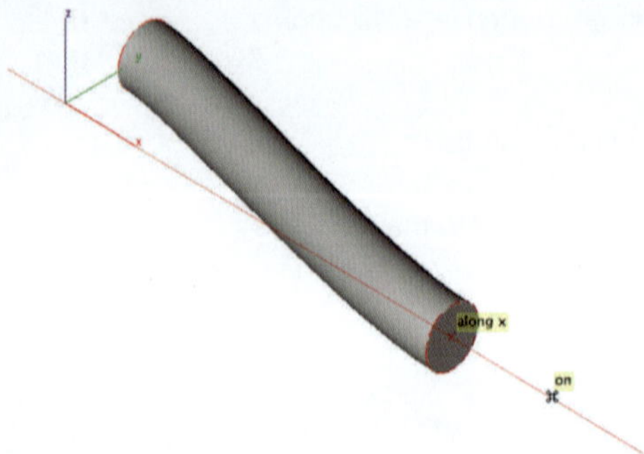

Figure 12.8

- Depress the Option key.
- Your body should now be mirrored forming a Y-shape similar to the one seen in Figure 12.9.

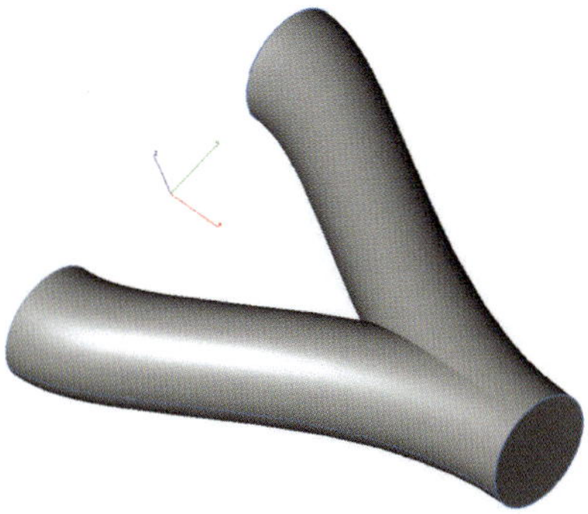

Figure 12.9 – Using Mirror tool

4. Adding Solid and Blending

- Select the *Add Solid* tool from the tool palette.
- Now select each part to join the two bodies.
- The *Add Solid* tool will join the bodies.
- Now, we will blend the intersection.
- Select the *Constant Blend* tool from the tool palette.
- Be sure to choose an appropriate sized blend. If the blend is too big, it will fail. We have used a blend with a radius of 0.5.
- Following the tool prompts, select the intersection to be blended.

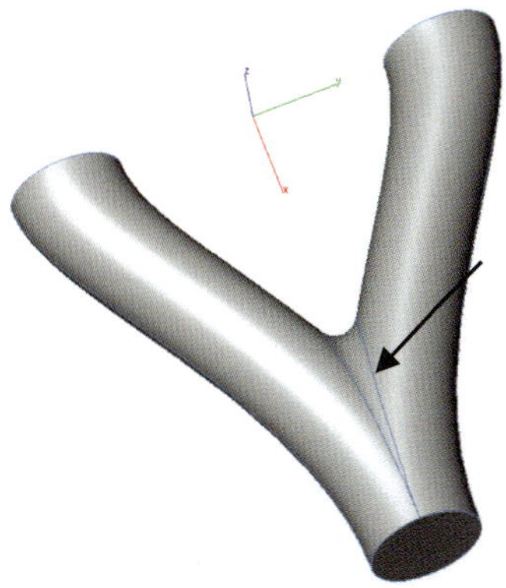

Figure 12.11 – Blending Intersection with Constant Blend tool

- Provided the input value is not too big, the fillet blend will run around the intersection.

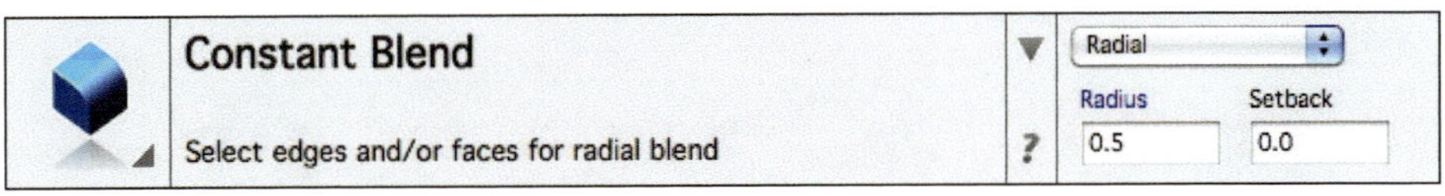

Figure 12.10 – Input appropriate Radius Value

5. Shelling

- Select the *Shell Feature* tool in order to hollow out the inside of the pipe.
- Enter an appropriate offset thickness for the wall of the Y Pipe into the Shell Feature top bar. We have used 0.2 for our offset thickness.

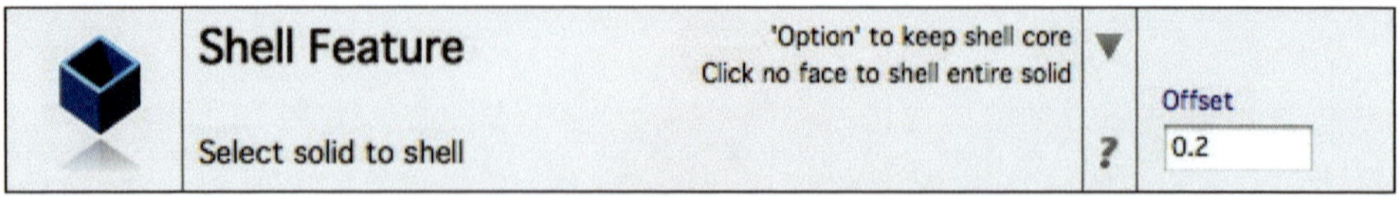

Figure 12.12 – Input the offset thickness into top bar

- Following the prompts, click the solid you wish to shell.
- Now press and hold the Shift key.
- Next, click the three faces we want to keep open while still holding the Shift key.

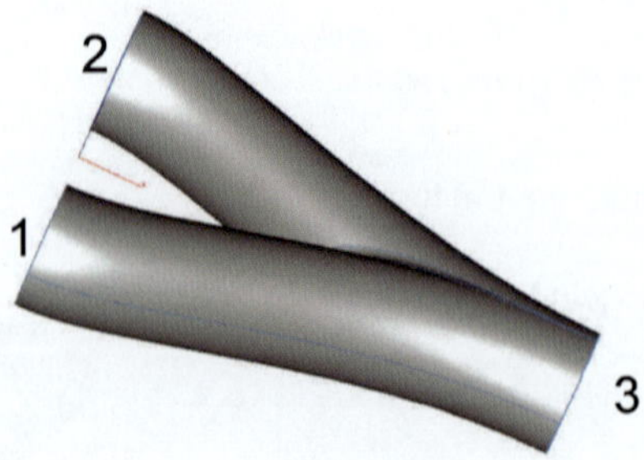

Figure 12.13 – 3 Open Faces

- If the program is unsure which face you are selecting, it will present you with an ambiguity pop-up. This appears when you select an object and there is not one clear face or object that the program can pick. You must select the appropriate entry yourself.
- If you wish to have a hollow object but no open faces, you can click on the background. If you only want to keep the hollowed out section, press the Option key.
- On releasing the Shift key, the shelled solid is created.

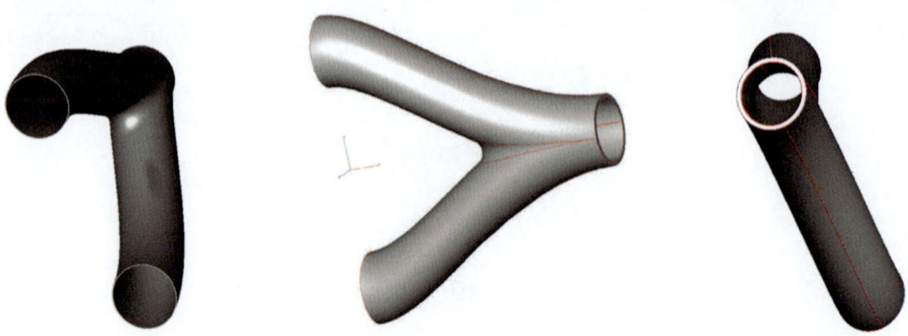

Figure 12.14 – Finished Y Pipe before rendering

6. Extra Touches

- You can add further realism to your design by photo rendering with materials. Figure 12.15 below shows an example rendering of the scene with ViaCAD Pro.

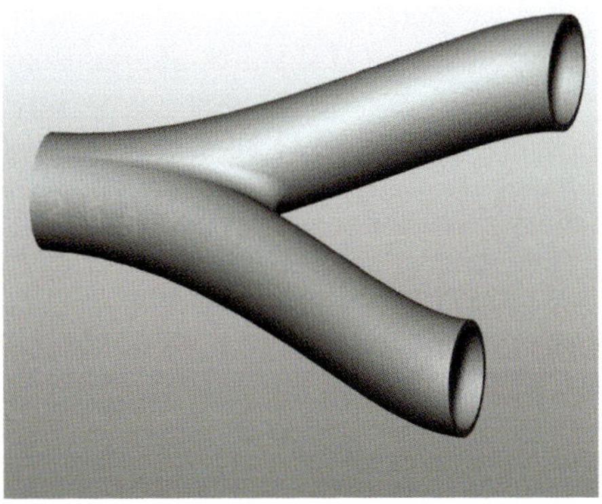

Figure 12.15 – Rendering of Pipe

Get the Look

Material: Aluminum Metal Cast

Background: Graduated White to Gray

Decals: Keyboard numbers

*Shadows on, anti-alias

- Additionally, try using Model to Sheet to generate 2D drawings of (and sections through) the Y-Pipe. Figure 12.16 displays an image generated using Model to Sheet.

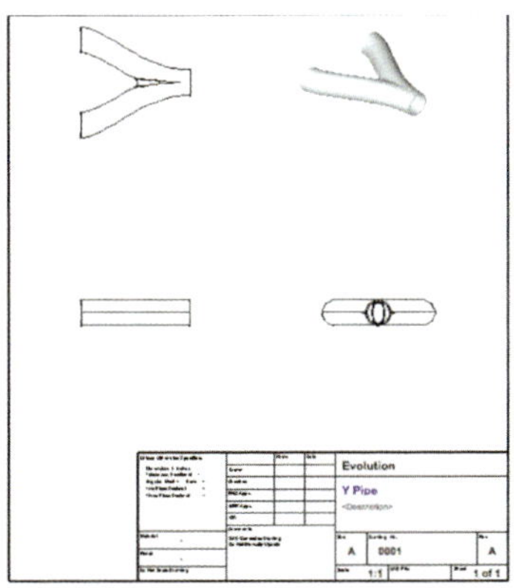

Figure 12.16 – Model to Sheet drawing of Y Pipe

Coffee Mug

Level: Intermediate

Description: In this tutorial, you will learn to draw profiles, to lathe, to shell, to join solids, and to fillet edges.

Key Tools: Line, Spline, Lathe, Shell, Blend, Extrude, and Add Solid

Overview:

Making the **Coffee Mug** can be broken down into the following processes:

1. Drawing the coffee mug body profile from which to create the 3D

2. Drawing the coffee mug handle profile

3. Using the *Solid Lathe* tool to generate the body of the Mug from its profile

4. Extruding the handle of the Mug from a closed profile

5. Joining the handle to the body of the Mug with the *Add Solid* tool

6. Shelling out the body of the Mug to an appropriate wall thickness

7. Blending the edges of the Mug and the intersection between the mug & handle

1. Drawing the Coffee Mug Body Profile

- Change the view to Front View by going to View and then selecting Front. Alternately, you can right-click on the drawing window and use the context sensitive menu.

- Start by right clicking on the origin to bring up the context sensitive menu.

- From this menu, select Construction Lines and then Horizontal to draw a horizontal construction line that represents the base surface on which the coffee mug will sit. Figure 13.1 to the right shows the context sensitive menu with the Construction Lines option selected.

- Next, begin constructing the body of the coffee mug by using the *Line* tool to draw the centerline of the mug body. This will typically start just above the horizontal base line and extend the height of the mug. However, you may find it easier to draw up from the base line and simply adjust the line later. Figure 13.2 below shows the centerline in red.

Figure 13.1 – Construction Lines

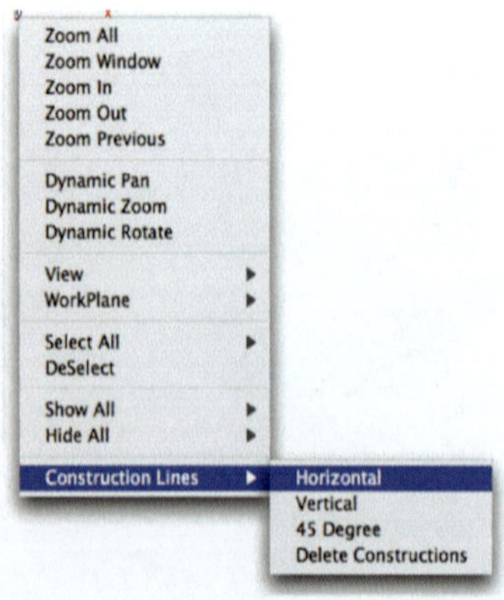

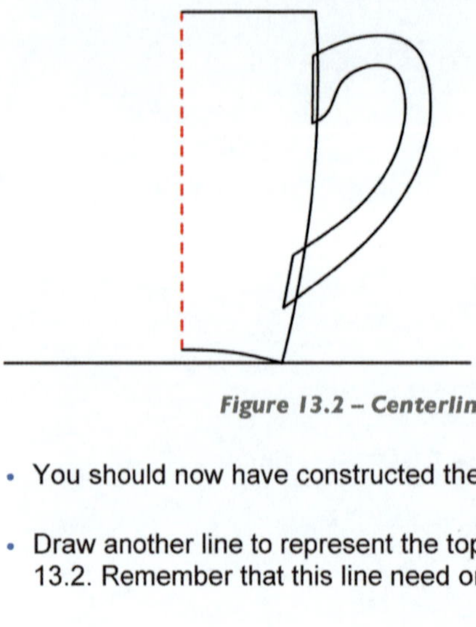

To quickly make lines of a given length, you can select the *Line* tool then left-click where you wish the line to begin. Click again (at an arbitrary distance from the first point) in the direction you want to draw the line. Then, type the line length into the text field of the *Line* tool top bar and press return.

Figure 13.2 – Centerline shown with mug and handle profiles

- You should now have constructed the base line and the centerline of the mug body.

- Draw another line to represent the top of the mug body, similar to the line shown in Figure 13.2. Remember that this line need only represent half the diameter of the mug.

- Use the *Tangent Points Arc* tool to draw the base of the mug profile:

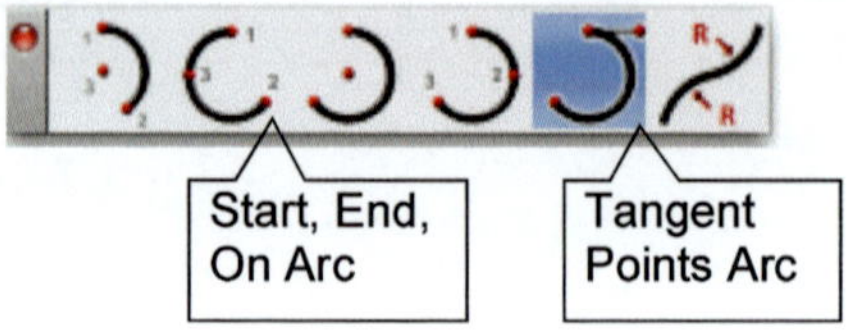

Figure 13.3 – Arc tools

- This tool requires 3 points.
- As long as the first 2 points are entered 'in-line' horizontally, a centerline tangent will be created.
- A centerline tangent is critical to create a smooth dished surface on the base of the mug.

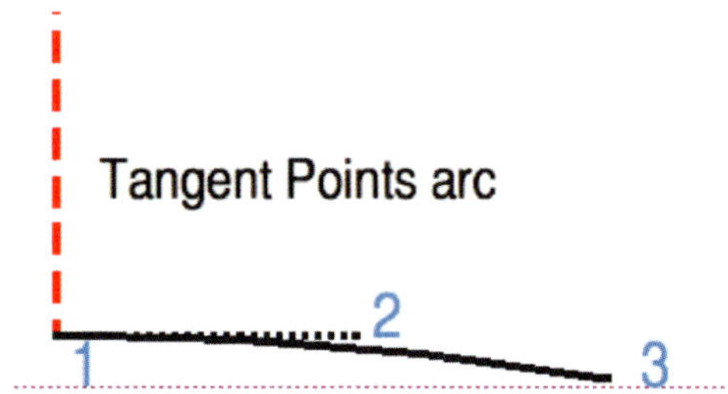

Figure 13.4 – Tangent Points Arc for Mug Base

- Use the *Start, End, On Arc* tool to complete the profile:

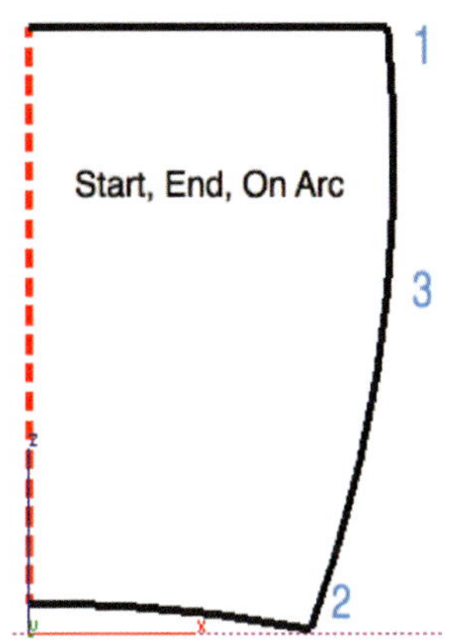

Figure 13.5 – Use the Start, End, On Arc tool to create the mug side profile

- Place points at both open ends of the profile, ensuring that you place them on the endpoints of the other curves.
- Then, click in between to determine the amount of curvature (the radius) of the arc.
- The radius value of the arc (in fact the defined values of any objects) can be adjusted in the Inspector dialog box. An even faster alternative would be using the Gripper to manipulate the 3rd point until a pleasing curvature is reached.

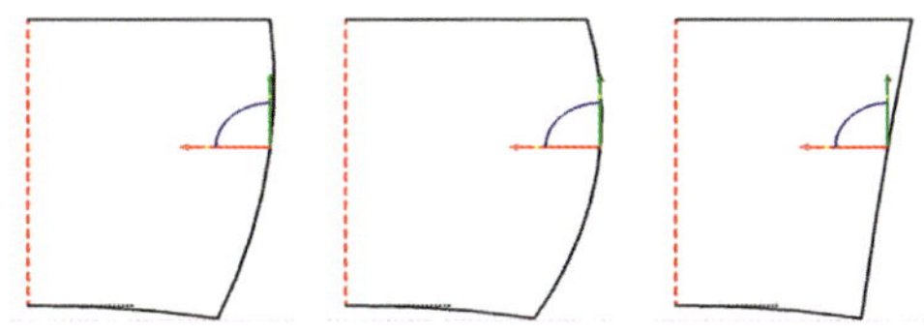

Original Moving Gripper Out Moving Gripper in

2. Drawing the Coffee Mug Handle Profile

- Use the *Interpolate Spline* tool to generate two curves that represent the inside and outside profile lines of the handle.
- To show the points of a spline, click Edit and select Show Points from the drop-down menu.
- Be sure that the splines overlap the mug body so there will be no gap between the handle and the body. Figure 13.6 shows an example handle profile. Notice the handle lines overlap the body.

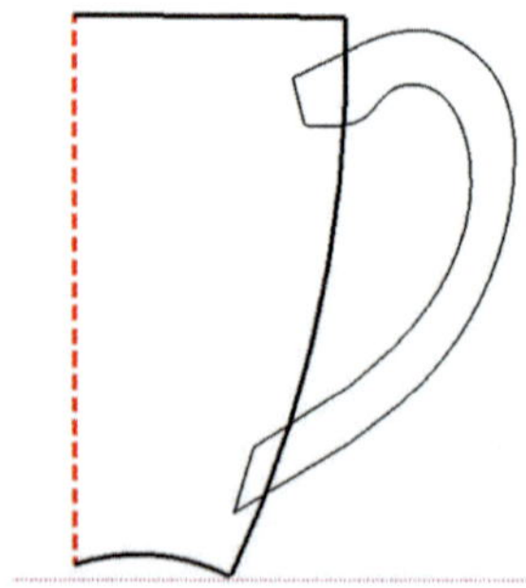

Figure 13.6 – Creating handle using splines

- When working with splines, you should use as few points as possible. In this case, four or five points should be sufficient.

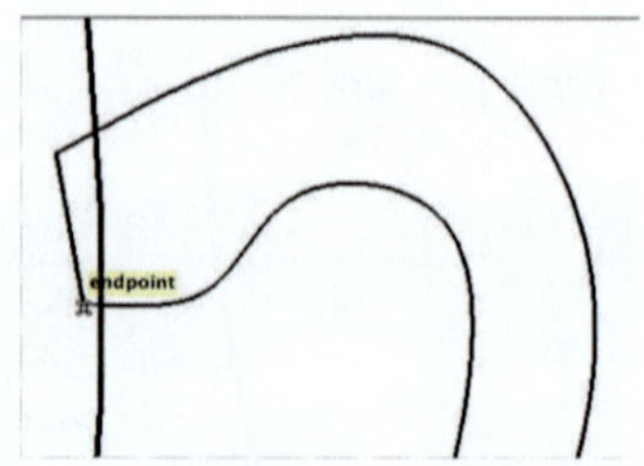

Figure 13.7 – Ensure that when connecting lines and curves the endpoints 'snap'

- When moving splines, you can nudge points using the Arrow keys on your keyboard. To enable nudging open Preferences and general set the desired nudge distance. More information can be found on nudging with your Arrow keys in Chapter 1 of this book.

- Close the profile using the *Line* tool. Be sure to snap to the spline end points. If you do not, a closed profile will not be created and the next operation will fail. You will be sure a snap has been achieved if the word endpoint appears next to your cursor. This can be seen in Figure 13.7 to the right.

3. Lathing the Body of the Mug

- Provided you have a closed profile (a series of lines / curves with no gaps), you should easily be able to generate a lathed solid.

Figure 13.8- Profile of body to be lathed by 360°

- Select the *Lathe Solid* tool from the toolbar.

- Following the prompts that appear under the tool name in the top bar, first select the curves that make up the closed profile.

- Instead of clicking one line at a time when selecting a profile, a profile can automatically be traced by right clicking on one of the curves that make up the profile. A contextual menu will appear. From these menu options, choose **Select Chain.** Provided your profile is good (there are no gaps, duplicate lines, or branched lines), the entire profile will be selected.

- Then select the axis about which to lathe. The tool defaults to 360° of rotation and zero draft angle as seen in Figure 13.9.

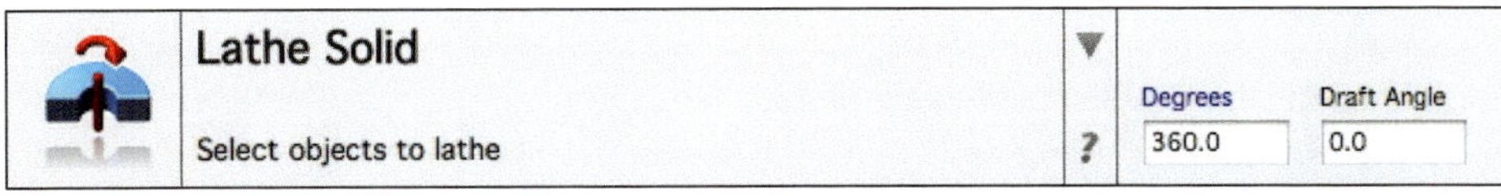

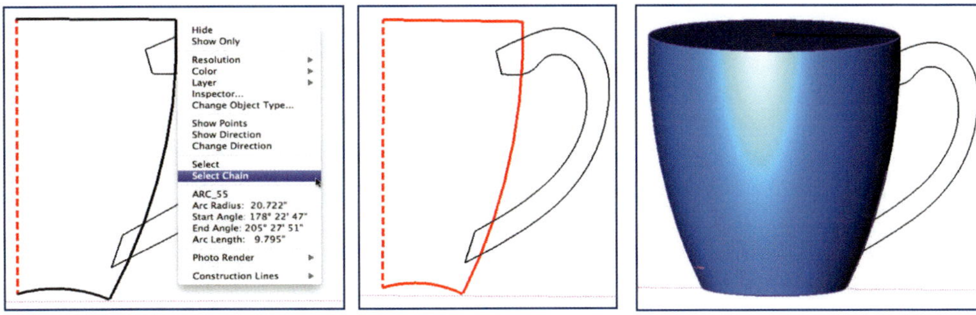

1 2 3

Figure 13.9 – Lathe Solid from profile

4. Extruding Mug Handle

- Next, hide the mug body and any other items that might complicate your view of the 4 curves / lines that make up the handle. To hide an object:
    - Right-click on the object to bring up the contextual menu.
    - Select Hide from the top of this menu.
- Now, choose the *Extrude Solid* tool from the toolbar.
- From the pull-down menu, select **Midplane**. This will extrude the handle equidistant either side of the profile.0

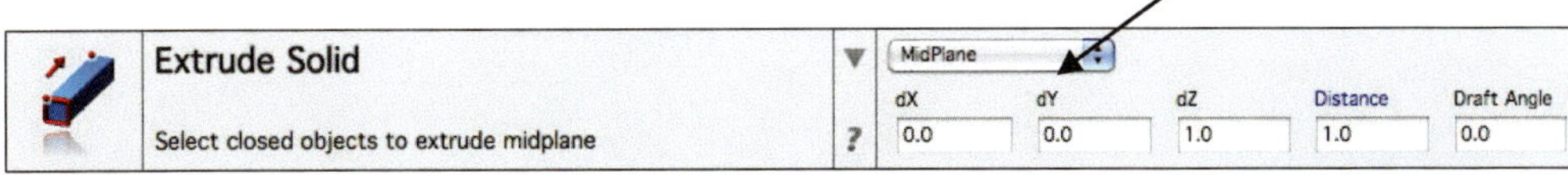

Figure 13.10 – Select Midplane and enter an appropriate distance

- Enter an appropriate extrude distance (the width you wish the handle to be).
- Then, following the prompts shown in the Extrude Solid top bar, select the closed objects you wish to extrude.
- As before, you can use the **Select Chain** command from the context sensitive menu to automatically trace the entire profile to save time.

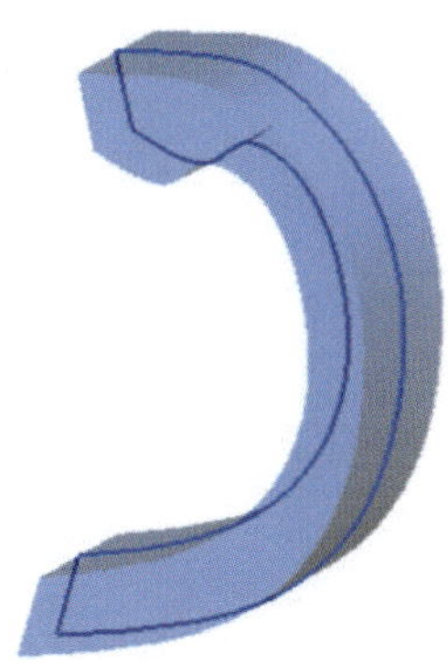

Figure 13.11 – Mug Handle Extruded

- Provided your profile is planar and has no gaps, the extrude will automatically be generated. It should resemble Figure 13.11.
- If you need to adjust the extrude distance, you can do so using the Inspector dialog box.
- Changing the profile curves from which the handle was extruded will update the shape of the handle.

5. Shelling Body of Mug

- Select the *Shell Feature* tool in order to hollow out the inside of the mug.
- Enter an appropriate offset thickness for the wall of the Mug into the Shell Feature top bar. We have used an offset of .250 inches.

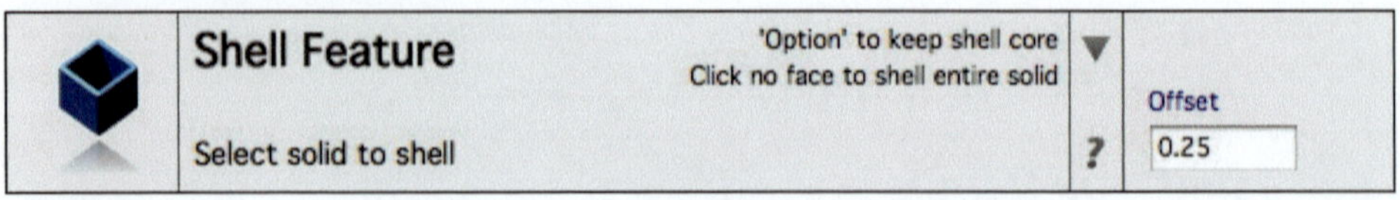

Figure 13.12 – Input the offset thickness into top bar

- Following the prompts, click the solid you wish to shell.
- Next click the face(s) you wish to leave open.
- If the program is unsure which face you are selecting, it will present you with an ambiguity pop-up. This appears when you select an object and there is not one clear face or object that the program can pick. You must select the appropriate entry yourself.
- You can press Shift to select multiple open faces. Additionally, if you wish to have a hollow object but no open faces, you can click on the background. If you only want to keep the hollowed out section, press the Option key.
- On releasing the Shift key, the shelled solid is created.

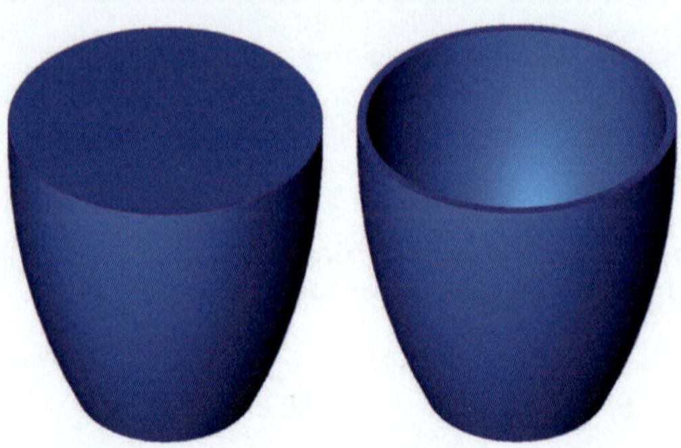

Figure 13.13 - Shell tool is employed to hollow-out the Mug Body

5. Joining Handle to Body

Figure 13.17 - Handle to Body Blend

- Now that you have both a Mug body and handle, you are ready to join them.
- Ensure that you have sufficient overlap between the two parts and that they are aligned in the plan (top) view.
- Choose the *Add Solid* tool.
- Following the prompts, select the objects to be joined. You should select the **body first** and then the handle. The order can be important in some instances, as the added part loses some qualities to the (first selected) master part.

Figure 13.14 - Joining the Handle to the Body

7. Blending

- Use the *Constant Blend* tool to soften the 4 long edges of the handle.

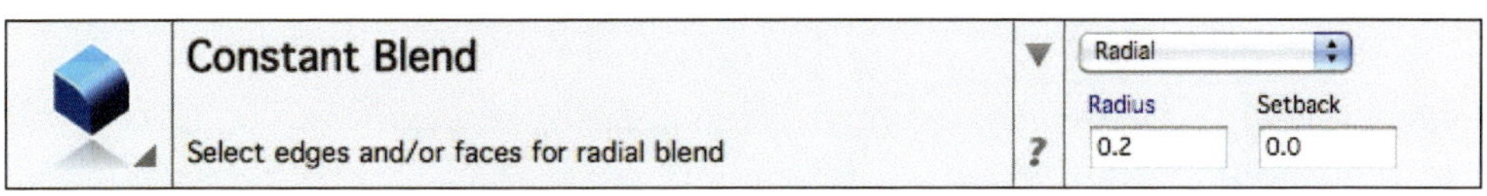

Figure 13.15 Constant Blend Top Bar

- It's important to use appropriately sized blends. If the blends are too big relative to the width and depth of the handle, the blends could fail or cusp on top of other blends.
    - o As a guide, therefore, begin with blends approximately half the width of the thinnest part of the handle.
- Following the tool prompts, select the edges and/or faces to be blended.
- Next use the *Constant Blend* tool again to soften the inside and outside edges on the top and bottom of the Mug body.

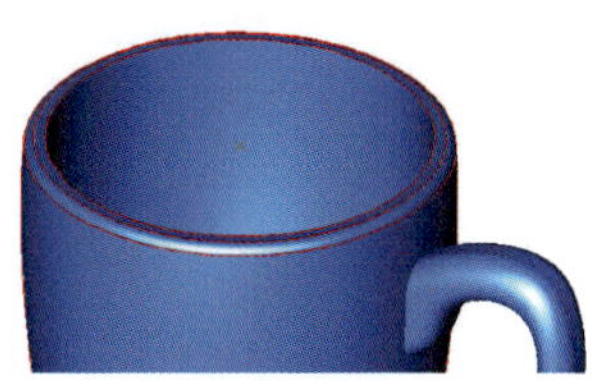

Figure 13.16- Blending edges on mug

8. Blending Intersection of Handle and Body

- Use the *Constant Blend* tool to blend the upper and lower intersections between the handle and the body of the mug.

- Again, be sure to choose an appropriate sized blend. Begin with blends approximately half the width of the thinnest part of the handle.
- Following the tool prompts, select the intersection to be blended between the body and handle.
- Provided the input value is not too big, the fillet blend will run around the intersection.

Figure 13.18 - Finished Mug before rendering

9. Extra Touches

- You can add further realism to your design by photo rendering with materials. Figures 13.19 and 13.20 below show example renderings of the scene using ViaCAD Pro.

Get the Look

Material: Ceramic Porcelain

HDRI: Studio/lwhdr_studio6_2k.hdr

HDRI Intensity: 2.30

*Shadows on, anti-alias

Figure 13.19

- Have fun with the rendering process and don't be afraid to experiment with some of the software's features.

Figure 13.20

Get the Look

Material: Cyan Plastic Polish

Decals: Photography Sunlight, Keyboard letters

HDRI: Studio/lwhdr_studio2 _2k.hdr

HDRI Intensity: 2.30

*Shadows on, anti-alias

- Additionally, try using Model to Sheet to generate 2D drawings of (and sections through) the coffee mug. Figure 13.21 displays an image generated using Model to Sheet.

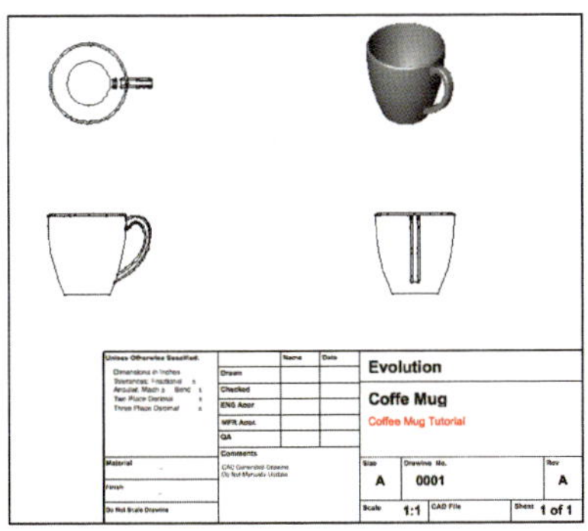

Figure 13.21 – Model to Sheet

IMPORTING SPLINES

Level: Intermediate

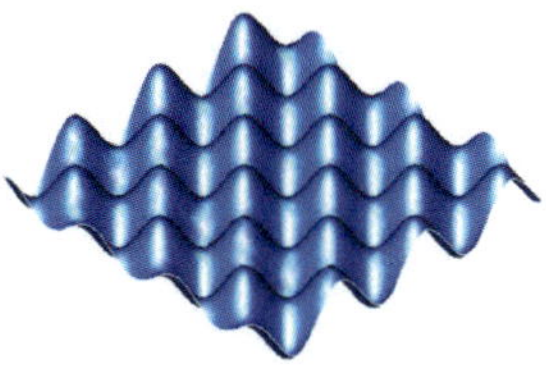 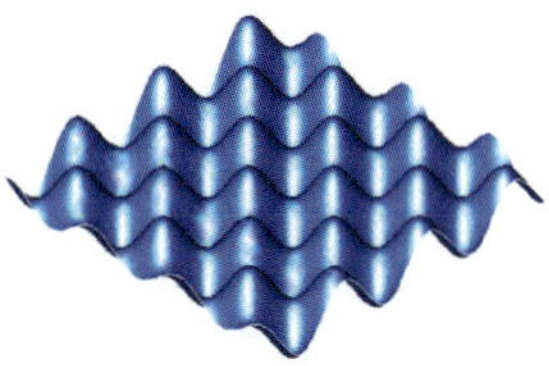 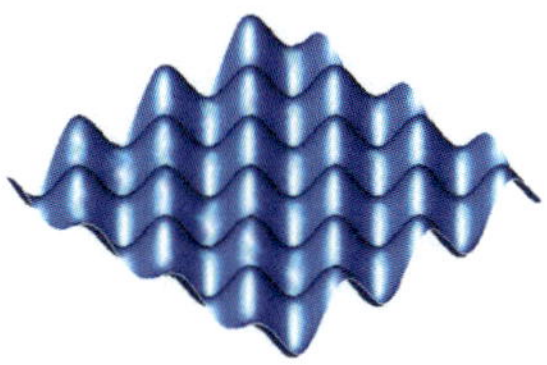

Description: In this tutorial, you will learn to import point, throughpoint, vectorspline, polyline, lawspline, and lawsurface splines.

Key Terms: The file format uses keywords to indicate the type of data to be imported. Supported keywords are displayed below:

POINT	Creates a point object
THROUGHPOINT	Spline that goes through provided point
VECTORSPLINE	Spline defined by spline control vertices
POLYLINE	A multisegment line
LAWSPLINE	A spline defined by vector functions
LAWSURFACE	A spline surface defined by vector functions

Overview: The Spline (.spl) file defines an ASCII file format that provides the ability to import a variety of splines directly into the program. The Spline import file feature is located under Import found under the File menu.

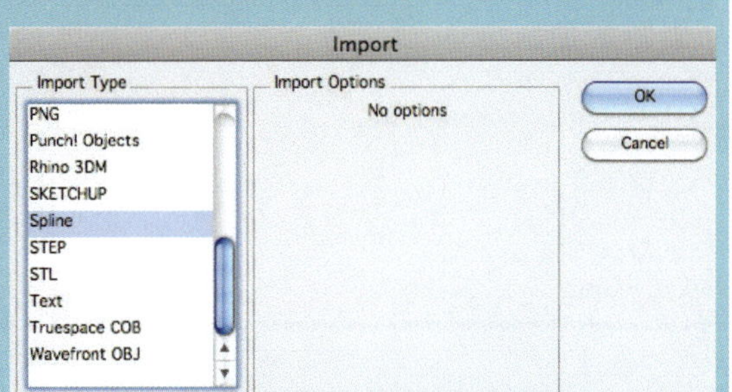

Figure 14.1

Comments, denoted with two forward slashes "//" at the beginning of the line, will not be processed by the reader. XYZ data is separated by spaces and may be either integer or floating point numbers.

Points

This keyword will create a collection of point objects. The keyword for this type is POINT followed by sets of xyz points. The points are terminated by either the end of file or another keyword.

Points Example

```
// creates 4 point entities
//
POINTS
   0.000000        2.386460      0.000000
   3.676037        3.216532      0.000000
   7.529947        2.386460      0.000000
   10.168393       4.313414      0.000000
```

Through Point Splines

A through point spline creates a B-Spline that interpolates or fits a set of points. The resulting B-Spline goes through the provided points. The keyword for this type is THROUGHSPLINE followed by sets of xyz points. The points are terminated by either the end of file or another keyword.

Though Point Splines Example

```
//This is an example of a through point spline
//
THROUGHSPLINE
10 10 0
11 11 0
12 11 0
13 10 0
//----File ends here
```

Figure 14.2

If no keyword is present in the file, the program will treat the entire contents of the file as points in a through point spline.

Control Point Splines

A control point spline creates a B-Spline that uses the provided points as the control polygon. The keyword for this type is VECTORSPLINE followed by sets of xyz points. The points are terminated by either the end of file or another keyword.

Control Points Splines Example

```
// Example spline that uses the provided points as
// control vertices of a bspline polygon
VECTORSPLINE
10      5       0
11      6       0
12      6       0
13      5       0
```

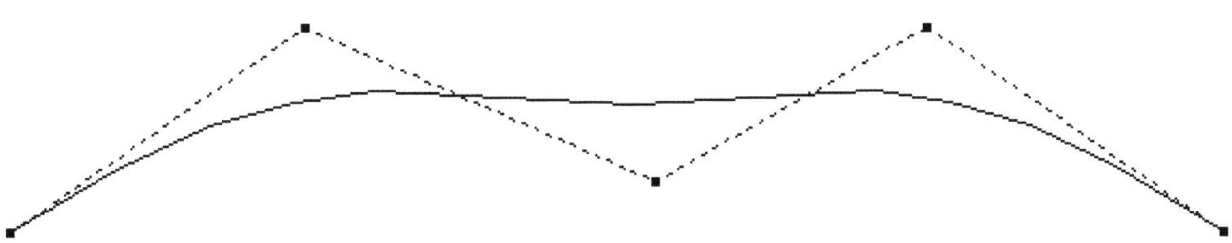

Figure 14.3

Polylines

A polyline creates a simple line entity that goes through set of points. The keyword for this type is POLYLINE followed by sets of xyz points. The points are terminated by either the end of file or another keyword.

Polylines Example

```
// Example polyline that uses the provided points as
```

```
// points for a single connected line
POLYLINE
10      2       0
11      3       0
12      3       0
13      2       0
14      3       0
```

Figure 14.4

Law Splines

A Law Spline creates a 2D or 3D B-Spline curve using an equation of the form:

$$f(t) = vec(x(t),y(t),z(t))$$

Three lines are used to define a law spline. The first line is the domain minimum value. The second line is the domain maximum. The third line is a line containing a 3D vector function for x,y, and z defined in the domain.

Law Spline Example

```
// Creates a spline from an equation
// In this example a circle at x=0,y=10
// first parameter is umin
// second parameter is umax
// third is vector function for x, y, z
LAWSPLINE
0
6.28
vec(cos(u),10+sin(u),0)


// Use LAWSPLINE to create a sin wave
LAWSPLINE
0
20
vec(u,sin(u),0)

// Use LAWSPLINE to create a helix
LAWSPLINE
0
40
vec(cos(u),-5 +sin(u),u/20)
```

Law Spline Example

```
// Use LAWSPLINE to create a elliptical
helix
LAWSPLINE
0
40
vec(2*cos(u),-10+sin(u),u/5)

// Use LAWSPLINE to create a ellipse
// x = 0, y = 5
LAWSPLINE
0
6.28
vec(2*cos(u),5+ sin(u),0)
```

```
// Use LAWSPLINE to create involute
curve at x=-20
```

```
LAWSPLINE
0
20
vec(-20 + .5*(cos(u) + u *sin(u)),.5*(sin(u)
- u *cos(u)),0)
```

```
// Use LAWSPLINE to create a funky
curve
LAWSPLINE
0
5
vec(5+0.1* (u^3) +abs(cos(u)^2),-5
+sin(u),sqrt(1+x)
```

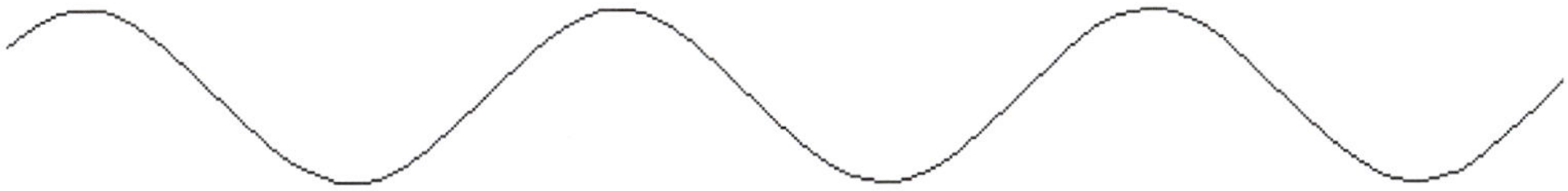

Figure 14.5

Law Surfaces

A Law Surface creates a 3D NURB surface using an equation of the form:

f(u,v) = vec(x,y,z)

Five lines are used to define a law surface. The lines are:

1. Domain minimum u value
2. Domain maximum u value
3. Domain minimum v value
4. Domain maximum v value
5. A 3D vector function for x,y, and z defined in the two domains

Law Surface Example

```
// Use LAWSURFACE TO create an "egg carton" surface
LAWSURFACE
20
40
20
40
vec(u,-30+v,2sin(u)*cos(v))
```

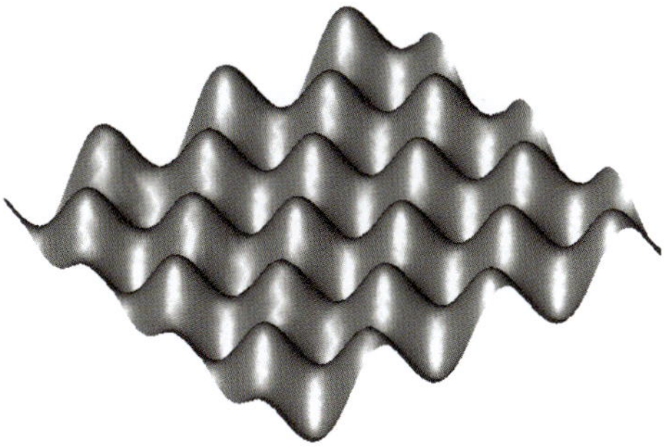

*Figure 14.6 – Law Surface Spline defined by f(u,v) = vec (u,-30+v,2sin(u)*cos(v))*

APPENDIX OF QUESTIONS

Glossary

3D Primitive — A basic geometric solid shape such as a sphere, block, torus, cone, and pyramid.

Absolute Coordinates — A way of inputting points based on ViaCAD's global coordinate system.

ACIS — A 3D modeling kernel developed by Spatial Inc. that provides a precision curve, surface, and solid modeling engine used by many commercial and research organizations as the core of CAD/CAM/CAE applications. Models can be shared precisely (no translation) using the SAT format to other applications using the ACIS engine.

Ambient Color — The color produced by ambient light and set in the Ambient Light Settings dialog box.

Ambient Light — Light that illuminates a model with equal intensity. Ambient Light is independent of location and direction. Ambient Light is turned on and off using the Ambient Light Settings dialog box.

Annotation — An object used to annotate a drawing such as text, dimension, symbols, and bill of material items.

Anti-Aliasing — Each pixel in the rendered image is calculated by averaging several neighboring pixels. The resulting image appears smoother.

Arc — A section of a circle limited by a start and end angle.

Arrowhead — An attribute applied to any curve type that adds an arrowhead, slash, or dot at the start or end of the curve. Use the Inspector to turn on/off an arrowhead.

ASCII — Abbreviation for American Standard Code for Information Interchange. This format is used to store text based file formats in most computer systems. Example ASCII files created by ViaCAD includes DXF, OBJ, STL ASCII, and SPL.

Associative Dimensioning — An intelligent link between a dimension and an object. The link also contains a set of rules that tell how the dependent object should update itself if something changes. The Smart Dimension tool creates associative dimensions.

Backup file	ViaCAD can be set to automatically backup your drawing and save it. This is a safeguard in case your file gets corrupted. It is saved with a .bak extension and located in your user documents folder.
B-spline	A blended piecewise polynomial curve defined by a collection of control points.
Bezier Spline	A polynomial curve defined by a collection of control points where each control point has an associated point to control the tangency.
CAD	Computer Aided Design. The process of creating drawings and models on a computer system.
CAM	Computer Aided Manufacturing. A type of computer application that helps automate a manufacturing process.
Conic	A class of curves that contains hyperbolas, parabolas, and ellipses. Conics are popular in the aerospace industry because of their smoothness and flexibility.
Coons' Patch	A NURBS surface with three or four sides.
Coplanar	Geometric objects lying in a common plane are said to be coplanar.
Cover Surface	A surface defined by the outlines of a curve boundary. The resultant surface may be created from one or more sides.
Cursor	Your cursor will change depending on what function it is performing in the program.
Curvature Analysis	Displays a curvature plot on a surface or solid.
Curve	A one dimensional mathematical object that describes length. Example curves include lines, circles, conics, and splines. A curve is a path in 3D space.
Defeaturing	A popular CAD/CAE simplification technique in which small or irrelevant features are suppressed within a CAD model for speeding-up downstream processes, especially finite element analysis.
Dialog box	ViaCAD uses a large number of dialog boxes to get information from you. You must know how input the information that it asks for.
DWG and DXF	File format used by CAD system to translate data back and forth to dissimilar systems. This interface provides ViaCAD the capability to share data with AutoCAD® and other

	systems which adhere to the DWG and DXF specification.
Edge	The curve boundary of a face. Edges can be used to define features such as fillets and chamfers.
Environment Map	Environment mapping is an efficient image-based lighting technique for approximating the appearance of a reflective surface using a pre-computed texture image. The Render Library dialog box provides access to a collection of Environment Maps.
EPS	Encapsulated PostScript (EPS) is a standard file format for importing and exporting PostScript files.
Extents	The outer boundaries of the objects you have drawn.
Extrude	Given a collection of curves, the Extrude tools will sweep these into a 3D surface or solid.
Flat Shading	A single, constant color across the extents of a facet, rather than smoothly interpolated colors.
Grid	This is pattern of lines or dots displayed on the screen to guide you. It can be toggled on and off by the Show Grid command.
Grips	Small 'handles' on objects that allow for quick editing.
Helix	A curve that spirals in 3D.
IGES	Abbreviation for Initial Graphics Exchange Specification. Used to transfer CAD data to other CAD systems supporting IGES. Later, this was replaced by STEP, which has better definition for solids.
Isolines	A display option for showing the iso parameter lines for a surface or solid.
Keyboard Shortcuts	Assign a key to a function for accelerating access to a particular command.
Layer	All objects are drawn on a layer. You can group objects (such as electrical) on a single layer and organize your drawing. Layers are created and edited using the layer manage tab in the Concepts Explorer dialog box.
Line	A straight path in 3D space defined by a start and endpoint.
Links	This is the associative relationship that exists between parent/child objects where a modification to the parent will

also modify the child.

LogiCusor — This is a method of intelligent snapping to precise points on an object.

Material — A collection of shaders used during rendering of an object's surface that determines an image's pixel color value. The shader types in a material include color, reflectance, displacement, transparency, and texture space.

Modify — A generic term used for changing an object's shape or position.

Moments — The name given to rotational inertia, which is the rotational analog of mass for linear motion. It appears in the relationships for the dynamics of rotational motion. Also known as Moments of Inertia.

Net Surface — A surface created from an MxN collection of curves

Normal — A three component plane equation that defines the angular orientation *but not the position* of a plane or surface.

NURBS — Non-Uniform Rational B-Spline. It is one of several forms available to modeling a curve or surface. The mathematical form describes the shaping and blending information.

Object — A CAD entity that describes a logical grouping for an individual or collection of entities. Example objects include points, lines, splines, conics, circles, polyconics, ruled, cones, and spheres.

Origin — The (0,0) point of your current co-ordinate system.

Ortho mode — This is a drawing mode that allows you to draw only perpendicular lines. It is toggled on and off by pressing the F8 key.

Pan — To move around drawing by dragging the drawing area around your screen.

Path — The specific folder where ViaCAD looks for, or saves files.

Perpendicular — Two lines, vectors, planes, etc., are said to be perpendicular if they meet at a right angle (90°)

Perspective — The appearance of things relative to one another as determined by their distance from the viewer.

Phong — A method of rendering that calculates pixel color based on

	interpolating normals.
Pick	To select an object by 'left-clicking' on it.
Plane	An infinite two-dimensional surface.
Plot	Also known as print. To make a hard copy of your drawing.
Point	A location in model space specified by the 3 coordinates x, y, and z.
Polar co-ordinates	A way of inputting points based on distance and angle. Use PrecisionPoint to specify polar coordinates.
Property	Any specific characteristic of an object such as layer, scale, linetype, start point, etc. Use the attribute inspector to change object properties.
Relative co-ordinates	A way of inputting points based on a starting point. Use PrecisionPoint to specify relative co-ordinates.
RHO	Used in defining a conic, it is the ratio of the center point – shoulder point distance and the center point – slope control point.
Selection Mask	A way of filtering out objects to select by type, layer, or color.
Smart Silhouette	A silhouette that displays only if it does not degrade the performance.
Snap	A data entry method that allows you to snap your cursor to precise points using LogiCursor. LogiCursor infers locations such as centers, midpoints, endpoints, and intersections from the current cursor location.
Solid	A three dimensional object that describes length, width, and height. Solids describe regions that define volumes. Example solids include sphere, square, cone, prism, and cylinders.
Spline	A piecewise parametric curve that consists of a collection of polynomial functions which describe a smooth shape.
Stitched Solid	A solid created from joining surfaces together.
Styles	Formatting that defines the look of text, dimensions, such as bold, italic, and underline.
Surface	A two dimensional object that describes length and width. Whereas a curve spans a length, a surface spans areas.

	Example surfaces include ruled, polyconic, fillet, and sculptured.
Uniformed Scaling	Scales an object equally in all directions.
Units	The basic drawing unit set for you drawing. For example, you can use inches or millimeters depending on your needs. To change the drawing units go to the Preferences Unit interface.
View	A particular area of your drawing.
Viewport	A separate 'window' on your drawing. You may have more than one viewport visible to see different areas of your drawing at the same time.
VRML	Virtual Reality Modeling Language (VRML) “a universal description language for multi-participant simulations.” (from VRML Mission Statement)
Wireframe	A CAD entity that represents length and perimeter. Curves such as lines, splines, conics, arcs, and circles are a class of wireframe entities.
Wizard	An easy step-by-step instruction set to help you set-up certain aspects of your drawing.
Z-Buffer	An accumulation buffer used in rendering to calculate what object is closest to the viewer.
Zoom	To view either a smaller section of your drawing (zoom in) or a larger section (zoom out)

INDEX

11017211R00152

Printed in Great Britain
by Amazon.co.uk, Ltd.,
Marston Gate.